British Idealism and International Thought

The Development of Human Rights

Nazlı Pınar Kaymaz

imprint-academic.com

With the support of

Society

Published in the UK by
Imprint Academic, PO Box 200, Exeter EX5 5YX, UK

Distributed in the USA by
Ingram Book Company,
One Ingram Blvd., La Vergne, TN 37086, USA

ISBN 9781788360234 Hardback

A CIP catalogue record for this book is available from the
British Library and US Library of Congress

Contents

Preface

This book is a revised version of my PhD dissertation that evolved and expanded throughout the years. The only thing I knew when I started my PhD was that I wanted to tackle the theoretical questions that underlay the concept of human rights and continued to discredit it through its inconsistencies. As a clueless and overconfident student, I was looking for a definitive theoretical answer that would prove and sustain the fact that human rights do exist. I was totally unaware of the existence of British Idealism as a school of thought. Following my adviser James Alexander's advice, I started reading T.H. Green's works on rights and then Bosanquet's works on the state and Ritchie's reflections on natural rights. During my research visit to Cardiff University's Collingwood and British Idealism Centre, I also became acquainted with the works of J.S. Mackenzie, J.H. Muirhead, Henry Jones, R.B. Haldane, and H.J.W. Hetherington. While I found abundant material to approach the topic of human rights in the works of all these writers, I also became aware that their thought and writing was a product of their time and it would be a mistake to directly translate their reflections on rights into a defence of human rights as we know it today. The biggest indicator of the futility of such a task was their approach to the matter of imperialism. There were passages in some of their writings that defended the imperial conduct of European powers and would totally discredit any argument that they were unconditionally supporting universal human rights. Thus, it became inevitable to deal at length with the historical specificities of the era they lived in and the political and international climate of which they were a part. When I started to pay attention not only to what they wrote, but also when and under which circumstances they wrote it, the picture became clearer.

The British Idealists' work was not a flawless and complete defence of universal human rights from the 1880s to 1930s. It was, rather, a story of intellectual evolution and growth that incorporated, through time, the necessary theoretical and conceptual tools that were indispensable for the recognition and maintenance of international human rights. Their thought was by no means perfect, but it is valuable today as it offers a viable way of taking human rights seriously. When Ritchie reflected on the merits of the French Revolution in 1892, he wrote, 'it is right to ask ourselves how our generation will be judged at the bar of history a hundred years hence... Will they be able to pardon our mistakes and our delusions, because of the spirit in which we tried to leave the world — not worse but a little better than we found it?'[1] Throughout this book, I tried to be as fair as possible to their work without glossing over the points where I did not agree with them. Of course, the reader will be the judge of my success in this regard.

I have been very lucky to study British Idealism in the 2010s when there already existed a considerable amount of literature on its political, international, and philosophical legacy. I learned the intricacies of the British Idealist line of thought by reading the works of scholars such as Maria Dimova-Cookson, Colin Tyler, William Sweet, and James Connelly. As a PhD student I benefited greatly from James Alexander's, Lars Vinx's, Daniel Just's, and Reşide Ömür Birler's criticisms and suggestions while developing the arguments that constitute the core of this work. I also had the chance to work under the supervision of David Boucher and Andrew Vincent in 2015 as a visiting researcher and benefited greatly from their guidance. I am especially indebted to David Boucher for his continuing support from 2015 onwards, both during my years as a PhD student and afterwards. In the writing of this book, I am most grateful to Peter Nicholson who read innumerable drafts of this

---

1 D.G. Ritchie (1892) '1792 — Year 1', *International Journal of Ethics*, 3 (1), p. 88.

manuscript and invested his valuable time in editing the language and the content of it. Without his expertise in British Idealism and his gracious support I would not have been equal to this task. I am grateful to Graham Horswell and the staff at Imprint Academic for their diligent work in preparing this manuscript for publication. I would also like to thank the editors of the *International History Review* for letting me use excerpts from an article of mine that was published in their journal.[2]

Lastly, I would like to offer my thanks to my family. I feel especially grateful to my husband, Timur Kaymaz, for his years' worth of love and encouragement. I dedicate this book to my late grandfather, Talat Gömbül, who probably never heard about British Idealism but it is his image that comes to my mind when I read and write about the pursuance of an ethical life.

---

[2] Nazli Pinar Kaymaz (2018) 'From Imperialism to Internationalism: British Idealism and Human Rights', *The International History Review*, published online.

Chapter 1

Introduction

A revival of interest in British Idealism is self-evident from the ever-expanding literature on their moral, political, and international theory as well as their metaphysics in the last thirty years. Although this literature is mostly dominated by a few names that can be perceived to be modern advocates of British Idealist philosophy, it is also possible to find references to well-known British Idealists in intellectual historiographies of the long nineteenth century. Especially T.H. Green's and Bernard Bosanquet's names are frequently mentioned in the historical accounts of British political thought in the Victorian and Edwardian eras. Yet, with a few exceptions, the 'modern advocates of British Idealism' confine their attention to the works of the best-known British Idealists. While such an approach has been useful to explain the philosophical basis of a political theory that has long been perceived as an historical eccentricity, today it unnecessarily limits the scope and character of the discussion. Furthermore, possibly due to the contemporary dominance of analytical philosophy, as well as the very limited time period Green produced his work in, there is a lack of interest in the historical specificity of the era during which British Idealism continued to develop and evolve. To have a broader understanding of British Idealism as an evolving school of thought, one firstly needs to broaden the focal point of research to include minor figures in the British Idealist school of thought in the discussion in a substantive way. Doing so automatically expands the timespan one deals with and enables one to observe several British Idealists' changing and varying reactions to major international phenomena. This study is an attempt to tackle the understudied field of post-Greenian British Idealist international theory.

This work offers an historical reading of the British Idealists' approach to international relations from 1900 to the 1930s. It starts with British Idealists' reflections on the British Empire and the general question of the legitimacy of imperialism. In the pre-Great War period the Boer War and its ramifications in the British intellectual arena constituted the larger picture in relation to which it is necessary to understand various British Idealists' respective positions on imperialism. While F.H. Bradley and D.G. Ritchie are separated from the rest of the school by their almost militaristic imperialism, the remaining names represent a more or less coherent 'sane', or moderate, imperialist vein. The sense one gets from a close reading of the British Idealists' writings during the period from 1900 to 1914 constitutes a striking contrast to the tone they adopted after the outbreak of the Great War. From 1914 onwards, the remaining British Idealists sound a unified chord in condemning imperialism and adopting an internationalist approach to international relations. With a focus on this shift, the main argument of this study emerges from the works of minor British Idealists who wrote extensively during and after the Great War on international relations. It pertains to a conviction that a closer look to this era would contribute greatly to a more nuanced understanding of British Idealist theory of human rights. While the Greenian theory of rights unarguably supplies the basis for such a theory, minor British Idealists' writings in the post-1914 period reveal how it is translated into a practical plan in a more receptive and internationalist intellectual arena by Green's students. It traces British Idealism's historical evolution in an era (1900–1930) that contains unprecedented international turmoil, reaching fruition at a time of intense intellectual endeavour to ensure future world peace and cooperation. Doing so enables one to identify an organic lineage from Green to his students that reflects on their shared understandings of the individual, the society, the state, and the international arena as well as the role and importance of rights.

I. Thomas Hill Green and
His Theory of Rights

The existing literature on the British Idealist theory of human rights is constrained in its scope due to its singular focus on the best-known British Idealists. While work on T.H. Green's theory of rights constitutes the bulk of the existing literature, attempts to defend Bernard Bosanquet from his historical New Liberal critiques encourages some scholars to investigate his approach to rights. Other well-known British Idealists, such as D.G. Ritchie and F.H. Bradley, remain as marginal figures in the literature so far as their work does not offer much to contribute to a theory of human rights. Such limitation of scope reflects on the availability of primary sources on the subject matter considering that the matter of 'human rights' did not have a central place in the writings of T.H. Green or Bernard Bosanquet. Although Green is known for the central place rights constitute in his political theory, he dealt with the matter of broadening the limits of rights beyond nations only in a subsection of his *Prolegomena to Ethics,* titled 'Duty to Humanity'. Green devoted this part of his work to defending the possibility of extending human community beyond national borders. He maintained that, due to the fact that all men are bestowed with reason and thus capable of striving for a common good, capable of communicating with others as 'I' and 'Thou', one can talk about a *potential* community of all men. He denied any categorical difference between the nation and 'universal human fellowship'.[1] The difference was only in terms of degree — the number of members and the vastness of space — and the difficulty in realizing such community was the same with every other community: ensuring preference of common good over private pleasure.[2] Green argued that, to the extent that human beings strive to overcome their selfishness, universal fellowship remained a

---

[1] T.H. Green (1906) *Prolegomena to Ethics,* Bradley, A.C. (ed.), Fifth Edition, Oxford: Clarendon Press, p. 252.
[2] Green, *Prolegomena,* p. 252.

possibility for mankind. His conviction in the potential of achieving a sphere of common good that encompassed all humanity was supported by his observation that each nation 'has maintained alike, under whatever differences of form, the institutions of the family and of property... a sort of common language of right, in which the idea of universal human fellowship, of claims in man as man... can find expression necessary to its taking hold on the minds of men'.[3] Thus, every man already had the idea and the habit of bestowing upon his fellow men certain rights and acting as a duty-bearer for their realization.

For Green, all it would take to go beyond the limits of nations and recognize rights in every human being would have been to broaden the scope of the sphere of the common good each individual perceived himself and others to be participants of. He strongly believed that by building upon the already existing notions of rights and duties recognized in communities, it would be possible to extend 'one system of law over many communities'.[4] Despite his adamant conviction regarding the possibility of human rights, Green had little to say on the institutional means through which they can be recognized and maintained. In the few pages Green discussed the necessity of increasing familiarity among men from different nations in his *Lectures on the Principles of Political Obligation*, it becomes apparent that for him an international institution with a capacity to maintain universal rights was a possibility, albeit a distant one. Instead, he hoped that 'free intercourse between members of one state and those of another, and in particular more freedom of trade' would enable individuals to be aware that not only their compatriots but all human beings were equal participants in a shared sphere of common good.[5] He maintained such occasions for intercourse were to be expected more frequently in the future as states—especially

---

3   Green, *Prolegomena*, p. 252.
4   Green, *Prolegomena*, p. 252.
5   T.H. Green (1895) *Lectures on the Principles of Political Obligation*, London: Longmans, Green, and Co., p. 178.

European ones — were reaching higher levels of organization which gave their citizens more freedom to travel and conduct business abroad. For Green 'the dream of an international court with authority resting on the consent of independent states' was realizable only after nations moved beyond their jealousies and egoistic interests through development of cordial relationships among their citizens.[6] Recognition and maintenance of rights among peoples from different states was first and foremost dependent on their willingness to recognize each other as equal right-bearers. While there was 'nothing in the intrinsic nature of a system of independent states incompatible' with the establishment of an international organization for the protection of rights, the first step was ensuring the emergence of a common will for its maintenance.[7]

Green died at a very young age, a few weeks short of his forty sixth birthday, in 1882. He did not witness the heyday of the imperialist sentiment in Britain at the very end of the nineteenth century that reached a climax with the Boer War in 1900 or the rise of internationalist arguments following the outbreak of the First World War. His reflections on the matter of rights first and foremost addressed the situation in Victorian Britain. As Duncan Kelly puts forward in relation with the overall Greenian political theory, his approach to rights was 'more concerned with relating a political theory of welfarism to a focus on individual character in the social context of later Victorian and Edwardian Britain, challenging the effects of unequal distribution of wealth and resources'.[8] His reflections on the nature of international relations were very much focused on the necessity of developing informal ties among individuals from different nation-states which he expected to lead to transcending national boundaries in recognition and maintenance of

---

6 Green, *Lectures*, p. 179.
7 Green, *Lectures*, p. 179.
8 D. Kelly (2010) *The Propriety of Liberty: Persons, Passions, and Judgement in Modern Political Thought*, Princeton; Oxford: Princeton University Press, p. 248.

rights. Deceased before the rise of internationalist sentiment in Britain, Green's approach to international relations was dominated by ethical cosmopolitanism that has clear reflections in some of the contemporary accounts of British Idealist understanding of human rights.

The wide range of positions taken by Green's numerous students on the matters relating to international relations led contemporary commentators to attribute various and sometimes conflicting positions to Green himself on the matter. In the past two decades alone, Green has been identified as a liberal imperialist, a Little Englander, and an anti-militarist internationalist.[9] Furthermore his theory has been associated with both communitarian and cosmo-politan approaches to human rights. David Boucher, for instance, related Green's work to the modern communitarian human rights theories.[10] Similarly, Samuel Moyn considered Green to be a communitarian.[11] Matt Hann, in contrast, arrived at a 'cosmopolitan human rights' interpretation by drawing on Green's conviction that it was possible and normatively desirable to extend the boundaries of the moral sphere beyond those of the nation-state.[12] I would suggest that while Green's work incorporated elements that would

---

[9]   J.L. Thompson (2008) *A Wider Patriotism: Alfred Milner and the British Empire*, London: Routledge, p. 3; J. Stapleton (2000) 'Political Thought and National Identity in Britain 1850–1950, in Collini, S., Whatmore, R. and Young, B. (eds.) *History, Religion, and Culture: British Intellectual History 1750–1950*, Cambridge: Cambridge University Press, p. 255; D. Bell (2016) *Reordering the World: Essays on Liberalism and Empire*, Princeton: Princeton University Press, p. 245; J. Morefield (2009) *Covenants without Swords: Idealist Liberalism and the Spirit of Empire*, Princeton: Princeton University Press, p. 24.

[10] D. Boucher (2011) *The Limits of Ethics in International Relations: Natural Law, Natural Rights, and Human Rights in Transition*, Oxford: Oxford University Press, p. 298.

[11] S. Moyn (2012) *The Last Utopia: Human Rights in History*, Cambridge, MA; London: The Belknap Press of Harvard University Press, p. 31.

[12] M. Hann (2014) "Who is My Neighbour?' T.H. Green and the Possibility of Cosmopolitan Ethical Citizenship', in Brooks, T. (ed.) *Ethical Citizenship*, Basingstoke: Palgrave Macmillan, p. 180.

support both a communitarian and a cosmopolitan approach to human rights, his immediate followers opted for the middle way position of internationalism in the years following the end of the Great War.

Green's theory of rights has been studied extensively as it offered a consistent whole which aimed to explain the source, justification, and functionality of rights. Green, as many other political theorists did, looked for the source of rights in certain attributes of human nature. He argued that the source of rights was to be found in men's moral nature and his morality was comprised of his rationality and sociability.[13] In this regard, the individual as a right-bearer existed only within a social context and he truly had rights only when he rationally acknowledged his fellow men as equal right-bearers with whom he cooperated for the realization of a common good. Green strongly denied the 'natural rights' perspective that attributed rights to human beings in a hypothetical 'state of nature' where they lived solitarily. Still, he used the term 'natural rights' with reference to the moral nature of men, which was apparent in the relations sustained in the social union of reasonable human beings. He argued that a man's moral nature was evident in his willingness to agree on a common good with his fellow men and to recognize the necessity of endowing each man with certain powers for its realization.[14] The recognition of these powers constituted the system of rights and duties, which existed in every known human community.[15]

The moral nature of man, according to Green, also constituted the justification for individuals' identification as right-bearers. An individual had rights not only because he was born moral and reasonable but also because his moral and reasonable nature required recognition of certain powers for their full realization. Thus, Green's

---

[13] S.M. Den Otter (1996) *British Idealism and Social Explanation: A Study in Late Victorian Thought*, Oxford; New York: Clarendon Press, p. 162.

[14] A.R. Cacoullos (1975) *Thomas Hill Green: Philosopher of Rights*, New York: Twayne Publishers Inc., p. 18.

[15] Green, *Prolegomena*, p. 238.

approach to rights, like his approach to liberty and politics, was not only deontological but also both consequentialist and teleological. The desired end was sustaining a social order in which all individuals had a chance to realize their full potential. This end, often called self-realization by Green, was put forward as a challenge to the hedonistic ethics that designated pleasure as the highest end for human beings.[16] Green maintained that instead of aiming for pleasure, which did not accumulate and/or improve the person but vanish at the instant of its acquirement, men were to aim for 'divine self-realisation'.[17] In that sense, rights were justified as the powers that made self-realization possible within a society composed of moral individuals pursuing their individual self-perfection as well as the common good of the social whole.

In addition to the central importance of the moral nature of men in substantiating and justifying rights, Green paid considerable attention to the social and historical processes of their actual emergence and development in societies. According to Green, rights were constituted first and foremost as 'right claims' to 'exercise a free activity' or 'acquirement of a certain power' on the condition that the same activity or power would be freely exercised by other members of the society. When members of a community 'socially' recognized this claim, their actions were duly and, in a sense, 'naturally' organized in pursuance of this common acceptance. A higher step of recognition occurred at the political level when the state took these social rights under protection by incorporating them into the legally acknowledged system of rights and duties. Thus, although rights did not come into existence through state recognition, their maintenance was mostly dependent on the existence of legal recognition and protection.[18] Though there is a lack of consensus in the literature, the common evaluation of Green's work points to a double-layered

---

16   Green, *Prolegomena*, p. 199.
17   Green, *Prolegomena*, p. 209.
18   Green, *Lectures*, pp. 145–46.

process of recognition. Recognition as 'consciousness' directly refers to men's moral character as capable of perceiving others' good in equal weight with his own. By recognizing each other as '*isoi kai homoioi*', men participate in a society that sustains a just system of rights and duties.[19] Recognition as 'response' or 'appropriate action', on the other hand, deals with the actual process of registering the necessity of having certain rights and acting in accordance with the principle of 'reciprocity of rights'.[20]

A decidedly large part of the literature on British Idealist theory of rights is marked by a consistent effort to incorporate the 'recognition' aspect of Green's rights theory into theories of human rights.[21] While this genuine attribute of Greenian rights theory dominates the secondary literature, the moral source and justification of rights have so far received limited attention. It is one of the major arguments of this work that the ideal of self-realization as well as the functional necessity of recognition constitutes an indispensable attribute of a British Idealist theory of human rights. Minor British Idealists' writings in the post-1914 era reveal the centrality of the moral condition of self-realization in the matter of universal human rights in addition to the more practical condition of recognition.

---

[19] Green, *Lectures*, p. 144.
[20] D.R. Nesbitt (2001) 'Recognizing Rights: Social Recognition in T.H. Green's System of Rights', *Polity*, 33 (3), p. 427.
[21] R. Martin (2013) 'Human Rights and the Social Recognition Thesis', *Journal of Social Philosophy*, 44 (1), pp. 1–21; R. Martin (2012) 'Natural Rights, Human Rights and the Role of Social Recognition', *Collingwood and British Idealism Studies*, 17 (1), pp. 91–115; G. Gaus (2006) 'The Rights Recognition Thesis: Defending and Extending Green', in Dimova-Cookson, M. and Mander, W.J. (eds.) *T.H. Green: Ethics, Metaphysics, and Political Philosophy*, Oxford; New York: Oxford University Press; D. Boucher (2011) 'The Recognition Theory of Rights, Customary International Law and Human Rights', *Political Studies*, 59 (3), pp. 753–71; M. Hann (2015) 'Double Recognition: Persons and Rights in T.H. Green', *Collingwood and British Idealism Studies*, 21 (1), pp. 63–80; Nesbitt, 'Recognizing Rights'.

II. Bosanquet, Bradley, Ritchie,
and Idealist Theory of Rights

Bernard Bosanquet (1848–1923), Frances Herbert Bradley (1846–1924), and David George Ritchie (1853–1903) were among the very early exponents of British Idealism to which they grew an affinity under the direct influence of Green. While Bosanquet was a student of Green in the 1860s at Balliol College, Oxford, Bradley attended Green's lectures as a student of University College.[22] David George Ritchie was tutored by Green when he entered Balliol College in 1874 after obtaining his MA degree at Edinburgh. Among these early converts, Bradley is known today as the best metaphysician amongst the British Idealists, and Bosanquet was deemed to be the most 'prominent defender' of the British Idealist theory of the state, which was not always meant as a compliment.[23] Ritchie, on the other hand, is often remembered as the theorist who aimed to achieve a synthesis between the two rival philosophical positions of his day: idealism and utilitarianism.[24] While it is possible to find various groupings and couplings of these three names under sub-divisions of idealist philosophy, for the purposes of this work the historical circumstances they witnessed and commented upon constitutes the bases on which their work is considered.

Bradley and Ritchie appear as persons of interest only in the first chapter of this work due to a lack of material on the subject matter from the 1900s onwards. In the case of Bradley, his lack of interest in political theory in general and international affairs in particular is explained with a general shift of interest he experienced from ethical

---

[22] F.H. Bradley (1999) *Collected Works of F.H. Bradley, Volume 1: A Pluralistic Approach to Philosophy 1865–1882*, Keene, C.A. (ed.), Bristol: Thoemmes Press, pp. 57–58.

[23] S. Collini (1978) 'Sociology and Idealism in Britain 1880–1920', *European Journal of Sociology/Archives Européennes de Sociologie*, 19 (1), pp. 10–12.

[24] D. Boucher and A. Vincent (2000) *British Idealism and Political Theory*, Edinburgh: Edinburgh University Press, p. 138.

theory to metaphysics as his work matured.[25] While Ritchie's reflections on international relations were considerably more abundant than those of Bradley, they also ended quite early — in 1903 — with his passing away. The situation in South Africa evidently attracted Ritchie's attention from 1899 onwards and constituted an opportunity for him to reflect upon and considerably change his perception of an ideal international order. The evaluation of Bradley and Ritchie's reflections on international relations up to 1903 shows that their support for an almost militaristic form of imperialism prevents their work from contributing to a British Idealist approach to human rights as it is developed here, even though they share the Greenian approach to civil rights with the rest of the British Idealist School.[26] In this regard, their approach to international relations in the pre-Great War period is discussed in this work as an example of an alternative version of British Idealism that does not support a human rights conception due to its overtly imperialistic and Darwinian approach to international relations.

Contrary to long-standing allegations regarding Bosanquet's deification of the state that rules out any authority above and beyond it, his reflections on the international affairs both before and after the Great War offer significant insights into the possibility of and conditions for a sustainable order of human rights. Although his work is marked by a long-maintained distrust towards supranational entities, his objection is neither unsubstantiated nor unconditional. On the contrary, his work from 1917 onwards reveals his growing support for the League of Nations. For instance, when Bosanquet

---

[25] Bradley's later work mainly focuses on the fields of logic and metaphysics. F.H. Bradley (1876) *Ethical Studies*, London: Henry S. King & Co.; F.H. Bradley (1883) *The Principles of Logic*, London: Oxford University Press; F.H. Bradley (1893) *Appearance and Reality*, London: Swan Sonnenschein; F.H. Bradley (1914) *Essays on Truth and Reality*, Oxford: Clarendon Press.

[26] D.G. Ritchie (1903) *Natural Rights : A Criticism of Some Political and Ethical Conceptions*, London : Swan Sonnenschein; Bradley, *Ethical Studies*, pp. 187–92.

republishes his monumental work *The Philosophical Theory of the State* with a new introductory section, 'How the Theory Stands in 1919', he states that the unifying activity was not limited within the state borders and the actual growth of the League of Nations was meant to lead to the integration of differences.[27] When combined with Bosanquet's adherence to a Greenian theory of rights with only minor revisions, his long-sustained ethical universalism along with his endorsement of cultural pluralism puts him amongst the names whose work inspires this study.

III. The Minor Figures: Mackenzie, Muirhead, Jones, Hetherington, and Haldane

It would have been a far-fetched attempt to deal with all the philosophers who were considered to be British Idealists at some point in a single work.[28] It would also not be productive as some of them were interested only in the metaphysics of idealism, while others outgrew idealism and adopted different and even opposing philosophical positions. Thus, limiting the scope of research to those names who witnessed the Great War — and commented on it — without diverging from the Greenian version of British Idealist political theory, this work focuses on the writings of Sir Henry Jones (1852–1922), John Henry Muirhead (1855–1940), Viscount Richard Burdon Haldane (1856–1928), John Stuart Mackenzie (1860–1935), and Hector James Wright Hetherington (1888–1965). These less known British Idealists were all taught by or worked under the supervision of T.H. Green, Bernard Bosanquet, or the great British Idealist of Glasgow University Edward Caird at some point in their lives and made extensive efforts to give Idealism their own interpretation in their philosophical endeavours. Yet, the contemporary literature remains mostly uninterested in the particular contributions these names

---

27 B. Bosanquet (1920) *The Philosophical Theory of the State, Third Edition,* London: Macmillan and Co. Limited, p. lix.
28 For a comprehensive account of British Idealism see: W.J. Mander (2011) *British Idealism: A History,* Oxford; New York: Oxford University Press.

made to Idealistic thought especially at a time of great international turmoil and intellectual transformation.

There may be two underlying presumptions that resulted in a lack of interest in the works of Jones, Muirhead, Mackenzie, Hetherington, and Haldane. 1) These minor figures among British Idealists were considered to be loyal followers of Green instead of original thinkers on their own capacity. Thus, their works were perceived to be restatements of Green's political theory that did not make any significant contribution to the overall understanding of British Idealist approach to international relations and human rights. 2) By the time these figures started earning their place in British intellectual circles, the Great War broke out, fatally wounding British Idealism as a philosophical school. Their reflections on the matter were received as desperate attempts to justify their pre-Great War position and they were deemed to be theoretically fallacious. Surely, both presumptions are reflective of the reality to a certain extent. For the first presumption, the intellectual biographies of these figures supply ample evidence. It is repeatedly pointed out that Jones, Muirhead, Mackenzie, and Hetherington were not original philosophers, and Haldane was not, strictly speaking, a philosopher. It was argued that in their works 'there was a loss—perhaps it was inevitable—of philosophical power and sheer intellectual excitement. The enthusiasm remained high, but it was spread pretty thin'.[29] Regarding the second presumption, the common conviction is that the First World War marked the end of the Idealist era in British intellectual circles.[30] Especially due to the disillusionment experienced with the state in particular and humanity in general

---

[29] P. Robbins (1982) *British Hegelians 1875–1925*, New York: Taylor & Francis, p. 107.

[30] Morefield, *Covenants without Swords*, p. 61; T. Gouldstone (2005) *The Rise and Decline of Anglican Idealism in the Nineteenth Century*, London: Palgrave Macmillan, p. 35; T. Brooks (2014) Introduction, in Brooks, T. (ed.) *Ethical Citizenship: British Idealism and the Politics of Recognition*, London: Palgrave Macmillan, p. 2.

after the Great War, British Idealists' advocacy of the moral character of the social, political, and international life was perceived to be dangerously naïve. Furthermore, at least some of the Idealists in Britain were viewed as representatives of Prussian militarism and seen as a corrupting influence on the long-standing tradition of British empiricism.[31] By the end of the Great War, the remaining British Idealists were side-line figures within the larger community of British intellectuals. In turn, this perception of insignificance for Jones, Mackenzie, Muirhead, Haldane, and Hetherington have led to an overall lack of attention to their works in the contemporary litera-ture on British Idealist theory of rights. When these minor figures received attention by contemporary scholars their role remained as supporting figures for the arguments of the major Idealists. This overemphasis on the continuity of the Idealist tradition from the main philosophers to their less capable followers led to the per-ception that British Idealism was an unchanging school of thought closed to outside influence. This work shows, on the contrary, that British Idealism reacted to both political and international phenomena taking place around them and to the shifts and variations of ideas within the larger circle of British intellectual thought. From the works of minor figures in British Idealism that were published from 1914 onwards it can be discerned that they were part of a wider movement from imperialism to international-ism in British intellectual circles and that this shift was very significant in terms of creating a favourable intellectual atmosphere for the transformation of Green's rights theory into an inter-nationalist theory of human rights by other British Idealists. Before moving onto the lengthy story of this transformation and its culmi-nation in a theory of human rights, it is helpful to have a look at the British Idealists who are the main actors in this work.

---

[31] T.C. Kennedy (1973) 'Public Opinion and the Conscientious Objector, 1915-1919', *Journal of British Studies*, 12 (2), p. 106.

Henry Jones was born on 30 November 1852 at Llangernyw, Denbighshire, Wales. He came from a family with very limited economic means. In 1870, he won a scholarship to Bangor Normal Teacher Training College and by 1873 he was the headmaster of a small country school in Brynamman, South Wales. In 1875 he won another scholarship, to Glasgow University where he planned to study theology. By that time, he was already registered as a Calvinistic minister. Under the influence of Edward Caird, however, his interest in theology gave way to a fascination with philosophy and metaphysics. In 1884, he became a Professor of Philosophy and Political Economy at the University College of North Wales. In 1894 he was appointed to Glasgow University's Chair of Moral Philosophy. During the First World War, Jones delivered a series of lectures at the Rice Institute titled the 'Obligations and Privileges of Citizenship'.[32] Especially in the second and third lectures he focused on the questions of international relations and war. He also wrote several essays and books during and after the Great War in which he strongly defended the necessity of forming a League of Peace.[33]

John Henry Muirhead was born in Glasgow in 1855. In 1875, Muirhead graduated from Glasgow University where he was greatly influenced by Edward Caird. Following his graduation, Muirhead won a scholarship to Balliol College, Oxford, where he met Green and his student and fellow idealist Richard Lewis Nettleship.[34] In 1888, he became a lecturer in Mental and Moral Science at Royal

---

[32] H. Jones (1919) 'The Obligations and Privileges of Citizenship — a Plea for the Study of Social Science', *Rice Institute Pamphlet – Rice University Studies*, 6 (3), pp. 119–42.

[33] H. Jones (1918) *Form the League of Peace Now: An Appeal to My Fellow Citizens*, London: The League of Nations Union. For a detailed account of his life and philosophical work see: D. Boucher and A. Vincent (1993) *A Radical Hegelian: Political and Social Philosophy of Henry Jones*, Cardiff: University of Wales Press; H. Jones (1922) *Old Memories: Autobiography by Sir Henry Jones, C.H.*, Jones, T. (ed.), London: Hodder and Stoughton Limited.

[34] D. Boucher (ed.) (1997) *The British Idealists*, Cambridge; New York: Cambridge University Press, p. xl.

Holloway College. In 1896, Muirhead acquired a professorship in the Philosophy and Political Economy Department of Mason College, Birmingham.[35] His publications during and after the Great War include *Rule and End in Morals* which is a restatement of Green's ethics, *German Philosophy in Relation to the War* which defends Hegelian idealism against its critics, and *Social Purpose: A Contribution to a Philosophy of Civic Society* which includes a chapter on the external relations of states. But, above all, Muirhead is mostly known as the editor of the 'Library of Philosophy'. The entry on Muirhead in *The Dictionary of Nineteenth Century British Philosophers* reads: 'Muirhead added little that was really new to the idealism he been taught, but he was an important example of an advocate for that worldview, and kept the idealist impulse alive until well into the twentieth century...'[36]

Richard Burdon Haldane's name was not included in the above-mentioned dictionary as there is no consensus on the question of whether he was a practical academic or a statesman with a particularly philosophical mind-set. Haldane was born in Edinburgh in 1856. During his studies in Edinburgh University he got acquainted with Hegelian philosophy and pursued his studies further in Gottingen under Hermann Lotze. Upon his return to Britain, Haldane became involved in politics and was elected MP for East Lothian in 1885. In 1905, after declining the positions of Attorney-general and Home Secretary, he accepted the War Office and was considered to be very effective in reforming the British army. In 1912 he was appointed Lord Chancellor. Haldane played an active role in the British mobilization for the Great War upon the request of Prime Minister Asquith. Yet his ties to Germany and German nationals fuelled a press campaign that accused Haldane of Prussianism. The campaign proved effective and he was left out of the coalition

---

[35] S. Brown (2005) *Dictionary of Twentieth-Century British Philosophers*, 2 Volumes, London: Thoemmes, p. 701.

[36] Brown, *Dictionary*, p. 702.

government that was formed in 1915. A considerable part of his written work was produced during and after the First World War.[37]

John Stuart Mackenzie was born in 1860, near Glasgow. In 1877, Mackenzie started his studies in Glasgow University where he was taught by Edward Caird and Henry Jones. In 1890, Mackenzie was elected to a Fellowship at Trinity College and in 1895 he secured a Professorship of Philosophy at University College, Cardiff.[38] It would not be an exaggeration to say that he was the most eclectic of the British Idealists. In his obituary published in *Mind*, Muirhead wrote that Mackenzie 'differed from contemporaries of the same school in the exceptional breadth of his reading, the hardly less exceptional range of his travels, and (perhaps as a consequence) in the singular hospitality of his mind for suggestions coming from different points of view from his own'.[39] After 1914, the ethical nature of the state and its rights and duties in international relations constituted a considerable part of his work. Although he put forward no fundamentally new theses, his reflections on the political questions of his time were exemplary of the British Idealist position especially after the Great War. Additionally, his reflections on the basis and scope of human rights in the 1920s constitute one of the primary sources of this study.

The youngest among these names, Hector James Wright Hetherington, was born in Cowdenbeath, Scotland. Between 1905 and 1910 he studied at Glasgow University where he was a student of Henry Jones. For the following four years he worked as Jones's assistant. In 1936, Hetherington became the Principal and Vice-Chancellor of Glasgow University and remained in this post until his

---

[37] R.B. Haldane (1918) *The Future of Democracy: An Address by Lord Haldane*, London: Headley Bros. Publishers; R.B. Haldane (1920) *Before the War*, London: Cassell And Company; R.B. Haldane (1922) *The Philosophy of Humanism and of Other Subjects*, New Haven: Yale University Press; R.B. Haldane (1921) *Reign of Relativity*, New Haven: Yale University Press.

[38] R. Metz (1938) *A Hundred Years of British Philosophy*, London: George Allen & Unwin, p. 313; Boucher, *The British Idealists*, p. xxxix.

[39] J.H. Muirhead (1936) 'J.S. Mackenzie (1860–1935)', *Mind*, 45 (178), p. 277.

retirement in 1961. Although Hetherington was an Idealist philosopher, writing was not his calling. He preferred focusing his energy
on his administrative duties. Still, the limited amount of written
work he produced contributes greatly to the formation of an internationalist approach to human rights. Most importantly, for the
purposes of this work, his *International Labour Legislation*, published
in 1920, offers important insights into the practical aspects of a
British Idealist theory of human rights.

IV. British Idealism and the Historiography
of Internationalism and Human Rights

The British Idealists' increasingly marginal position within the
intellectual sphere after the Great War significantly limited their
direct impact upon the later theories of human rights. It was their
distant cousins, international idealists like Alfred Zimmern and
Gilbert Murray, who dominated the intellectual sphere during the
twenty years crisis and who receive much more attention in contemporary histories of the inter-war period. Still, paying attention to
the 'internationalist' adaptation of Green's theory of rights by the
younger Idealists contributes to our understanding of human rights
and internationalism by filling a void at the intersection of two literatures: the history of the idea of human rights and the historiography
of intellectual thought on internationalism at the end of the long
nineteenth century. While the first literature predominantly deals
with the post-war (connoting the Second World War) period, the
second literature rarely pays attention to the concept of human rights
during the years following the Great War. Thus, the younger
Idealists' international approach to human rights remains
unexamined.

In his study of the recent historiography of human rights, Devin
Pendas argues that the field is marked by 'a clear lack of consensus…
about even the most elementary contours of the subject' and the
most basic question in regards to the origins of human rights proves

to be the most contested one.[40] The history of the concept of human rights has been traced back to the works of ancient Greek and medieval philosophers as well as to religious texts such as the Bible and the Koran.[41] Alternatively, the American and the French Revolutions and the Enlightenment idea of the 'rights of man' that they promoted have been considered to be predecessors of the concept of human rights by those who perceive it as 'part of a long and honourable tradition of dissent, resistance, and rebellion against the oppression of power and the injustice of law'.[42] A radical break from the accepted historiography of the idea of human rights is offered by Samuel Moyn in *The Last Utopia: Human Rights in History*. Moyn contends that a more accurate understanding of human rights needs to focus on a 'much more recent timeline' going back only to the 1970s, during which human rights emerged as the dominant utopian project 'to make the world a better place'.[43] Although in a later piece, Moyn acknowledges the continuity of ideas from past to present in shaping our understanding of human rights, his reading does not attribute an essential importance to the source of human rights idea from 'Greek philosophy and monotheistic religion, European natural law and early modern revolutions, horror against American slavery and Adolf Hitler's Jew-killing'.[44] In line with Moyn's reading, the literature on human rights takes the post-war period during which several human rights declarations, including the Universal Declaration of Human Rights of 1948, are articulated as the decisive point in

---

[40] D.O. Pendas (2012) 'Toward a New Politics? On the Recent Historiography of Human Rights', *Contemporary European History*, 21 (1), pp. 95–96.

[41] D.N. Stamos (2015) *Myth of Universal Human Rights: Its Origin, History, and Explanation, Along with a More Humane Way*, London; New York: Routledge, p. 12.

[42] C. Douzinas (2007) *Human Rights and Empire: The Political Philosophy of Cosmopolitanism*, New York: Routledge-Cavendish, p. 13.

[43] S. Moyn, *The Last Utopia*, p. 7.

[44] S. Moyn (2013) 'The Continuing Perplexities of Human Rights', *Qui Parle*, 22 (1), p. 96.

its emergence if not as its genesis.[45] The post Great War period on the other hand — with a couple of exceptions — does not receive such attention from the historians of the idea of human rights, mostly due to the marginal position occupied by the concern for human rights during the years following the Great War.

Here, it is necessary to acknowledge that rights or human rights was not a popular topic of discussion in the period when British Idealism was a prominent force in British intellectual circles. The natural rights theory had been under attack for more than a hundred years on multiple fronts. Bentham and his utilitarian disciples were criticizing natural rights for being an imaginary construct in political theory. When utilitarian philosophy became the dominant philosophical position in Britain by the mid-nineteenth century, the importance traditionally attributed to natural rights by liberal thinkers was replaced by an emphasis on the primacy of liberty in political organization.[46] By the end of the nineteenth century, utilitarians, led by Mill, were recognizing the value of rights in pursuing the moral end of 'happiness' and defending their protection, but their recognition remained a conditional one.[47] Furthermore, rights were perceived as a possible threat to the level of 'liberty' attained in the society by utilitarian thinkers so far as their protection was strictly dependent on the existence of laws, and law by definition was an encroachment on the 'natural' liberty of individuals.[48] An alternative attack on 'natural rights' came from the Marxist front. In a well-known passage of *On the Jewish Question* Marx wrote: 'None of the so-called rights of man, therefore, go beyond egoistic man... that is, an individual withdrawn into himself, into the confines of his

---

[45]   S.-L. Hoffmann (2010) *Human Rights in the Twentieth Century*, New York: Cambridge University Press, p. 14; E. Hafner-Burton (2013) *Making Human Rights a Reality*, Princeton: Princeton University Press, p. 46.

[46]   W. Sweet (2005) *Idealism and Rights: The Social Ontology of Human Rights in the Political Thought of Bernard Bosanquet*, 2nd ed., Lanham: UPA, p. 12.

[47]   Sweet, *Idealism and Rights*, p. 35.

[48]   D. Beetham (1995) 'Introduction: Human Rights in the Study of Politics', *Political Studies*, 43 (1), p. 2.

private interests and private caprice, and separated from the community.'[49] Marx's objection to the rights of man was related to the conception of man as an isolated being in natural rights theories. He argued that these rights were both the product and the servers of an atomistic perception of man with selfish interests that is conceptually positioned in an antagonistic relation to the rest of the society.[50] Faced with criticism from two directions the natural rights theory was discredited by the end of the nineteenth century. In recognition of the disrepute the theory of natural rights had been experiencing, Ritchie started his book *Natural Rights* by saying 'when I began, some three years ago, to write a paper on "Natural Rights," which has grown by degrees into the present volume, I had a certain fear that in criticising that famous theory I might be occupied in slaying the already slain'.[51] While the 'natural rights' theory was not a tenable position anymore, alternative theories of rights were not readily emerging in this period, except in the works of British Idealists.

The historians of intellectual thought interested in the history of internationalism, however, find plenty of material to work with in the final decades of the long nineteenth century as well as during the years that followed the outbreak of the Great War.[52] The final years of the Great War, marked by a boom in the literature on the possible designs for a world federation or a league of peace, prove to be of special interest to intellectual historians. Works by the New Liberals such as Leonard Hobhouse and J.A. Hobson, members of the Fabian

---

[49] K. Marx (1844) *On the Jewish Question*, Deutsch-Französische Jahrbücher, p. 13.

[50] M. Hann (2016) *Egalitarian Rights Recognition*, London: Palgrave Macmillan UK.

[51] Ritchie, *Natural Rights*, 'Preface'.

[52] M. Mazower (2009) *No Enchanted Palace: The End of Empire and the Ideological Origins of the United Nations, Lawrence Stone Lectures*, Princeton: Princeton University Press; D. Bell (2007) *Victorian Visions of Global Order: Empire and International Relations in Nineteenth Century Political Thought*, Cambridge: Cambridge University Press.

Society like Bernard Shaw, and the participants of Alfred Milner's Round Table offer insights into the conditions envisioned for ensuring future international peace and order through establishing a stable and cooperative international society. In this literature, internationalism and imperialism are not perceived to be mutually exclusive positions but their primacy within the intellectual mind-set is thought to be inversely associated. While imperialists' hopes for a cooperative international order in the pre-Great War period is limited within the boundaries of the 'civilized nations', from 1915 onwards the vocabulary of civilization experiences a steady decline in popularity, leaving its place to the concepts of national autonomy and self-government in accordance with the rising internationalist sentiment.[53] This shift in intellectuals' approach to non-European peoples is not perceived to be a sincere and complete detachment from the imperialist sentiments they entertained only a couple of decades earlier. Susan Pederson argues, for instance, the mandates system of the League of Nations under which 'mandated territories were not better governed than colonies' was the result of a 'potent brew of liberal internationalism, imperial humanism, and sheer territorial acquisitiveness'.[54]

While it remains impossible to measure the sincerity of the change of sentiment towards non-European peoples among liberal intellectuals, a profound shift can be observed in the way international relations were discussed in Britain in the years following the outbreak of the Great War. According to Casper Sylvest, the most significant characteristic of this change was the move from moral internationalist arguments to institutional internationalist ones in the 1920s.[55] The moral internationalist position, which emphasized the

---

53 D. Bell (2007) *The Idea of Greater Britain: Empire and the Future of the World Order, 1889–1900*, Princeton: Princeton University Press, p. 96.

54 S. Pedersen (2015) *The Guardians: The League of Nations and The Crisis of Empire*, Oxford: Oxford University Press, pp. 4–27.

55 C. Sylvest (2005) 'Continuity and Change in British Liberal Internationalism, c. 1900–1930', *Review of International Studies*, 31 (2), p. 269.

'need for a new international consciousness' that can 'assure progress, order, and continuity internationally', was superseded by a growing interest in international mechanisms and international law in this period.[56] This was also the period during which British Idealism lost its prominence within the British intellectual sphere. In an intellectual environment that focused on the topics of specific 'policy objectives' on the matters of 'disarmament, international legislation, and peace' the remaining British Idealists continued to work with the highly metaphysical language they inherited from T.H. Green.[57] While this disparity between their moral way of theorizing and the institutionalist turn within the intellectual sphere led to their further marginalization in the 1920s, it also enabled them to put forward a unique approach to internationalism and human rights.

Apparently, the post-war writings of the British Idealists fall in the blind spots of the literatures on the historiography of human rights and international relations. Still, their study offers important insights into the political, international, and intellectual circumstances that enabled the emergence of an internationalist approach to human rights. First, theirs was a singular position amongst other British philosophical schools of thought of their time in the central importance attributed to rights in their thought system. The political philosophy of T.H. Green served in this period as a reviving force for the concept of rights by constructing an alternative to the discredited theory of 'natural rights'. T.H. Green and other British Idealists who adopted his theory of rights offered a new approach to rights that was capable of meeting the criticisms of both the utilitarians and the Marxists. Second, these Idealists' transition from imperialism to internationalism came with an underlying conceptual shift from cultural monism to multiculturalism. Following a period of 'supposed' monism that perceived cultural, social, and political

---

[56] Sylvest, 'Continuity and Change', pp. 266–68.
[57] Sylvest, 'Continuity and Change', p. 278.

differences as a symptom of inadequate compliance with the ideal of civilization, their post Great War writings show their recognition of the existence and necessity of cultural particularities of communities in a cooperative world order. In their attempt to reconcile these particularities with a universal morality, they used Green's theory of rights, which is based on the universal ideal of 'self-realization' that can be pursued in various cultural and political settings.[58] Thus, it can be argued that the 'classical' internationalist position adopted by Mackenzie, Jones, Muirhead, Hetherington, and Haldane in the years following the Great War serves as a 'middle ground' between communitarianism and cosmopolitanism.[59] It also constitutes a nuanced approach to human rights insofar as it puts forward a universal moral justification for the recognition of human rights based on the ideal of 'self-realization' while acknowledging the possible variations in its application in each particular community.

The importance attributed to the historical transition from imperialism to internationalism in the evolution of the British Idealists' approach to human rights in this work does not necessarily preclude the universal character of human rights. This study also does not aim to offer an alternative point of origin for the idea of human rights, nor does it claim that the younger generation's internationalist approach to human rights had a significant impact on contemporary human rights theories. This work simply draws attention to a unique approach to human rights that first emerged under special political and international conditions. It highlights the conditions which forced a group of thinkers belonging to the Idealist school of thought to deal with the newly (re-)emerging problem of reconciling cultural multiplicity with moral universality. Consider-

---

58   M. Dimova-Cookson (2006) 'Resolving Moral Conflicts: British Idealist and Contemporary Liberal Approaches to Value Pluralism and Moral Conduct', in Dimova-Cookson, M. & Mander, W. (eds.) *T.H. Green*, Oxford: Clarendon Press, pp. 292–317.

59   P. Lawler (2005) 'The Good State: In Praise of 'Classical' Internationalism', *Review of International Studies*, 31 (3), p. 432.

ing the same issue still constitutes the bulk of the problem regarding theories of human rights, the internationalist approach maintained by these thinkers offers a significant alternative to prioritizing either the universal or the particular. As internationalism has been offered as a middle-way solution or a third option to the cosmopolitanism–communitarianism divide in the recent human rights literature, the example set by these thinkers may contribute to recent attempts to develop an internationalist theory of human rights. Although Moyn argues that internationalism is 'merely one form of cosmopolitanism', the central position occupied by the nation-state in the Idealist understanding of human rights points to a different outcome.[60] Based on the specific example of an internationalist approach to human rights detailed in this work, it is maintained in line with Lawler that while an internationalist order of human rights requires states to act 'in a cosmopolitan minded manner' it does not aim to supersede the international system of nation-states for a unified world order.[61]

The structure of this book simply follows the historical flow of the story that it aims to unravel. In the following — second — chapter several British Idealists' approach to international order and imperialism is scrutinized in the pre-Great War period. This chapter offers insights into the pioneering British Idealists' perceptions of the nature of international order from 1870s onwards while also trying to locate the positions of minor Idealists in relation with their more prominent counterparts. Some of the British Idealists' reflections on the Boer War offer valuable insights into their perception of the British Empire and imperialism in this time period. The third chapter focuses on the impact of the Great War on the British Idealists' attitude towards international order and to the question of war and peace. Works produced by Muirhead, Haldane, and Henry Jones

---

[60] S. Moyn (2014) 'The Universal Declaration of Human Rights of 1948 in the History of Cosmopolitanism', *Critical Inquiry*, 40 (4), p. 371.
[61] Lawler, 'The Good State', p. 431.

supply ample material to perceive the source and nature of the shift
in their ideas due to their disillusionment with imperialism and
'Western Civilization'. The fourth chapter deals with British
Idealists' resurfacing optimism at the end of the Great War, mostly
based on the hope that a League of Nations would ensure cooperation among equal and independent nations. In this period, by
putting emphasis on the compatibility of true patriotism and true
humanism, British Idealists try to discern the underlying unity of
humanity under the apparent multiplicity of particular cultures.
Their reflections from this period create the basis for the internationalist approach to the question of prevention of war as well as
to the establishment of a moral basis for a universal order of human
rights. The fifth chapter identifies the main tenets of the internationalist theory of human rights that can be discerned from the
post-1914 writings of the British Idealists. Special attention is paid to
Mackenzie's list of human rights, which is quite comprehensive in its
scope. This chapter also discerns the impact of Greenian political
philosophy on the internationalist position occupied by the minor
idealist thinkers in the post Great War era.

While pursuing the development of an internationalist approach
to human rights constitutes the main purpose of this work, a number
of supplementary arguments emerge that are also worth attention
and further scrutiny in the future. One of the most striking is
Bosanquet's apparent impact on minor British Idealists in appre-
ciating the particular contributions of all peoples to the overall
experience and development of humanity. Contrary to the allegations that Bosanquet's approach to international sphere was not conducive to a human rights theory, his emphasis on cultural pluralism
constitutes an indispensable part of an internationalist approach to
human rights as other Idealists developed it in the 1920s. Another
important argument this study upholds is in regard to the relation
between British Idealism as a school of thought and the British
liberal intelligentsia, especially from 1900 onwards. While reading
works of British Idealists in this period in isolation from the general
British intellectual thought may mistake the evolution of their think-

ing under adverse and rapidly changing circumstances as confusion and inconsistency, locating them within the larger intellectual evolution in Britain shows that their evolution was not unique. Far from being deviant figures from the larger intellectual society, most British Idealists were part of the mainstream position as liberal imperialists before the Great War and as internationalists and supporters of the League of Nations following its outbreak. Still, their similarity to the mainstream intellectual positions does not mean that they were unoriginal thinkers. They were unique in the sense that they inherited a very specific theoretical framework through which they continued to reflect on political and international phenomena. The centrality of rights in their theoretical position made their work unique in the post-1914 period. While the majority of liberal intellectuals were focused on the questions of international arbitration and reduction of armaments, British Idealists' works contained a pristine example of an internationalist theory of human rights.

Chapter 2

British Idealists

International Relations, Imperialism, and the Second Boer War

The Second Boer War (1899–1902) proved to be a very strong incentive for many British intellectuals to elaborate on their views on imperialism in general and on the British Empire in particular. Ironically enough, it was not a war between a colonized people and their colonizers; it was a war between two European powers that claimed a right to rule over the same part of Africa. The issue of control over parts of South Africa historically constituted a source of tension between the Dutch and the British forces in the region and caused the First Boer War in 1880. Following an uneasy agreement after the defeat of British forces in 1881, South Africa was partitioned between independent Dutch — the Transvaal and the Orange Free State — and British — Cape and Natal — settlements. For those who supported the British, the Dutch were disrespecting the rights of their non-Boer citizens by denying them the right to vote. While these non-Boer citizens included native Africans, the British were particularly interested in the voting rights of those who came from British descent. The Dutch, on the other hand, argued that the British were interested in the voting rights of their citizens only because they aimed to take control of the gold and diamond mining industries in Dutch settlements by having more British voters than Boer ones. The Second Boer War broke out in 1899 following the ultimatum of the President of the Transvaal, Paul Kruger, in which

he demanded that the British forces leave the borders of the Trans-
vaal and the Orange Free State in 48 hours.[1] While in the rest of
Europe support for the Boer forces prevailed, in Britain, Kruger's
ultimatum was received as a just cause for war against the Boer
Republics in South Africa.[2] Coupled with the understanding that
Africans were gravely mistreated within the Boer Republics, the
British war effort was justified in the eyes of the general public.
Thus, use of military force against the Boer militia was endowed
with the moral conditions defined by *ius ad bellum* in line with the
prevailing understanding of the just war theory.

As the war effort prolonged and the much-anticipated victory
was continually delayed, the British public started to question not
the justification of the war but the methods that were used to achieve
success against the Boer forces. This was mostly thanks to the efforts
of the New Liberal intellectuals who proved to be the most vocal
among the pro-Boers in Britain. Especially the publication of news in
regard to the use of 'scorched earth' policy by the British army
against the Boer farmers raised questions in regard to the moral
quality of the war effort. As the news of the suffering of the civilian
population in South Africa due to the burning of Boer farms reached
Britain not only the morality but also the legality of the British war
effort under the 'civilised war customs of the 1899 Hague Convention' began to be put under scrutiny.[3] Equally important was the
work of the Committee of Ladies and especially of Emily Hobhouse
in publicizing the atrocities committed in the refugee camps in
which Boer women, children, and the elderly were gathered by the

---

[1] For a detailed account of the British-Boer controversy that precedes the
    Second Boer War see: A. Porter (ed.) (2001) *The Oxford History of the
    British Empire: Volume III: The Nineteenth Century*, Oxford: Oxford Uni-
    versity Press, pp. 603–83.
[2] P.M. Krebs (1992) ''The Last of the Gentlemen's Wars': Women in the
    Boer War Concentration Camp Controversy', *History Workshop*, 33, p. 50.
[3] B. Nasson (2002) 'Waging Total War in South Africa: Some Centenary
    Writings on the Anglo-Boer War, 1899–1902', *The Journal of Military
    History*, 66 (3), p. 826.

British forces. Hobhouse reported upon her return from South Africa that those refugees who were known to have relatives among the Boer combatants were penalized by reductions in their rations.[4] Though the conditions of the camps were improved following the recommendations prepared by the Committee of Ladies, methods adopted by the British forces in South Africa raised considerable concern in British public opinion. After all, 'it was one thing to celebrate... the battlefield heroism displayed at Paardeberg, but quite another to remain comfortable with the burning of Boer farms and the herding of Boer civilians into squalid and disease-ridden "concentration camps"'.[5] Although Kruger's ultimatum supplied the British Empire with an acceptable justification for going into war, the methods adopted by the British Army especially towards the end of the war did not satisfy the dictates of *ius in bello*.[6]

Still, the intellectual support for imperialism during the Boer War came from various and seemingly divergent groups in Britain. While Bernard Shaw pushed Fabians to stand with the imperial cause, they were not the only socialists who supported the war against the Boer forces.[7] The well-known pro-Boer New Liberal thinker J.A. Hobson explained socialists' position on the matter as follows:

> Some liberals with socialistic leanings and a few professed socialists support the South African War and the imperialism it embodies... as follows: if an individual member of society, owning land, neglects to develop its natural resources or so uses it as to make it a public nuisance, or refuses permission to the public to utilise it for fair compensation, it is admitted that society has a right to compel him to refrain from such neglect or abuse and to deprive him of the control of his property if he resists... The Transvaal, it is contended, was such a State; it would not develop its resources properly nor would it

---

4   Thompson, *A Wider Patriotism*, p. 64.

5   C. Williams (2013) "Our War History in Cartoons is Unique': J.M. Staniforth, British Public Opinion, and the South African War, 1899–1902', *War in History*, 20 (4) (November 1), p. 493.

6   C. Greenwood (1983) 'The Relationship between Ius ad Bellum and Ius in Bello', *Review of International Studies*, 9 (4), p. 221.

7   J. Alexander (2009) *Shaw's Controversial Socialism*, Gainesville: University Press of Florida, p. 156.

let others develop them; its backward civilization was a contamination and a menace to the States around it.[8]

While some socialists' support for the Boer War strengthened the
imperialists' hand by being a proof of 'cross-party support' for the
war, those leftists who were pro-Boer were too disillusioned with the
political and cultural atmosphere in Britain to put up a strong opposition. While members of the Labour Party and some local Socialists
groups were supporting the Boer forces in this war, they were too
disheartened and too disorganized to create an anti-war front in
Britain.[9]

On the Liberal side, support for imperialism was not scarce
either. Although, for the post-colonial mind, liberal values constitute
a stark contrast with an imperial outlook, the liberal imperialist
position was populated by many prominent liberal intellectual
figures by the end of the nineteenth century.[10] To put it simply, the
liberal imperialists usually defended the imperial agenda for they
believed it would benefit humanity through spreading enlightenment to backward corners of the world. Bernard Porter argued:
'Liberal imperialists like Richard Haldane, Sir Edward Grey and
Herbert Henry Asquith were men whom all but the most hidebound
Conservative imperialist could trust…'[11] Reportedly, Haldane was
actually one of the first liberal public figures who expressed his
support to the British Governor in South Africa, Alfred Milner,
through a private letter when the news of the impending war
reached Britain. Haldane wrote in his letter to Milner, who was

---

8   J.A. Hobson (1902) 'Socialistic Imperialism', *International Journal of Ethics*,
     12, p. 44.
9   G. Hinton (2015) 'Newcastle and the Boer War: Regional Reactions to an
     Imperial War', *Northern History*, 52 (2) (September 1), p. 293.
10   K. Mantena (2010) *Alibis of Empire: Henry Maine and the Ends of Liberal
     Imperialism*, Princeton: Princeton University Press; T. McCarthy (2009)
     Race, Empire, and the Idea of Human Development, Cambridge: Cambridge
     University Press.
11   B. Porter (2004) *The Lion's Share: A Short History of British Imperialism,
     1850-2004*, 4th ed., Harlow: Pearson/Longman, p. 201.

accused by some for sabotaging the negotiations and hastening the outbreak of the war, 'Transvaal Ultimatum is published this morning! Do not think that... Liberals as a whole have misunderstood your policy. On the contrary, I am satisfied that four-fifths of our people really follow and assent to it'.[12] Such support from Haldane was consistent with the considerable amount of importance he attributed to maintaining a strong and united British Empire as a civilizing force in the world and with the general liberal imperialist position. Even though liberal imperialism was not as strong as it was in the first half of the nineteenth century, it was still influential. Its ethical legitimacy was traditionally found in Mill's liberal defence of the Empire and with every challenge it faced it developed new defensive argumentations.

It was the New Liberals who directed the strongest criticism to imperialist policies pursued in South Africa in the Liberal Camp. Among them Hobson was the earliest and the most enthusiastic critic of the Boer War. Others joined him as well, as they perceived the British Empire's failure in delivering the promised outcome: an easy victory that would serve humanity. In a collected edition published in 1900, for instance, G.H. Perris argued against the 'arrogance' of British imperialism as it was evident in their hostility towards the Boer, which created an animosity among nations that required each nation to maintain a large navy and army. Similarly, in 1905 L.T. Hobhouse wrote: 'Imperialism was to give us a cheap and easy victory, it gave us nearly three years' war. It was to sweep away the abuses of a corrupt, incompetent and over-expensive administration. The present administration of the Transvaal is more costly than the former, and more completely in the hands of the capitalists...'[13] According to Hobhouse the only acceptable position in regards to the British Empire at that time was to accept the naked fact 'that we

---

12 G.H. Perris (1900) 'The New Internationalism', in Coit, S. (ed.) *Ethical Democracy*, London: Grant Richards, p. 54.
13 L.T. Hobhouse (1905) *Democracy and Reaction*, New York: G.P. Putnam's Sons, p. 41.

are maintaining a distinct policy of aggressive warfare on a large scale and with great persistence'.[14] The only outcome that can be expected from ignoring these facts was introducing 'an atmosphere of self-sophistication, or in one syllable, of cant into our politics which is perhaps more corrupting than the unblushing denial of rights'.[15] Still, Hobson's and Hobhouse's strong criticisms of the British Empire did not culminate into a total refutation of imperialism in general. And in this regard the expectations of the British Idealists like Henry Jones or Muirhead from a true empire—as it is explained in the following pages—were not so much different from the type of imperialism the New Liberals were willing to support.[16] Still, the New Liberals did not find the mitigating position adopted by mainstream Idealists on the matter of imperialism critical enough. Hobhouse, who proved to be a persistent critic of British Idealism for decades to come, argued that when the British Idealist theory was judged not by its profession but by its fruits, it became obvious that it was no more than a fiction, and a dangerous fiction for that matter. He maintained that idealist philosophy proved to be a useful tool for those who tried to find reasons for ignoring the wrongs committed by the British Empire.[17]

Contrary to Hobhouse's assumptions, British Idealists did not constitute a unified front on the matter of imperialism and the Boer War. Still, there were recognizable patterns of argumentation that allow us to discern two different approaches to the matter from Idealist thinkers. There was Bradley and Ritchie's position that combined Hegelian idealism with evolutionary ethics and justified a process of natural selection in the international arena. This seems to be the correct target for the criticism Hobhouse directed towards the British Idealist school of thought in general. The second position was the mainstream Idealist one that followed Green's teaching and

---

14 Hobhouse, *Democracy and Reaction*, p. 28.
15 Hobhouse, *Democracy and Reaction*, p. 28.
16 Boucher and Vincent, *A Radical Hegelian*, p. 154.
17 Hobhouse, *Democracy and Reaction*, pp. 77–78.

substituted the grounds on which the Idealist perception of international order evolved during and after the Great War. While Green himself cautioned against the potential adverse effects of imperialism on the international order and the relations among European states long before the Boer War, his students were less concerned about its possible ramifications. Although these British Idealists did not give unconditional support to the imperial policy pursued by the British government, they still advocated a 'true' form of imperialism that depended on education of and communication and cooperation with subject peoples rather than mere military occupation.

I. T.H. Green

Although Lee Thompson notes in the introductory chapter of his book on Alfred Milner that Green was 'credited with laying down the philosophical foundations of Liberal Imperialism', there is no evidence that Green's liberalism was an imperialist one.[18] While some of Green's students from Balliol College—including Alfred Milner—turned out to be ardent supporters of the British Empire, Green himself was not an open advocate of the Empire. On the contrary, in his reflections on the international order, Green expressed his distrust towards an imperial mind-set and warned against the militarist nationalism it might lead to in the future. Furthermore, for Green, use of military power was always a moral wrong regardless of the end it was supposed to serve. For him, a war waged against an 'inferior civilization' would not have been morally permissible even if it resulted in the elevation of all humanity into a higher level of civilization.

In his major works Green seldom dealt with popular issues in politics and international relations. He often referred to instances from the Greek polis, the Roman Empire, and English history when he wanted to substantiate his philosophical argumentation with concrete examples while at the same time avoiding passing moral

---

18 Thompson, *A Wider Patriotism*, p. 3.

judgment on these events. A similar caution can be observed in his evaluation of contemporary ideas and institutions. In his *Lectures,* he admits his hesitancy to judge: 'we are not, indeed, entitled to say that it could have been brought about in any other way. It is true to say (if we know what we are about in saying it) that nothing which happens in the world could have happened otherwise than it has.'[19] The British Empire, for Green, was an institution in existence and criticizing its existence was a futile endeavour. Still, Green's scepticism towards the moral legitimacy of imperialism as well as his concern for its potential negative impact on international relations can be discerned from his remarks on the Ottoman Empire and Russian Czarism. Furthermore, in his *Lectures,* Green identifies imperialism as one of the most immediate threats to peace among European powers.

For Green every human community was based on the dictates of the same moral principles and development of a system of rights and obligations in every society was almost a natural outcome of man's moral nature. But Green recognized a difference between Christian nations and others in terms of the degree to which they developed an adequate and egalitarian system of rights and obligations in their societies. He argued in his *Prolegomena*: 'However retarded, equality before the law has at length been secured, at least ostensibly, for all full-grown and sane human beings throughout Christendom.'[20] There were factors inherent in the doctrine of Christianity that led to this end, the most important of which was a universal interest in the betterment of all mankind. Christianity, especially in the distinct rational form it attained through Hegelian philosophy, offered the mind-set in which the particular (individual) had the means to identify himself with the universal (humanity).[21] An essential point

---

[19] Green, *Lectures,* p. 169.
[20] Green, *Prolegomena,* p. 243.
[21] T.H. Green (1997) *Works: Vol. 5 Additional Writings,* Nicholson, P.P. (ed.), Bristol: Thoemmes Press, p. 182; C. Tyler (ed.) (2008) *Unpublished Manu-*

to take into account is that for Green it was not the established church and theology of Christianity that distinguished Christian nations from others in terms of their moral advancement.[22] On the contrary, a singular interest in dogmatic forms of Christianity tended to overshadow the 'living stream of christian experience', which supplied the bases for Christian citizenship.[23] The essential moral significance of Jesus was based on the fact that he as an historical and eternal figure represented the unity of the divine with nature and humanity and in doing so set forth the ideal of Christian life and citizenship.[24] In other words, it was the example of Jesus who embodied the capacity of mankind for moral progress and perfection that set the Christian citizen's duty to strive towards that ideal in his own life both as an individual and as a part of a social whole. Such a consciousness of unity of the individual with the universal distinguished the Christian citizen and constituted the basic premises which European communities were founded upon.

Green's emphasis on the centrality of Christendom in the development of European civilization was not based on a prejudice towards other religions. Rather, he perceived an intrinsic link between the Christian creed and the way European civilization evolved to surpass other civilizations. Based on his reflections on Britain's position *vis-à-vis* the Russo-Turkish animosity in the 1870s, it would not be wrong to designate the Turkish Empire as an antithesis of European values in Green's mind. In a number of speeches he delivered, Green was highly critical of the possibility of England being 'enlisted in a foolish war with Russia in defence of some imaginary British interests, but really on behalf of this Turkish

---

scripts in British Idealism: Political Philosophy, Theology and Social Thought, 2nd ed., Exeter: Imprint Academic, p. 6.

22 For a detailed discussion of Green's reflections on Christian theology see: Gouldstone, *Rise and Decline of Anglican Idealism in the Nineteenth Century*.

23 R.L. Nettleship (ed.) (1888) *Works of Thomas Hill Green, vol. III: Miscellanies and Memoir*, London: Longmans, Green, and Co., p. 170.

24 Green, *Prolegomena to Ethics*, p. 238.

despotism, which was a scandal to humanity'.[25] Although Russia itself was despotically governed by the absolute coercive power of the Czar and the habitual obedience of its people, it was still possible to call it a state.[26] Whereas the Turkish Empire failed to meet any of the requirements of being a state so long as it was merely a power 'which denies the simplest personal rights to the greater part of its subjects'.[27] And, although Russia itself was counted as a state 'by a sort of courtesy on the supposition that the power of the Czar… is so far exercised in accordance with a recognised tradition of what the public good requires as to be on the whole a sustainer of rights', it was not on the same level of despotism with the Turk.[28] Green argued that Russia was in a process of change and progress, which was exemplified in the emancipation of 40,000,000 serfs in the last fifteen years. Furthermore, Russian aggression towards the Turks was not based only on strategic interests but also on Russia's concern for the demise of the Christian populations who lived under the Turkish dictatorship.[29]

Although Green maintained his objectivity towards historical phenomena that brought both Turkish despotism and European civilization into being, he maintained that these two specific forms of social and political organization represented different stages of civilization. Europe itself was still not a thoroughly organized political life, but it was not to be equated with Turkish despotism. So, Green argued, it was England's responsibility to ignore its selfish interests in the region — which comprised a desire to weaken Russian power — and to offer support to the rising nations of Eastern Europe against a despotic empire. Green did not perceive this duty simply as one based on Christian brotherhood but as a service to the

25   Green, *Works: Vol. 5 Additional Writings*, p. 302.
26   Green, *Lectures*, p. 101.
27   Green, *Works: Vol. 5 Additional Writings*, p. 319.
28   Green, *Lectures*, p. 137.
29   Green, *Works: Vol 5 Additional Writings*, pp. 299–300.

interests of mankind.[30] The honour and interests of England required the country to stand against a despotic power that continually violated the rights of its defenceless citizens. Overall, what distinguished the European civilization from Turkish despotism was not a mere religious difference. Rather, it was the way society was organized and positioned *vis-à-vis* the state. While in Europe states functioned as a means of maintaining and reconciling rights, Turkish despotism, erroneously called a state, was not party to a system of political rights and obligations. The relationship was more like the relationship between a slaveholder and his slaves, and for similar reasons to those that prohibited Green from considering a slaveholder as a political leader, the power residing over the Turkish despotism was not to be considered a legitimate state.

Green's criticism of the Turkish Empire was primarily based on the arbitrary authority it held over its minorities without representing their will. Following Maine's classification of empires, Green argued that there was a categorical difference between the empires of the East and the British tenure of India.[31] The Eastern empires were tax-collecting empires that used the most violent form of coercive power without administering or maintaining the customary law of its population. Under such circumstances such an empire remained an arbitrary sovereign whose only relation with the population under its control was in regards to collecting taxes and sometimes recruiting soldiers.[32] To the extent that its 'sovereignty' was based on pure coercive power without any representation of the general will of the people it ruled, it was to be considered as a despotic political entity. The other category of imperial rule was a law-giving or rule-maintaining empire. This category was exemplified by the Roman Empire in history and its legitimacy was based on

---

[30] Green, *Works: V. 5 Additional Writings*, p. 319; C. Tyler (2006) *Idealist Political Philosophy: Pluralism and Conflict in the Absolute Idealist Tradition*, London: Continuum, p. 101.

[31] Green, *Lectures*, p. 99.

[32] Green, *Lectures*, p. 100.

the support it received from the peoples under its rule. Although such empires did not necessarily employ a representative body, they were 'firmly grounded on the good-will of the subjects', and the subjects had a strong interest in the maintenance of the imperial order.[33] Such difference in the relation between the ruling power and its subjects constituted the grounds on which a tax-collecting empire was distinguished from a law-giving/maintaining empire.

Following his discussion of the types of empires, Green maintained British tenure in India was a middle-case between a tax-collecting and a law-giving/maintaining empire. The British government was a law-giving power in India only to a very limited extent; its main role was maintenance of the customary law of the Indian people. Furthermore, the British government's role not only as a tax-collecting military power but also as the maintainer of the customary law invoked in the Indian people an 'habitual obedience' to its rule.[34] So far as the British government used its coercive power to maintain the customary law, its power was not to be considered illegitimate. Customary law was, by definition, an expression of the Indian people's general will, and the English government was serving its Indian subjects by upholding it. Clearly, Green perceived the law, like many other Victorian intellectuals, 'as a gift that England could bestow on other nations at lower rungs in the hierarchy of civilisations'.[35] So long as the imperial government was receptive of the demands of the colonized peoples, Green perceived this paternalistic relation as morally acceptable.

Still, even the British Empire as a law-maintaining power in India was not righteous enough to escape from Green's criticism. In his memoir written by Nettleship, it was noted that Green constantly expressed his contempt for 'so called "national honour" and imperial

---

[33] Green, *Lectures*, p. 101.
[34] Green, *Lectures*, p. 101.
[35] Bell, *Victorian Visions of Global Order*, p. 92.

greatness'.[36] It was not necessarily the rule of foreigners over another population that earned Green's contempt for empires. He believed that such a political organization was indicative of a certain kind of patriotism; a patriotism dominated by a 'special military sense' and surely that kind of patriotism was not marked by the 'temper of the citizen dealing with fellow-citizens, or with men who are themselves citizens of their several states'.[37] Such militarist nationalism shared its roots with tribalism that was based on the rule of feudal chiefs or the rule of privileged classes that was 'ultimately' based on coercion.[38] But, in addition to the non-ideal form of rule the 'inferior populations' were subjected to under imperialism, such an international order also prevented 'European mankind' from organizing itself thoroughly into a legitimate political order.

According to Green, the militant patriotism that prevailed in Europe both hampered the development of moral and civic national unity in European states and prevented the establishment of a peaceful international order. In his *Lectures*, Green identified five primary causes that required European states to maintain standing armies, and thus barred the establishment of a peaceful international order among states that are organized around the principle of civic nationalism. Two out of these five causes were directly related to the existence of empires, be they tax-collecting Eastern empires or the British 'tenure of a great Indian Empire'.[39] According to Green an international order organized through empires was prone to turn Europe into a great military camp for two specific reasons. On the one hand, the existence of empires that were not based on the principle of citizenship or *civitas* in close proximity to European states posed a constant threat of violence, especially towards the

---

[36] R.L. Nettleship (1906) *Memoir of Thomas Hill Green, Late Fellow of Balliol College, Oxford, and Whyte's Professor of Moral Philosophy in the University of Oxford*, London: Longmans, Green, p. 17.

[37] Green, *Lectures*, p. 176.

[38] Green, *Lectures*, p. 176.

[39] Green, *Lectures*, p. 177.

newly arising Eastern European nations. The existence of European empires, on the other hand, bestowed a military character upon these states that did not originally belong to their nature and brought them into hostile relations with their European counterparts.[40] According to Green, the unprecedentedly large standing armies of European states were not to be considered as a sign of their success in national organization, but as an indicator of their failure in realizing a civic form of nationalism. Like all animosity that occurred among states, imperial aggression was also a result of the erroneous idea that the good that was to be sought was a material one. For Green the search for imperial aggrandizement was only a new expression of the same delusion that 'the gain of one nation must mean the loss of another'.[41] Based on this erroneous understanding of 'the good', states were striving to exclude their counterparts from their markets and to appear stronger than their rivals both economically and militarily.

There are a couple of points that can be discerned from the issues that are raised so far regarding Green's approach to humanity, imperialism, and international order. Firstly, Green perceived the condition of the international order at the end of the nineteenth century in a relatively negative light. He thought states still operated mostly in accordance with national vanities, jealousies, and rivalries as a result of human wickedness that was to be superseded in the future thanks to mankind's inherent moral potential. Aggression among states was not to be considered as the natural order of the international arena. On the contrary, it was a sign of humanity's failure in going beyond its 'less worthy' desires and realizing its 'higher nature'. Secondly, Green believed that the inherent morality of mankind found its highest form of expression in Christianity, or in its restatement in Hegelian philosophy. It surely was not the complete manifestation of the Spirit on earth, yet it was the highest level

---

40   Green, *Lectures*, p. 177.
41   Green, *Lectures*, p. 166.

of moral development humanity was able to achieve towards the end of the nineteenth century. Green called this moral sentiment towards self, family, country, and humanity 'Christian citizenship', and it was this sentiment of moral duty to work towards personal and social progress engrafted in European civilization that distinguished it from others. Spreading such a form of morality to other societies was not perceived to be problematic by Green, although he had serious misgivings about the use of colonization for that end.

II. Bernard Bosanquet

Bosanquet, like his teacher Green, rarely commented on the issue of imperialism or the nature of the British Empire. Essentially, it was not until after the Great War that Bosanquet got truly interested in the issues of international relations and peace. In 1910, when he wrote a second introduction to his masterpiece *The Philosophical Theory of the State,* Bosanquet merely mentioned a movement towards a sentimental unity of mankind, especially effective in European civilization. He wrote, 'Europe is full today of the ethical and democratic demand for real progress, guided by the actual interests and emotions of mankind; for a future to be moulded by and for humanity'.[42] And in the original text of the same book, published in 1899, it is possible to find a few pages from which one can vaguely discern his approach to the concept of humanity.

Bosanquet recognized the concept of humanity as an 'inescapable' level of unity which would have a place in any 'tolerably complete philosophical thinking' but his discussion on humanity's actual existence as a social unity reflected a high level of reservation.[43] Although humanity was necessarily a universal idea, its actuality was very much dubious because 'according to the current ideas of

---

[42] Bosanquet (1920) *Philosophical Theory of the State,* p. xl.
[43] B. Bosanquet (1899) *The Philosophical Theory of the State,* London: Macmillan and Co, p. 328.

our civilisation, a great part of the lives which are being lived and have been lived by mankind are not lives worth living, in the sense of embodying qualities for which life seems valuable to us'.[44] In other words, Bosanquet thought, although every human being had the potential to be part of humanity, in actuality their potential was realized only to a limited extent if it was realized at all. As there was a huge gap among nations in terms of developing a civilization adequate for realizing human potential, it was impossible to talk about a universal human experience or a general will of humanity.[45] Bosanquet maintained that European civilization was an adequate expression of human nature and it was superior to other forms of civilizations in which men led lives that could not be considered to be fully human.

Like Green, Bosanquet argued that Christianity was the 'complete and energetic conception of life which the growth of ages has developed as the civilisation of Christendom'.[46] It was a combination of the Pagan virtues that it inherited from ancient Greece and the Roman Empire such as temperance, courage, and justice, and genuinely Christian virtues of faith, hope, and charity, that made Christian morality superior.[47] For Bosanquet Christian civilization was the highest step in the ladder of civilization against which other cultures were to be judged. In an article published in 1895, he argued that the savage religions reflected man's impulse to strive towards a civilized religion. Although they were quite inadequate embodiments of such a religion, they became meaningful in what they implied to civilized men. Bosanquet wrote: 'even the relics of genuine savagery, though nothing in themselves, become something to us as first stammering statements of the riddle which,

---

44   Bosanquet (1899) *Philosophical Theory of the State*, p. 328.
45   Bosanquet (1899) *Philosophical Theory of the State*, p. 329.
46   B. Bosanquet (1893) *The Civilization of Christendom, and Other Studies*, London : Swan Sonnenschein; New York: Macmillan, p. 99.
47   B. Bosanquet (1999) *Some Suggestions in Ethics*, Sweet, W. (ed.), vol. 16, Bristol: Thoemmes, pp. 224–25.

comparatively speaking, we have read.'[48] Thus, a considerable part
of mankind could not be perceived to be on an equal footing with the
European man in terms of realizing their human potential. Yet it was
of vital importance to bear in mind that all those who were called
man were different from animals to the extent that they carried the
human potential to realize a better version of themselves. There was
no essential difference between 'Jew and Gentile, Greek and bar-
barian, Mussulman and infidel, Christian and heathen…' except the
degree to which these civilizsations enabled their members to reach
their full potential.[49] As the idea of man was not maintained with
reference to its lowest common denominator but to the highest
possible realization of man's nature, humanity referred not to a brute
enumeration of man but to an ideal unity that was to be actualized
through man's self-realization.

A nuance Bosanquet introduced to the idealist discussion on
'levels' of civilization was a certain type of relativism regarding the
value and effectiveness of civilizations. Clearly, he took the
Christian/European civilization in which he was raised to be the
highest type of civilization realized by humanity to his day. Yet he
was aware that one's perception towards one's own culture was very
much dependent on the particular way he experienced and made
sense of life. As early as 1899, he acknowledged 'the probability that
to every people its own life has seemed the crown of things, and the
remainder of mankind only the remainder'.[50] For Bosanquet, it was
quite understandable that individuals' perception of the best possible life was shaped by the culture in which their personalities
developed. It was for this reason 'every people, as a rule, seems to
find contentment in its own way of life'.[51] He was aware of the
possibility that his belief in the superiority of the European way of

---

[48] B. Bosanquet (1895) 'The Evolution of Religion', *International Journal of Ethics*, 5 (4), p. 433.

[49] Bosanquet (1899) *Philosophical Theory of the State*, p. 330.

[50] Bosanquet (1899) *Philosophical Theory of the State*, p. 331.

[51] Bosanquet (1899) *Philosophical Theory of the State*, p. 332.

life was based on the particular way he evaluated 'the good' for humanity. So far as he was aware of this possible bias in his own understanding, he was reluctant to argue for an objective superiority of his own civilization. On the contrary, he advised caution in regards to the 'general theory of progress' and argued that 'one type of humanity cannot cover the whole ground of the possibilities of human nature'.[52] By acknowledging the inherent plurality of human experience, divided into different nations and civilizations, Bosanquet warned his fellow idealists from committing to a goal of covering 'the whole ground of human nature'.

Still, Bosanquet did not offer a substantial criticism of imperialism or the British rule over its colonies. He noted the impossibility of forming a general will amongst peoples who do not share a common experience of life, but he did not challenge Britain's claim to rule over other civilizations. On the contrary, in the first edition of his *The Philosophical Theory of the State* he argued that the relation between England and India was beneficial in demonstrating the common tissue that unites the whole humanity although there were various ways in which it finds a concrete shape in different communities. He wrote:

> Such a relation as that of England and India brings the matter home. Englishmen cannot make one effective self-governed community with the Indian populations. It would be misery and inefficiency to both sides. But our State can recognise the primary rights of humanity as determined in the life of its Indian subjects, and enforce or respect these rights, whether India be a dependency or an independent community.[53]

For Bosanquet, a close relation among various civilizations was beneficial not for unifying human experience across the globe but for introducing a common awareness and appreciation of the vast number of values each civilization developed in their midst. Forming 'a universal society including the entire human race' would have

---

[52] Bosanquet (1899) *Philosophical Theory of the State*, p. 332.
[53] Bosanquet (1899) *Philosophical Theory of the State*, p. 330.

been possible only through such insemination of values spreading from each and every human community.[54] From such a perspective, he wrote in 1893: 'in the future a real unity of all mankind must surely come to pass; and the task completed by each race or religion will then be appropriated by the others.'[55]

Still, to his mind, Christendom as the Western races practised it offered something fundamental for human experience that others failed to offer: the belief in development.[56] Although he refrained from calling the civilization of Christendom the highest or the best, he argued that it was something 'essentially different' from others. And this essential difference made the Western races 'history-making races of the world'.[57] This quality, which was most clearly expressed in Christian religion, was embodied in the fine art, science, politics, social action, and philosophy of the Western races.[58] Bosanquet did not advocate spreading these Western values to other cultures and civilizations by means of colonizing them, as he thought an organic process of value insemination was preferable. Still, he maintained that it was legitimate to claim one's own civilization to be the best, until it was possible to talk about a state of mind that is common to whole humanity. He argued:

> The respect of States and individuals for humanity is then, after all, in its essence, a duty to maintain a type of life, not general, but the best we know, which we call the most human, and in accordance with it to recognise and deal with the rights of alien individuals and communities. This conception is opposed to the treatment of all individual human beings as members of an identical community having identical capacities and rights.[59]

Bosanquet's position regarding particular civilization's relation to humanity as a whole neither justified nor condemned imperialism as

---

[54] Bosanquet (1899) *Philosophical Theory of the State*, p. 330.
[55] Bosanquet, *Civilization of Christendom*, p. 99.
[56] Bosanquet, *Civilization of Christendom*, p. 84.
[57] Bosanquet, *Civilization of Christendom*, p. 72.
[58] Bosanquet, *Civilization of Christendom*, p. 72.
[59] Bosanquet (1899) *Philosophical Theory of the State*, p. 331.

a means for the development of mankind. Yet the fact that human experience was particularized in each society and that an unforced form of acquaintance with other civilizations was preferable in forming a common understanding of humanity was an essential point in Bosanquet's reasoning. Arguably, Bosanquet preferred a unity of societies around the common values of humanity that was enriched by every society's particular contributions. Maintaining these particular experiences was necessarily threatened by the efforts to spread a certain form of civilization by force.

Bosanquet's reflections on international order and imperialism prior to the Great War suggest not a deviation from Green's position but an improvement of it. Both Green and Bosanquet perceived a tendency in human nature to move towards greater and greater unity that would only end in the unity of mankind. For Green it was a unity of sentiment that would abolish the difference between my neighbour whom I personally know and a human being who lives on the other side of the world, and I do not have a reasonable chance to meet. Green thought the difference between civilizations seemed to be more of a matter of degree than being a particular expression of human nature. As each state and nation that formed cleansed itself from its jealousies and prejudices, a cooperative international order would emerge as the basis of the moral and sentimental unity of societies. What Bosanquet added to Green's vision of such international cooperation was the importance of particular values that were to be added by each culture to humanity as a whole. While Green attached great importance to the shared moral potential of humanity, Bosanquet attributed an equal amount of value to the particular ways each society realized that potential. Such difference in emphasis did not result in a fundamental discrepancy in the way they understood the nature of international order or humanity in general. Both Green and Bosanquet perceived a 'better' expression of human potential in the civilization of Christendom and they shared, at least, a distrust of the imperial agenda of ruling other nations as a means for humanity's overall progress.

III. F.H. Bradley

Bradley, who has the reputation of being the best metaphysician among the British Idealists, had a great impact on his fellows. Bosanquet stated that one of the two most influential works on the development of his philosophical thinking was Bradley's *Ethical Studies*.[60] Yet his Idealism is often distinguished from other British Idealists' as he was 'far more conservative' and his stricter interpretation of Hegel's work was criticized by other Idealists like Jones and Mackenzie.[61] Without going into a detailed overview of Bradley's metaphysics, it suffices to say that Bradley tended to tip the balance between the particular and the Absolute in favour of the Absolute, and this tendency often led him to focus on the perfect revelation of the Absolute and to overlook the importance of the dialectical process of development that led to it. Mackenzie perceived such a tendency in Bradley's view of Reality and argued: 'With Mr. Bradley... the process appears to be non-essential, and the self-contradiction is merely something to be got rid of.'[62] It was and still is a common criticism of idealism that it favours the universal over the particular, and it leads to a partial blindness towards the sufferings of the individual as long as it serves the community. Such criticism does not hold ground against those British Idealists who saw an irreplaceable interdependence between the particular and the universal, or the good of the individual and the communal. But Bradley's position can be distinguished from such Idealists' to the extent that he sometimes overlooked the morality of the process through which progress is achieved as long as it served humanity to approximate to the Absolute. The main difference between his

---

[60] B. Bosanquet (1917) *Social and International Ideals: Being Studies in Patriotism*, London: Macmillan, p. 33.

[61] J. Bowle (1954) *Politics and Opinion in the Nineteenth Century*, London: Jonathan Cape, p. 275; J.S. Mackenzie (1894) 'Mr. Bradley's View of the Self', *Mind*, 3 (11), p. 334.

[62] J.S. Mackenzie (1894) 'Review of *Appearance and Reality*, by F.H. Bradley', *International Journal of Ethics*, 4 (2), p. 247.

position and that of other British Idealists regarding imperialism seems to originate from such a divergence in their metaphysics. Bradley's emphasis on the Absolute was reflected in his devoted support of the Empire and his belief in the vitality of its success for the progress of humanity.

Bradley's article 'The Limits of Individual and National Self-Sacrifice' was published in 1894. It was a provocative piece that harshly criticized humanitarian sentimentalism in national and international politics and offered instead to employ all means necessary for the progress of humanity. According to Bradley, humanitarian sentimentalism was 'inconsistent, deficient, and in part downright false'.[63] It was false because it was based on the false assumption that all men had equal value; that all men should be governed by law; that all men have equal rights. It was a doctrine of 'universal love and self-sacrifice' that originated from an erroneous combination of Christianity and nationalism.[64] Bradley argued that the claim for unconditional equality of all men was related to a perception of the universe without a moral end. Yet for him there was an end towards which history was unfolding. Thus he argued: 'when there is an end and a worth in this world men become unequal, for they must realise the end in different degrees.'[65] From his point of view the worth of each man was to be decided by his contribution to the progress towards the end. Of course, it was desirable that all men contributed equally to humanity's progress but that was not the case. Based on the idea that men were unequal in relation to their contribution to humanity's progress, Bradley argued that self-sacrifice became moral and necessary for certain individuals and nations under certain circumstances. Self-sacrifice became moral for an individual when he gave up his own existence for the betterment of something that was

---

63 F.H. Bradley (1894) 'The Limits of Individual and National Self-Sacrifice', *International Journal of Ethics*, 5 (1), p. 19.
64 Bradley, 'Limits of Individual and National Self-Sacrifice', p. 19.
65 Bradley, 'Limits of Individual and National Self-Sacrifice', p. 18.

worth more than his life.[66] For instance, Bradley argued, 'abolishing the existence' of criminals within a country would be morally right for the betterment of the society.[67] After all, they could not be considered as valuable members of the society who contributed to its progress, and their elimination would contribute to the general well-being of the society.

It can be seen that Bradley's emphasis on the primacy of the Absolute was reinforced by the quite popular discussions on eugenics as a possible solution for social and political evils. In another article published the same year, Bradley discussed the merits of Darwinism in its application to society. For Bradley, society was an organic whole, and individuals were its parts that can be discarded if they were deemed to be harmful to the whole.[68] He argued there was nothing to be set 'against the unlimited right of the moral organism to dispose of its members...' except superstition and prejudice.[69] Mutual assistance and cooperative action were also tools of evolution and they superseded competition as a means of progress only in most developed organisms. So far as society was such a developed form of organism, social evolution would be sustained through benevolence, charity, and mercy. But such principles of cooperation were not absolute, they were dependent on the conditions that prevailed, and they were only 'secondary and subject to the general end'.[70] When the general end required it 'ethical surgery' was the most benevolent form of action. Bradley argued that a very simple question was to be asked to determine the morality of 'ethical surgery': 'on which side lies the balance of harm?'[71] For instance, in the case of the drunkard or the lunatic, Bradley wrote, violating their

---

[66] Bradley, 'Limits of Individual and National Self-Sacrifice', p. 17.

[67] Bradley, 'Limits of Individual and National Self-Sacrifice', p. 20.

[68] F.H. Bradley (1894) 'Some Remarks on Punishment', *International Journal of Ethics*, 4 (3), p. 272.

[69] Bradley, 'Some Remarks on Punishment', p. 276.

[70] Bradley, 'Some Remarks on Punishment', p. 280.

[71] Bradley, 'Some Remarks on Punishment', p. 282.

rights was not a great source of harm to the society. But letting them stunt the societal progress under the disguise of respecting their rights was harmful to the overall organism. Quite passionately, he stated: 'I am disgusted at the inviolable sanctity of the noxious lunatic. The right of the individual to spawn without restriction his diseased offspring to the community, the duty of the state to rear wholesale and without limit an unselected progeny—such duties and rights are to my mind a sheer outrage on Providence.'[72] Apparently, the importance Bradley attributed to the communal well-being of the society was strengthened with the Darwinian meta-phor of the social organism and in turn gave rise to a line of thinking that would legitimate stripping certain individuals of their rights as long as it supposedly served the interests of the society.

Bradley applied a similar set of premises to international relations when he reflected on the morality of 'national self-sacrifice'. The formula he maintained was the same: 'the end is general perfection, and for this end, certainly, self-sacrifice may be required'.[73] He argued that defending absolute equality and rights of nations was even more erroneous than defending absolute equality and rights of individuals within a community. In a community, individuals might have similar rights and duties, as they would perceive each other as partakers of the same ideas and values. Thus, when the necessity occurred a member of a community would willingly sacrifice himself so that his 'life survives in the whole, and that the common spirit gains' by it.[74] But the same principle could not be applied to nations so far as they remained races and embodiments of ideas alien to each other. As there was not a higher unity for which self-sacrifice would be morally legitimate, each state was responsible for protecting its own existence, sometimes at the expense of others. Another differ-ence between the individual and the nation revealed itself in the lack

---

72 Bradley, 'Some Remarks on Punishment', p. 283.
73 Bradley, 'Limits of Individual and National Self-Sacrifice', p. 24.
74 Bradley, 'Limits of Individual and National Self-Sacrifice', p. 22.

of an executive authority in the international arena. A community, being an organized whole, had institutions that had the authority to decide the morality of 'eliminating' a drunkard or preventing him from having children. Such decisions would be based on law and they would be supported by force if and when it became necessary. Yet, Bradley argued, there was no international sovereign and there might never be one. In this lack of authority, it was the responsibility of the powerful nations to act on their best judgments. For the realization of the end, i.e. 'the development of humanity', nations who had the force were justified in exterminating or 'making use of both men and nations' when they judged such course of action necessary. Bradley was aware that his argument could be used to justify almost anything, and it might have turned out to be harmful for the development of humanity. Still, he argued that it was important to understand that in some cases individuals and/or nations would be not only justified in but morally bound to take such extreme measures for the attainment of the moral end. He summarized this point as follows:

> Leaving... abstract considerations, if we take the case of criminals within and savages without the community, it surely may be right to abolish their existence. The principle we act on no doubt can be mis-used by the immoral. It can furnish a pretext for blind persecution or selfish aggrandisement. And the progress of humanity being furthered by the diversity of its elements, it is desirable in general that individuals should develop their natures. And this shows a presumption against the extinction or hindrance of man or nation. But it does not prove that in some cases we are not morally bound to accomplish it.[75]

Bradley's deviation from the mainstream Idealist position regarding international relations and imperialism seems contradictory to the general view that places him in the camp of absolutist Idealists along with Bernard Bosanquet. Being absolutist Idealists, both of them may be expected to attribute greater importance to the whole rather than its parts and thus favour the state above the individual and the

---

[75] Bradley, 'Limits of Individual and National Self-Sacrifice', p. 20.

moral end above the means that leads to it. Yet the tone of difference between Bradley and Bosanquet was noted before and expressed by Muirhead:

> With all their theoretic agreement there was certainly a deep-seated difference of temperament which, I have elsewhere suggested, might be indifferently described as 'that between rationalistic and mystic, radical and conservative, simple and complex, classic and romantic,' and which manifested itself in their attitude to some of the practical problems of daily life in politics and religion.[76]

This deep-seated difference revealed itself in their approaches to international order quite sharply as Bosanquet attributed great importance to the particularities of every culture that contributes to the progress towards a human community and Bradley emphasized the importance of humanity as an absolute end that was to be achieved through whatever means necessary.

IV. D.G. Ritchie

Ritchie adopted an approach similar to Bradley's on international relations and applied it to the specific case of the Boer War. But, unlike Bradley, Ritchie's reflections on states' rights over the individual did not focus on states' capacity to exterminate or to punish the criminal, the drunkard, or the lunatic for the higher good of the community. On the contrary, Ritchie emphasized the state's duty to educate the children, treat the sick, and aid the poor for their own betterment as well as for the betterment of the social organism. Although, like Bradley, he utilized the metaphor of the body while commenting on the nature of the relation between the individual and the society, he argued that pursuance of the common good could not be thought apart from the good of all the parts that constituted the whole. Thus, against Bradley's and Spencerian evolutionists' arguments in favour of the elimination of the weak for the good of the

---

[76] J.H. Muirhead (1942) *John Henry Muirhead: Reflections by a Journeyman in Philosophy on the Movements of Thought and Practice in His Time*, London: G. Allen & Unwin, p. 102.

social whole, Ritchie focused on the social causes that led to the emergence of weak individuals in the first place. According to him, natural selection was already present in British society, especially among the poor. But it was not an effective way of pursuing the common good as it meant permanently injuring a certain part of the body while giving free rein to another. While Bradley accepted the moral permissibility of eliminating the 'weaker' parts of the society, Ritchie was looking for ways to strengthen their position within society.[77]

While Ritchie's approach to social and political phenomena was fairly stable over the years, his reflections on international relations evolved considerably. In a book chapter published in 1883, Ritchie ended his piece by expressing his hope for the recognition of international law based on international moral ideals. According to Ritchie, the order of the world made the existence of independent nations necessary but their relations with each other were to be developed further in time. The last sentence of this chapter read: 'in any case we must recognise that the civilisation of the world is not now entrusted, as of old, to one keeper only; and history should teach us that no nation has the right to say "surely we are the people; and wisdom will die with us."'[78] In this statement resonated Bosanquet's emphasis on the value of each particular civilization and undesirability of creating a monolithic human civilization. Yet in another article, published in 1891, after dealing at length with the possibility of a complementary relation between national sovereignty and international law, he applied the principle of natural selection to nations. He argued that international law was not—at

---

[77] For that reason, for example, he supported universal free education: D.G. Ritchie (1891) *The Principles of State Interference: Four essays on the Political Philosophy of Mr. Herbert Spencer, J.S. Mill, and T.H. Green*, London: Swan Sonnenschein & Co., pp. 116–17.

[78] D.G. Ritchie (1883) 'The Rationality of History', in Haldane, R.B. and Seth, A. (eds.) *Essays in Philosophical Criticism*, New York: Burt Franklin, p. 158.

least not yet — *Lex* but *Jus* as the community of nations was merely an idea and not a legal or political institution.[79] As *Jus*, these laws were only customs that were enforced 'through the consequences of violations'.[80] These consequences entailed the natural anger and hatred of the nations wronged and not 'regular judicial penalties'.[81] In that sense, the international order was still in a state of nature or a 'state of war' under a law that is merely customary and not legal. Within such an order it was the vigorousness of the nations that ensured their survival. Yet his identification of vigorousness as the condition of a nation's survival brought with it the possibility of merging into a militarist form of nationalism that Green warned about in his discussion of imperialism.

Ritchie's oscillation between the ideal of international law based on international morality and the conception of international order functioning through 'natural selection' came to an end with the beginning of the Second Boer War. Starting from 1900, he wrote several articles on the matter, most of which were meant to serve as answers to Hobson's criticism of the British Empire and its materialistic passions that led to war in South Africa. According to Hobson, the war was brought about by a handful of mine owners of British descent and it was made popular by a kept press in Britain. The argument that the British were trying to free the 'Kaffir' from Dutch oppression was not reflective of reality. It was only the Christian missionary who had a 'view of the native, as a man and a brother with a soul and body of his own and a right to determine his own destiny'.[82] According to Hobson, such a perception of the native races was not popular among British settlers any more than it was popular among their Dutch counterparts. The humanitarian argu-

---

[79] D.G. Ritchie (1891) 'On the Conception of Sovereignty', *The Annals of the American Academy of Political and Social Science*, 1, p. 410.

[80] Ritchie, 'Sovereignty', p. 410.

[81] Ritchie, 'Sovereignty', p. 410.

[82] J.A. Hobson (1900) *The War in South Africa: Its Causes and Effects*, New York: The Macmillan Company, p. 283.

ment was merely a cover for the capitalistic passions of the white races in South Africa. It was so, not only in the case of South Africa but in all the lands the British Empire seized control of. The real driving force behind the British Empire, Hobson argued, was 'the organised influences of certain professional and commercial classes which have certain definite economic advantages to gain by assuming this pseudo-patriotic cloak'.[83]

From Ritchie's perspective, freeing South African colonies from the inefficient ways of Dutch administration and production was a service to humanity as well as a natural outcome of the Dutch civilization's inferiority. He argued that the British Empire was 'a far healthier "organ of humanity" than the independent domination of a backward race'.[84] Thus, the moral responsibility in South Africa rested on Mr. Kruger and his friends; they were not to stand in the way of Great Britain 'for the future democracy and for the growth of the idea of Federation—the only means of diminishing wars in the world and of securing peace'.[85] Against this argument, Hobson's answer was clear: a single nation was not authorized to judge the efficiency of other nations and to act on its own judgment of the matter. Such an action would only be ethical if and when an International Court as representative of the general will of nations deemed it inevitable. When such an authority was absent, only the 'clearest evidence of necessity' would force a nation to take arms against another.[86] Against Ritchie's claims that widening the British Empire was the best course of action to reach a World Federation, Hobson argued that imperialism, by breaking the nationalistic spirit of small peoples, was destroying 'the means of attaining in the future

---

[83] J.A. Hobson (1900) *Capitalism and Imperialism in South Africa*, New York: The Tucker Publishing Co., p. 28.

[84] D.G. Ritchie (1900) 'The South African War', *The Ethical World*, February 3, p. 71, in Nicholson, P.P. (ed.) (1998) *Collected Works of D.G. Ritchie Vol. 6: Miscellaneous Writings*, Bristol: Thoemmes.

[85] D.G. Ritchie (1900) 'Another View of the South African War', *The Ethical World*, January 13, p. 20, in Ritchie, *Miscellaneous Writings*.

[86] Hobson, 'Socialistic Imperialism', p. 48.

that solid federation of civilised peoples which is the only hopeful security against the recrudescence of barbarism in the shape of war'.[87]

There is fair ground to argue that Ritchie's unshakable belief in the righteousness of the British Empire in the South African conflict and its leading role on the way to a World Federation led him to move away from British Idealist positions on key matters. For the British Idealists, war was always a sign of states' incomplete fulfilment of their function, a sign that there was a defect in the way they were maintained. They all perceived that there was always a moral wrong committed in the act of war although it was not always possible to pinpoint the party or the parties in the wrong. In his reflections on the Boer War and especially in his replies to Hobson, Ritchie distanced himself from this position considerably. In his comments on Hobson's *The War in South Africa* Ritchie wrote: 'Mr. Hobson thinks federations can only arise in peace and from within. Has any federation in the history of the world, except the still incomplete Australian federation, ever come into existence save through the shock of war, or been composed of members none of whom have ever fought against each other?'[88] He added, war was better than a 'long period of political scheming and vituperation' as it had an instant cleansing effect. From such a perspective he was thankful to Mr. Kruger whose ultimatum had ended the possibility of further Conventions and made war inevitable in South Africa. Ritchie had increased hope in the future of South Africa as he expected that, after an arduous struggle, the British Empire would found a unified South Africa under British rule.

Ritchie's comments as the war progressed became more forceful in their support of war as a means of progress. In an article published in September 1900, he wrote, 'the "soul" that "goes marching

---

[87] Hobson, 'Socialistic Imperialism', p. 55.
[88] D.G. Ritchie (1900) 'Mr Hobson's Book and the Coming Settlement', *The Ethical World*, March 10, p. 146, in Ritchie, *Miscellaneous Writings*.

on" is not the spirit of state-rights and of a narrow local and racial "independence," but the spirit of progress and consolidation asserting itself, where necessary, by blood and iron'.[89] In 'The Moral Problems of War', he argued that 'nations are to one another in the same position as individuals who have no state over them'.[90] As they were in a state of nature there was no moral order by which to pass judgment on particular nations' actions. The only criterion was—in a similar fashion to Bradley's point—whether a specific action was serving the good of humanity through taking humanity closer to the ideal of a world federation. With a reference to the Hebrew prophets' Divine Justice and Hegel's motto that 'the real is rational', he argued that the rise and fall of nations was part of a larger movement, which we cannot discern through our limited understanding.[91] Thus, he stated, 'I do not think we are entitled to pronounce on the right and wrong of particular wars in the light of abstract and arbitrary intuitionalist theories'.[92] He argued that it was necessary to recognize wars as a 'harsh form of dialectic' or as a 'rough means of solving hard problems'.[93] War, after all, was sometimes the only means of effective action against reactionary and antiquated types of rule. Regarding the acquisition of lands that were already inhabited by 'lower races', Ritchie defended the motives of the European civilization which he identified as 'to suppress the slave trade, and to defend fellow-citizens'.[94] According to Ritchie, the lower races were already living under the tyranny of African despots, and although such acquisition usually brought with it some harshness and ill treatment of the natives, it also created considerable problems for the

---

[89] D.G. Ritchie (1900) 'John Brown's Body', *The Ethical World*, September 9, p. 613, in Ritchie, *Miscellaneous Writings*.

[90] D.G. Ritchie (1901) 'The Moral Problems of War—in Reply to Mr. J.M. Robertson', *International Journal of Ethics*, 11 (4), p. 495.

[91] Ritchie, 'Moral Problems of War', p. 505.

[92] Ritchie, 'Moral Problems of War', p. 505.

[93] D.G. Ritchie (1901) 'War and Peace', *International Journal of Ethics*, 11 (2), p. 149.

[94] Ritchie, 'War and Peace', p. 153.

Empire. Ritchie maintained that the abstract principles of national sovereignty and non-intervention sounded nice, but they were not tenable maxims in the international arena.

In *War and Peace,* Ritchie's ideal international order was transformed again, from a World Federation of States to the rule of 'a few great "Empires"'.[95] He argued that a federation of civilized nations was a desirable order of international relations, but the world was inhabited by races who were 'unfit for constitutional government'.[96] When these races were left to their own devices they quickly turned into black anarchies, and although these races had the potential to develop themselves, it was happening at a rather slow pace. It was 'as "inevitable" that vigorous and enterprising white races should overflow into other lands, as it is that water should run downhill'.[97] From such a perspective Ritchie asked: 'May not a few great "empires," in which self-governing federated communities control the less advanced races, represent a higher stage — more likely to be stable, less exposed to war, and preparing the way for a federation of the world?'[98] His answer was in the affirmative: 'Our federation of "free states" will have territories under it, which must be governed more or less despotically by a trained and capable service. This is a federation of the world, which is not an altogether visionary ideal.'[99]

The empires that were to rule the world in Ritchie's ideal of an order of great empires were different from what liberal imperialists generally condoned. Ritchie's envisioned world order was to be based on brute force rather than on law of the general will of the nations. In that sense, Ritchie's conceptualization of the empire fell short of what Green expected a 'law-giving' or 'law-maintaining' empire to be, as it did not take into consideration the established customs and rules of the peoples it ruled over. It was rather

---

[95] Ritchie, 'War and Peace', p. 150.
[96] Ritchie, 'War and Peace', p. 157.
[97] Ritchie, 'War and Peace', p. 153.
[98] Ritchie, 'War and Peace', p. 150.
[99] Ritchie, 'War and Peace', p. 157.

considered to be an authority that ruled peoples for their own good but against their will when deemed necessary. It was a position that was hard to reconcile with the basic presumptions of idealistic political philosophy as it severed the vital link between the legitimacy of a political authority and its dependence on the general will and consent of the peoples it ruled over. It would not be unfair to say that Ritchie was aware of this discrepancy and that is why he called such a rule 'more or less despotic'.[100]

Ritchie was not a deviant figure in the British Idealist school of thought when his work on political philosophy is concerned. Yet his approach to international relations in general and his understanding of imperialism in particular was not representative of the British Idealist position. His deviation from the teachings of Green can be explained with his engagement with the Fabian Society at the time. Especially, Ritchie's emphasis on the Dutch incompetence to manage the natural resources of South Africa reminds one of Shaw's arguments in defence of the Second Boer War. Similarly, Ritchie's singular hostility towards Hobson—whose arguments were rejected by the Fabians thanks to Bernard Shaw's intervention—points to a possible alignment of Ritchie with the Fabian Society rather than other Idealists on the matter of the Second Boer War.[101]

V. Muirhead, Mackenzie, and Jones

Muirhead, Mackenzie, and Jones were the exponents of the main line of thinking in British Idealism regarding imperialism and the British Empire at the end of the nineteenth century, as T.H. Green was no longer alive and Bosanquet was not commenting on the matter at length. They recognized the atrocities committed by the British, especially during the expansion period, but they also recognized a capability on the part of the British Empire in terms of civilizing the subject races, spreading European values, and consequently bringing

---

[100] Ritchie, 'War and Peace', p. 157.
[101] Alexander, *Shaw's Controversial Socialism*, p. 159.

humanity together in pursuance of human progress. They felt that they were members of a generation that carried great responsibility all around the globe due to the circumstances they could not control, circumstances that arose mostly out of actions that were not morally justifiable. Yet they also believed that 'there was always room for repentance', and under the circumstances 'to retire from tasks it has undertaken, however thoughtlessly at the time, [was] the poorest sort of corporate repentance' the British could engage in.[102] Although the success of the British in this mission would not have cancelled all the wrong committed by the Empire, it would have bestowed the Empire with a moral identity without which it would remain an exploitative colonizer of the world. Their emphasis on the inescapability of the moral duty to prevent 'disintegration' of 'native societies' through responsible and responsive government was in line with the general liberal imperialist position at the time.[103]

For Mackenzie, Muirhead, and Jones, a sudden realization that England was not a small island anymore fundamentally altered the way the British people perceived their relation to the colonies and dependencies by the end of the nineteenth century. Obviously, the British Empire was around for quite a time before the realization of a duty towards the subject races awoke. Mackenzie expressed this sentiment in his article when he wrote in 1900, 'so we woke up, almost on a single day, to realise, as we had never realised before, that we have ties and obligations that carry us round the world...'[104] Muirhead argued that this awakening was a result of a general change in the way British people saw their relation to the world. Utilitarianism both in its philosophical capacity and practical

---

[102] J.S. Mackenzie (1900) 'The Source of Moral Obligation', *International Journal of Ethics*, 10 (4), p. 477.

[103] K. Mantena (2007) 'The Crisis of Liberal Imperialism', in Bell, D. (ed.) *Victorian Visions of Global Order: Empire and International Relations in Nineteenth Century Political Thought*, Cambridge: Cambridge University Press, p. 131.

[104] Mackenzie, 'The Source of Moral Obligation', p. 469.

application shaped the way citizens of the mother country perceived its colonies until the end of the nineteenth century. From a utilitarian perspective, colonies were important so far as they provided material wealth for the mother country, and Adam Smith showed that they actually did not supply such wealth.[105] Thus, during the nineteenth century British people lost their interest in the value and future of their colonies.[106] The change of mentality in regards to British colonies occurred when a larger shift occurred in 'nothing less than the Spirit of the Century'.[107] Muirhead argued Goethe was the first prophet of this new sentiment, the sentiment that in industry, organization, and civilization lay the future of humanity and it was the mission of Europe to spread those values around the world. Germany at the time was not ready to undertake this duty but England was.[108] According to Muirhead, the attempt to civilize the subject races of the British Empire was an improvement on the part of English people. He argued the history of the British Empire was to be divided into two phases in terms of its approach to subject races. There was the first phase, under the philosophical influence of utilitarianism, during which the English nation did nothing for the development of the 'negro or Indian'.[109] In this phase the Empire was interested solely in the material wealth it derived from their territories without a regard for the conditions of the native peoples. Yet England's attitude towards their subject races changed at the end of the nineteenth century as they 'began to think of the negro as a fellow Christian...'[110]

Though Muirhead, Mackenzie, and Jones believed in the imperial mission of the British people that became clear in the second phase

---

[105] J.H. Muirhead (1900) 'What Imperialism Means', *Fortnightly Review*, LXVIII, reprinted in (1902) *Philosophy and Life and Other Essays*, London: Swan Sonnenschein and Co., p. 82.

[106] Muirhead, 'Imperialism', p. 81.

[107] Muirhead, 'Imperialism', p. 83.

[108] Muirhead, 'Imperialism', p. 84.

[109] Muirhead, 'Imperialism', p. 92.

[110] Muirhead, 'Imperialism', p. 92.

of the imperial mind-set, they thought substantial reform was necessary in imperial administration to make it more responsive and conciliatory to the peoples they governed all over the world. After all, force was only a temporary and non-ideal solution for imperial hardships. Muirhead quoted Edmund Burke in his article to press this point: 'A nation is not governed which is perpetually to be conquered.'[111] The 'true empire', in addition to being a tool for the civilizing mission of the subject races, was also to be a moral unity of all the peoples that constituted it. It was — or ought to be — something more than a 'fiscal unit', or a financial partnership. According to Jones, the unity of the Empire was 'represented as consisting of two strands — unity of sentiment and a unity which privileged commercial relations expected to bring; good feeling *plus* sound business'.[112] Thus, downplaying the sentimental aspect of the Empire was an injustice to the potential of the British Empire in furthering the sentimental unity of mankind. After all, it was thanks to this newly emerging sentimental unity that the colonies were no longer pictured as 'fruits that drop off when they are ripe', but as 'leaves and branches that nourish while they spread the influence of the tree, or, better still, of the banyan tree, whose branches root themselves in the ground and add support to the parent system'.[113]

For Muirhead as well as for Jones and Mackenzie, the task of the British Empire in regard to its colonies was clear yet challenging — it was a task of immensely wide extent. It was so, because 'it [was] concerned not with the government of a few million Europeans in accordance with European traditions, but the reconstruction of the moral, industrial, and political ideas of some four or five hundred million souls of every race and religion and at every stage of civilisation except our own'.[114] There were serious impediments to the execution of this civilizing mission that was undertaken by the

---

111 Muirhead, 'Imperialism', p. 91.
112 Jones, *Working Faith of the Social Reformer*, p. 131.
113 Muirhead, 'Imperialism', p. 87.
114 Muirhead, 'Imperialism', pp. 89–90.

British Empire by the end of the nineteenth century. It was vital, for its future success, to ask: 'Are these nations fit for the education we are giving them? Have they capacity enough to make it worth our while to give it? Granting that they have the capacity, are we setting about the task of developing it in the right way?'[115] Muirhead's and other Idealists' answer to the question—whether or not the subject races have the capacity to understand and adopt European values— was a confident yes. After all, at the heart of Idealist philosophy was the conviction that every man had the moral and rational capacity to realize a higher version of himself if he is given the necessary powers. Differences in race and religion were not indicators of inferiority or superiority of groups of people in a permanent sense. It was rather a sign of their position in the evolutionary ladder of civilization, and it was possible to progress or regress on that scale. European nations were obviously at the top in the ranking of civilizations, and with persistent education and administration other nations had the capacity to follow in their footsteps. According to Muirhead, Egypt was the shining example of what the British Empire was capable of achieving as long as 'the good of the subject' was perceived to be the 'first object of government'.[116] When the best intelligence of the British people was deployed to the pursuance of the moral end, success was ensured in foreign as well as in home policy.

Still, two obstacles were to be overcome by the English people if they wanted to achieve any results in this huge endeavour. The first was to accept that the highest degree of civilization could not be taught to the 'savage' in a short period of time. According to Jones: 'Few things have entailed such waste of ethical force, which is man's very lifeblood, as the neglect of this simple practical maxim... We seek to engraft straightway the elevated thoughts of the Christian

---

[115] Muirhead, 'Imperialism', p. 93.
[116] Muirhead, 'Imperialism', p. 92.

religion upon crude and barbarous civilisations.'[117] A sudden rupture in the way a people lived, thought, worked, and believed would lead to adverse consequences the reformer did not aim for and it would most probably end in violence.[118] Thus, it was necessary not to fight against the current of the order of things and accept that 'morality, whether personal or social, can be acquired only step by step'.[119] Instead of forcing subject races to adopt the European ideas and values overnight, the British Empire was to educate its peoples so that they themselves would recognize the desirability of adopting them.

The second obstacle was strongly related to the first, and it was a limitation on the part of the English nation. Muirhead argued it was a mistake for the Empire to not trouble itself to understand its subject races' customs and traditions. The most serious impediment to the mission of civilizing these peoples was the fact that there was no organic link between their established customs and the European ideals which they were expected to adopt. Imposing such ideas and values on a race that could not assimilate them into their way of life was not only ineffective but also disruptive. According to Muirhead, this was the main reason for the British Empire's failure so far in its civilizing mission, although it provided all the necessary materials for the children of the Empire. As European values and ideas were not naturally assimilated by the subject races, two distinct reactions to their sudden introduction occurred. They either totally rejected the legitimacy of European ideas and developed hostility towards the mother country, or they strived to adopt these ideas to no avail. While the problem with the first reaction was clear enough, it was the second form of reaction that posed an even greater challenge to the civilizing mission:

---

[117] Jones, *Working Faith of the Social Reformer*, p. 26.
[118] Jones, *Working Faith of the Social Reformer*, p. 26.
[119] Jones, *Working Faith of the Social Reformer*, p. 26.

Education in the case of the latter class consists of a thin veneer of
European ideas sufficient to destroy the beliefs and sentiments that
gave the mind a hold on the realities of life, but wholly insufficient to
provide it with anything that can take their place.[120]

The result was a superficial adaptation to European values that did
not endow these individuals with the teachings of civilization while
severing their organic connection with the values of the society they
lived in. This was an outcome of English people's ineptitude in
dealing with 'more delicate tasks' such as 'education and social
reconstruction, requiring higher refinements of insight, tact, and
sympathy' that prevented the British Empire from educating the
subject races in European values.[121]

While these Idealists were aware of the shortcomings of the
Empire in its mission to 'civilize' humanity, they did not perceive it
as a failed attempt or as an impediment to international peace or
moral progress. On the contrary, they were quite confident in the
British Empire's ability to transform itself in order to better meet its
obligations to its daughter states such as Canada and Australia and
to its colonies such as India in the future. It was, after all, natural to
stumble on the way to the realization of a great empire the like of
which was never founded before. The English nation itself was in a
process of development in which it was learning the heavy duty of
civilizing the world. To that end Mackenzie wrote: 'we need not be
surprised that the consciousness of the obligations of empire does
not at once come upon us as a matured and sobered sense of duty.'[122]
For Mackenzie, Muirhead, and Jones, the duty of the British Empire
was an obvious one: transforming itself from a colonizer to a true
empire and to serve humanity by elevating other races to the level of
European civilization. In that sense, they overlooked Bosanquet's
contribution to the discussion of civilization that put emphasis on
the singularity of every society and the undesirability of creating a

---

[120] Muirhead, 'Imperialism', p. 94.
[121] Mackenzie, 'The Source of Moral Obligation', p. 470.
[122] Mackenzie, 'The Source of Moral Obligation', p. 470.

monolithic human civilization. For them, the moral duty of advancing humanity as a whole by spreading the ideas and values of a higher civilization overshadowed the particular contributions each society can make to humanity on its own terms. Their approach to 'subject races' reflected not a racist prejudice that located them at a sub-human level, but a belief that they were not yet developed enough to know how to realize their human potential. In other words, these writers thought, the subject races were not different from European peoples in terms of potential, but their level of civilization was not conducive to pursuing a truly human life. Thus, these peoples were judged only potential right-bearers, like children, who can be trusted with full rights and duties only after they were educated enough to know how to use them morally.

Muirhead, Jones, and Mackenzie agreed that the history of the Empire contained ample evidence of wrongdoing on the part of Britain. The Empire itself was grown 'out of actions often thoughtlessly, perhaps imprudently or even wickedly, undertaken'.[123] The imperial mission in its totality was not singularly guided by the love of humanity; it was often tainted by the vanity and greed of individuals. Although the British Empire was not the only party that committed itself to the lower passions of human nature, from time to time, it 'relapse[d] to lower standards—by the contention, for instance, that empire is empire, and that such an end sanctifies almost any means'.[124] In recognition of those failings, Mackenzie contended that 'we have, no doubt, like others, had great faults, made great mistakes, even, I am afraid, committed what can hardly be called less than great crimes'.[125] But the idea inherited from Green that there was no point in questioning what could have been done differently in the past resonated in the writings of Jones, Mackenzie, and Muirhead on the matter of the British Empire. Thus Muirhead

---

123 Muirhead, 'Imperialism', p. 88.
124 Mackenzie, 'The Source of Moral Obligation', p. 470.
125 Mackenzie, 'The Source of Moral Obligation', p. 477.

argued: 'how did the circumstances in which we find ourselves arise?' was not a relevant question; the question to be asked was 'what do these circumstances require of us?'[126] According to him, forfeiting imperial responsibilities would be the greatest crime against humanity. The situation in which Britain found itself at the end of the nineteenth century required it to embrace its duties all over the world and advance itself towards what he called a form of 'true imperialism'.[127] And according to Mackenzie, the spirit of imperialism was to be found neither in 'Little Englandism' nor in 'Jingoism'. It rather meant the solemn acceptance that Britain have its 'part to play with others in the great task of advancing humanity... in the promotion of peace, liberty, justice, and enlightenment'.[128]

So long as the citizens of the mother country carried the imperial crown, which to some seemed more like a 'crown of thorns', Britain was fulfilling its duty to its dependencies and colonies.[129] Admittedly, it was not an easy task, but the future of the British Empire was promising according to Muirhead and Mackenzie. Muirhead believed Britain had the capacity and the determination to prove that it was equal to the challenge at hand. He wrote: 'The case of Egypt has shown what British administration can achieve when it has the courage to grasp and undertake all that the situation requires for this object, when it is prepared to bring the best intelligence of the nation to bear on the task it has undertaken, and when, without flinching from the policy the circumstances dictate, it uses every opportunity to conciliate the better elements of European opinion.'[130] From a similarly optimistic perspective Mackenzie argued that when the opposition against this new form of political unity subsided, the positive outcome of the Empire in terms of unifying humanity and

---

[126] Muirhead, 'Imperialism', p. 88.
[127] Muirhead, 'Imperialism', p. 88.
[128] Mackenzie, 'The Source of Moral Obligation', p. 477.
[129] Mackenzie, 'The Source of Moral Obligation', p. 477.
[130] Muirhead, 'Imperialism', p. 96.

spreading European values would become clear even to the most fervent critics of the British Empire. He wrote:

> If we truly grasp the situation before us, if we see clearly where our obligations lie, we shall, I am convinced, find nothing but good in the breaking down of our insularity, in the widening of our horizon, whether it be in Africa, in India, or Australia, or it may be, nearer at home, in Ireland. If we seize the situation in the right spirit, there is every hope for us still, that when 'the tumult and the shouting dies' there will be some fruit of our labours that is not wholly vain, an honour that is not rooted in dishonour, a flag that is something better than a 'commercial asset'.[131]

Both Mackenzie and Muirhead wrote their work under consideration here in 1900 and possibly as a response to the ongoing discussions on the legitimacy of the Boer War in Britain. More than 40 years later, Muirhead wrote in his memoir that the Boer War was an imperial war that did not unite the nation for the cause of the Empire. Muirhead himself was openly critical of the imperial policy that led to the Boer War.[132] In his memoir of Bosanquet, Muirhead noted: 'Bosanquet, like Edward Caird, the master of Balliol and other leading British Idealist philosophers, was strongly "pro-Boer"'.[133] Similarly, Henry Jones recognized that Britain was not free from 'blatant imperialism' and 'reckless greed' that caused conflict with the subject races and with other European nations, explicitly referring to the Boer War.[134] Still, their misgivings regarding the Empire's motivation to go to war with the Dutch republics in South Africa did not result in a general mistrust towards the British Empire or imperialism in general. While some of them, mostly on private occasions, expressed discontent with the aggressive attitude of the

---

[131] Mackenzie, 'The Source of Moral Obligation', p. 477.

[132] Muirhead, *Reflections of a Journeyman in Philosophy*, p. 112.

[133] J.H. Muirhead (ed.) (2014) *Bernard Bosanquet and His Friends: Letters Illustrating the Sources and the Development of His Philosophical Opinions*, Oxon: Routledge, p. 95.

[134] Jones, *Working Faith of the Social Reformer*, p. 184.

government in this particular case, they continued to foster hopes for the evolution of a better and more efficient imperial organization.[135]

VI. Conclusion

Towards the end of the nineteenth century the place of the British Empire in the world became a hot topic of discussion in the political, intellectual, as well as scholarly circles of England. Not only British Idealists from their seats at various universities but also members of intellectual societies and journalists throughout the country were engaged in a fierce argument about the nature and aims of the British Empire. Obviously, one's position in regard to the Boer War did not directly implicate his position on the question of the Empire in general.[136] The Boers, as white Protestants, did not fit the usual stereotype of imperial enemies. Still the war gave rise to a long-sustained controversy about the moral legitimacy of imperialism and its possible repercussions for international order and peace. Among the British Idealists, only Ritchie exhibited an openly hostile stance towards the Boer. His position on the matter of the Boer War showed that he perceived the Boer as representatives of an insufficient and ineffective European force that prevented the British Empire from making better use of the natural sources of the land and governing the people. The natives of South Africa were 'savages' who needed to be taken under control either through acculturation into European values or through use of force. Although Bradley did not directly comment on the Boer War, his general reflections on the matter of imperialism make one think that he would have supported the British cause as a more straightforward way towards ensuring humanity's overall progress. In the other camp of the British Idealists were self-proclaimed pro-Boers such as Muirhead. They did not openly express their disdain for British aggression in South Africa

---

[135] Boucher and Vincent, *A Radical Hegelian*, p. 147.
[136] Williams, "Our War History in Cartoons is Unique': J.M. Staniforth, British Public Opinion, and the South African War, 1899–1902', p. 492.

towards the Boer in their writings. Still, it is possible to infer that like 'a handful of pro-Boer intellectuals' in Britain, they respected the 'rights of the small nations' so long as they belonged to the European civilization.[137] For them, the Dutch settlers would have been representatives of European civilization who were unjustly attacked by another power that was superior to them only in terms of military power. The native Africans on the other hand would have belonged to a civilization that was — temporarily — inferior to the European one and thus in need of protection and education as subjects of European colonizers.

Except for Bradley and Ritchie, the British Idealists that we have dealt with in this chapter neatly fitted into the 'liberal imperialist' mind frame that was dominant in England by the end of the nineteenth century. In *Reordering the World*, Duncan Bell defines liberal imperialism as a set of ideas that maintained 'liberal states have a right (even a duty) to spread "civilization" to the purportedly non-civilised peoples of the world… that empire is only legitimate if it is primarily intended to benefit the populations subjected to it'.[138] From the liberal imperialist perspective 'any other benefits' that were acquired through colonization were 'derivative and incidental'.[139] British Idealists were mostly in line with the liberal imperialist position that had been a popular justification for the Empire in the last two centuries. Still, there were certain variations in the way they adopted the main liberal imperialist line of argument into their own thought systems. One of the variations that can be perceived in liberal imperialist thought in general and among British Idealist in particular was related to the question regarding the future of the Empire. Was the Empire a prominent aspect of international order, or was it a temporary fix until such time that the colonized peoples

---

[137] J.S. Ellis (1998) "The Methods of Barbarism' and the 'Rights of Small Nations': War Propaganda and British Pluralism', *Albion: A Quarterly Journal Concerned with British Studies*, 30 (1), pp. 49–75.

[138] Bell, *Reordering the World*, p. 104.

[139] Bell, *Reordering the World*, p. 104.

acquired the ability to rule themselves as civilized nations? It can be discerned from the above discussions that some Idealists, like Bosanquet, treated the Empire as a temporary order of things that was to be superseded when the civilizing mission was achieved in the future.[140] Whereas Muirhead's reflections on the matter reveal that he perceived the Empire as a permanent state of international order; even when the colonized peoples were civilized, they were expected to uphold their organic relations with the mother country as in the example of the 'banyan tree'.[141]

An additional difference of emphasis can be perceived in the importance attributed to the economic benefits of the Empire for Britain and for the world. As it has been argued above, a singular focus on the economic benefits of the Empire was condemned by the British Idealists as an outdated and erroneous approach to the question of imperialism. The main focus by the end of the nineteenth century was the civilizing duty of the European peoples towards the colonized peoples in Asia, Africa, and the Pacific. While Muirhead faithfully followed this line of thinking and paid no attention to the material aspect of the matter, Henry Jones perceived the economic benefits and industrial developments achieved through the colonies as an important contribution of the Empire. Obviously, it was not 'solely, or even primarily' the economic benefits derived from imperialism that justified colonization for Jones. Thus, he defined the benefits of the Empire as 'good feeling *plus* sound business'.[142] Possibly, Jones's emphasis on the importance of the commercial relations can be understood as similar to Green's faith in the power of developing commercial relations among peoples as a way of creating good-will and cooperation among nations. Jones's interest in the economic aspect of colonization as a positive incentive for making good use of natural resources all around the world is a

---

[140] Bosanquet (1899) *Philosophical Theory of the State*, p. 330.
[141] Muirhead, 'Imperialism', p. 87.
[142] Bell, *Reordering the World*, p. 102; Jones, *Working Faith of the Social Reformer*, p. 131.

persistent one as he dwelled on this point throughout his tour of Australia in 1908.[143] Although the developments in production in colonized territories were not the main justificatory cause for colonization, it was an important one for Jones. Thus, he said in a speech delivered at Sydney University: 'Australia, in spite of its vast extent of rich soil and its mountains veined with gold, was a poor continent, of no account in the world's mart, so long as its inhabitants were savage.'[144]

While the British Idealists' arguments were mostly in line with the general liberal imperialist mind-set, their writings from the 1900s show that they did not necessarily believe that the civilizing mission of the Europeans was a good enough moral reason for colonization. Although they clearly defined the civilizing mission as a 'duty' of the Europeans as the more civilized nations, they adopted an apologetic language when they dealt with the origins of the British Empire. Mackenzie, Muirhead, and Jones described the British Empire as a legacy of the British national history that contained a fair amount of immoral conquest. Thus, the Empire was a 'crown of thorns'; a burden for the English people that they were morally bound to carry. But more importantly, it was not possible to undo the immoral acts committed in the past during the colonization period. On the contrary, the only available moral action was to ensure that the Empire served the interests of the peoples that were already colonized. This was a curious position to occupy. While the civilizing mission was not perceived strong enough to justify the conquest of another people, it was still defended as the moral justification for keeping the colonies that were already under British rule.

This attitude adopted by Muirhead and Mackenzie especially fits in very well with what Karuna Mantena defined as an 'alibi' rather than a moral justification for the British Empire. Mantena argues in

---

[143] See for example: H. Jones (1909) *Idealism as a Practical Creed*, Glasgow: James Maclehose and Sons, p. 55.

[144] Jones, *Idealism as a Practical Creed*, p. 53.

'The Crisis of Liberal Imperialism', as 'different forms of rebellion, resistance and instability in the colonies' challenged the British Empire in the second half of the nineteenth century, the civilizing mission argument also started to lose its convincing power. Thus 'rather than as a willed and purposive moral project, empire was instead deemed a practical necessity arising from the nature of colonised societies themselves'.[145] For the British Idealists the civilizing mission constituted a justificatory argument because it was already introduced into the social and political structure of the native peoples. Abandoning these peoples was believed to be counterproductive as the Empire already disturbed their organic development and it was impossible for these societies to go back to a pre-British Empire order. Thus, it was the need of these peoples for the presence of the Empire as a social and political stabilizing force that justified its authority. Additionally, deferring the moral responsibility to a previous version of the British Empire absolved its present state from the moral responsibility of justifying its existence. Mackenzie's argument that the British people woke up one morning to realize that they were in possession of colonies all over the world, or Muirhead's choice of wording when he wrote that the Empire was a 'situation Britain found itself in', are clear examples of this attempt to escape moral responsibility.[146] By severing the link between the 'British Empire as a conquering power' and the 'British Empire with a duty to civilize the peoples under its rule', Muirhead and Mackenzie were forfeiting the quest of morally justifying the existence of the 'British Empire' as a whole.

Overall, Muirhead's, Mackenzie's, and Jones's alignment with the liberal imperialist mind-set was in line with Green's contention that 'Christian citizenship' constituted the highest moral consciousness achieved by humanity and that moral progress was in the nature of

---

[145] K. Mantena, 'The Crisis of Liberal Imperialism', p. 131.
[146] Muirhead, 'Imperialism', p. 88; Mackenzie, 'The Source of Moral Obligation', p. 469.

humanity. Yet, they ignored Green's warning that imperialism was prone to give rise to international jealousies and militarization. Evidently, they were not isolated in their support for the Empire; they were part of a large and fragmented front that consisted of liberals, socialists, and conservatives that 'differed over the forms of empire they defended, the intensity of support they offered, and perhaps most significantly, the justificatory arguments that they articulated'.[147] Even among these three Idealists of the same generation there was not an absolute agreement on the details of the justificatory argument. Still, what they put forward neatly fitted in what Bell called the 'ideal typical justificatory strategy' of the 'civilizing argument'. Yet when the Great War proved Green right, they gradually distanced themselves from their previous imperialist position and adopted a position, more similar to Bosanquet's, by focusing on the importance of people's particularities in the formation of a cooperative human unity.

---

[147] Bell, *Reordering the World*, p. 19.

Chapter 3

From Empire to Commonwealth

British Idealists' Trial with the First World War

Like many British liberal imperialists of the nineteenth century, British Idealists were forced by the Great War to investigate the roots of European militarization that led to this great catastrophe. But unlike other British intellectuals, they were also burdened with the task of proving that their position was not inherently linked to 'Prussian state-worship and militarism'. During the war they made several attempts to negate the accusation that Hegelianism in Germany was responsible for the Great War. Instead, they argued, it was the distortion of Hegelianism through its contamination with materialistic arguments that gave rise to Prussian militarism and the Great War. Von Bernhardi and Treitschke's works were the most obvious examples of this distorted version of Hegel's work and evidently they were not similar to the works of British Idealists—the true heirs of Hegel's political philosophy. Still, their recognition of the materialistic roots of German militarism that is fuelled by the enthusiasm for the establishment of a German World Empire brought with it the necessity to exercise self-criticism. Starting with Henry Jones—and with the exception of Viscount Haldane—they recognized the materialistic and immoral nature of imperialism and distanced themselves from the language of civilization and progress they used previously in defence of the Empire. Rather, they moved on to defend the necessity of transforming the Empire into a commonwealth composed of free and equal nations. By the end of the Great War, they were again in line with the general liberal senti- ment in Britain that abandoned the goal of sustaining a vast empire with the purpose of 'civilizing' subject peoples and moved on to emphasize the necessity of establishing a commonwealth consisting mainly of the settler colonies of Canada, Australia, South Africa, and New Zealand. In this period, the future of the dependent colonies constituted an unsavoury discussion topic and it was glossed over through voicing an unqualified intention to liberate them as soon as possible.

The majority of the articles published in the *International Journal of Ethics* on the matter of the Great War from 1915 to 1918 maintained that the war was the outcome of Great Powers' imperial ambitions that had been hidden behind a veil of false morality until 1914. In these articles, the Great Powers were no longer spoken of as benevolent forces of civilization but as aggressive forces that pose a considerable threat to the security and survival of smaller nations.[1] The imperialistic claim of civilizing the barbarians was no longer accepted as a legitimate reason to claim dominion over other peoples. The doctrine of the 'white man's burden' was decreed as intolerable as the German's 'conviction that *Deutschtum* is to be the salvation of the world'.[2] As the 'dominant race' became ready to 'sicken at the talk of 'the white man's burden', as nothing but so much tyrannical can't', British as well as the American intellectuals began to envision a new world order.[3] The new order, be it a World- Parliament, a European concert, or a League of Peace, was expected to put an end to the pre-Great War practice of forming alliances and

---

1   H.T. Weeks (1918) 'An International War Chest', *International Journal of Ethics*, 29 (1), p. 27.
2   H.A. Overstreet (1918) 'Ethical Clarifications through the War', *Inter- national Journal of Ethics*, 28 (3), p. 333.
3   F.M. Stawell (1915) 'Patriotism and Humanity', *International Journal of Ethics*, 25 (3), p. 299.

counter-alliances to maintain a balance of power among the Great Powers. Furthermore, in this new order, the dominant values of the civilized nations, after which they had been striving, were to be redefined so as to enable increased cooperation among independent nation-states. The goal was to ensure that, at the international level, values of 'self-direction' and 'equality' replaced the imperialistic 'line of superior–inferior class rule'.[4]

Both the British Idealists and their fiercest critics were part of this newly popularized anti-imperialistic sentiment and the quest to envision a new world order. In *The World in Conflict*, Hobhouse wrote: 'the catastrophe of 1914 was not for the observer of currents of public life in any way a bolt from the blue. It was the climax of a time of stress and strain, the final eruption of forces that had been shaking the world for two decades.'[5] The forces that shook the world were generated by the 'ideas of world domination based on racial superiority' and they were not specific to the German mind-set. Referring to the Boer War, Hobhouse argued against the notion that only German imperialism was militaristically aggressive and noted: 'that any such suggestion is possible in England only shows how short are the political memories of men. It is less than twenty years since very similar notions enjoyed a brief but disastrous ascendancy in this country, under the name of Imperialism.'[6] Similarly, Hobson condemned all the Great Powers in their 'cravings' for 'places in the sun', and asked, 'can we confidently assert that no other State has in the past harboured such designs, or may not harbour them again?'[7] According to Hobson, the international order before the Great War that was defined by the 'pursuit of the Balance of Power' was 'seen

---

[4]   J.H. Tufts (1918) 'Ethics and International Relations', *International Journal of Ethics*, 28 (3), p. 311.

[5]   L.T. Hobhouse (1915) *The World in Conflict*, London: T. Fisher Unwin Ltd, pp. 15–16.

[6]   Hobhouse, *World in Conflict*, p. 52.

[7]   J.A. Hobson (1915) *Towards International Government*, New York: The Macmillan Company, p. 14.

to be nothing else than an idle feint'.[8] Like Hobhouse, Hobson recognized the end of the Great War as a critical juncture for the realization of a wider and ethical international order. In 1916 he wrote, 'I believe that, as the product of the war, there will exist a greatly strengthened common will for peace, for peace at almost any price' in its aftermath.[9] He added that if each state had a strong conviction regarding the necessity of forming an international organization for its own security as well as the security of other states, a world federation would strengthen the common will of humanity.[10]

Although the British Empire itself emerged from the Great War with larger territories, the war struck a deadly blow to British liberals' faith in the imperial project as a means of civilizing the world. This was the result of a combination of factors that were experienced not only by the intellectuals but also by the general public, the peoples in the dependent colonies, and the soldiers who fought the war. For the British soldiers it was a first time experience to see the territories they ruled over and to fight alongside soldiers from these distant lands; it was an opportunity to put a face on their 'imperial subjects'.[11] To the peoples who fought for Britain, the war revealed the importance of their contribution to the war effort and led them to seek equality in government, as they were expected to give equal service in the battlefield.[12] Concessions were already made to certain colonies during the war and there was a general trend of demanding more autonomy from the mother country in all

---

8   Hobson, *Towards International Government*, p. 23.
9   J.A. Hobson (1916) 'Is International Government Possible?', *The Hibbert Journal*, 15, p. 203.
10 Hobson, 'Is International Government Possible?', p. 203.
11 H. Tinker (1977) *Race, Conflict and the International Order*, London: Macmillan Education UK, p. 39.
12 E. Manela (2007) *The Wilsonian Moment: Self-Determination and the International Origins of Anticolonial Nationalism*, Oxford: Oxford University Press, p. 12.

the colonies.[13] But most importantly, the rhetoric adopted during the war in condemnation of Germany put unparalleled emphasis on nations' right to freedom and self-determination.

Dissemination of these values made it impossible to defend the Empire through the 'civilizing' argument. Thus, a considerable section of liberal imperialists, instead of totally abandoning the imperial project and demanding de-colonization, devoted their allegiance to the idea of a 'British Commonwealth' that was imagined as a family of free nations.[14] According to Bernard Porter, supporters of the Commonwealth in Britain in the post Great War period were 'antediluvian imperialists, romantics, humanitarians and Fabian socialists; people who in former times had positively welcomed the Empire for what they believed to be its contribution to the good of mankind, or else wished at least to see its successor making up for the bad it had done'.[15] Such re-conceptualization of the Empire necessitated one further alteration in the way liberals understood and condoned imperialism. Re-branding the Empire as a commonwealth, a family of nations, necessitated paying increased attention to settler colonies, and ignoring so far as possible the dependent colonies that did not easily fit into this picture. Although the tendency to focus on the settler colonies while thinking about the British Empire was present in the last quarter of the nineteenth century, the dominant vocabulary used by the liberals in the aftermath of the Great War made overlooking the existence of dependent colonies a practical necessity.[16]

In this period a new set of values such as self-determination, national sovereignty, international cooperation, and community of nations replaced the vocabulary of civilization, progress, and

---

[13] B. Porter (2004) *The Absent-Minded Imperialists: Empire, Society, and Culture in Britain*, Oxford: Oxford University Press, p. 256.

[14] Porter, *Absent-Minded Imperialists*, p. 276.

[15] B. Porter (2016) *Empire Ways: Aspects of British Imperialism*, London: I.B. Tauris, p. 25.

[16] Bell, *Victorian Visions of Global Order*, p. 281.

educating the 'savages' or the 'barbarians'. Thus, reflections on the future of dependent colonies focused on the distant goal of granting national liberty to the peoples who achieved a certain level of social and political maturity. The end pursued by the Commonwealth was not to keep the colonies under British rule but to set them free to become equal and cooperative members of the international community of nations.[17] This obviously did not mean that British liberals totally abandoned the belief in their civilizational superiority. It rather meant that colonizing and ruling foreign peoples was no longer perceived to be a feasible or defendable method of civilizing the rest of the world.

I. Mackenzie, Jones, Muirhead, and Haldane from 1900 to 1914

The previous chapter shows that prominent British Idealists were 'imperialists' to varying degrees by the end of the nineteenth century. Bradley and Ritchie were the fiercest advocates of the imperial cause amongst this school of thinkers. Although they occupied a marginal position in the overall British Idealist approach to the issue of imperialism, they constitute a great example of what Idealism was transformed into when the link of mutual good between the parts and the whole was severed. When the whole was constituted not as an aggregate of its parts but as an independent and supreme end, its parts became expendable. This hard-line imperialist British-Idealist position faded in the years following the Boer War as Ritchie died in 1903 and Bradley was no longer interested in international relations.

For the rest of the Idealists, a 'true empire' became morally legitimate not only with reference to the end it served but also with the means it employed for its realization. In 1898, Bosanquet argued for instance against the contention that a plausible end justified the means used in its pursuance. He argued that a unification achieved

---

17 Porter, *The Absent-Minded Imperialists*, p. 282.

by the 'rule of blood and iron' was doomed to be a fragile and short-lived one and its morality was questionable to say the least. The desirability of an end was not a satisfactory criterion in judging the morality of an act because 'all ends are laudable to those who desire them, it would be held to follow simply and absolutely that might is right'.[18] Minor figures among the British Idealists also embraced the ideal of a 'true empire' which was to found its unity on the educated will of the nations and their economic, technological, and moral cooperation with each other. The Boer War was a sign of the British Empire's failure to constitute a 'true empire', yet it was not a reason to dismiss the possibility of reform in the future. If the British people proved capable of fulfilling their duty to mankind and formed a 'true empire', all of the nations living under its flag were to benefit from such an enormous achievement. Although, following the Boer War, the issue of imperialism temporarily lost its popularity in public and scholarly discussions, British Idealists continued to reflect on the matter in their books, lectures, and speeches in the years that preceded the Great War.

In 1906, Mackenzie delivered a series of lectures as the Dunkin Lecturer in Sociology at Manchester College, Oxford, under the title of 'Humanism'.[19] It constituted one of the most extensive studies of the concept of humanity as a larger unity than particular nations conducted by a British Idealist. In a prefatory note to the book in which the lectures were collected, Mackenzie stated: 'the subject of "Humanism" was selected, as having a special interest at that particular time and place.'[20] The special interest in humanism was due to what can be called the spirit of the time they were living in because the 'modern conception of the political life is so completely

---

[18] B. Bosanquet (1898) 'A Moral from Athenian History', *International Journal of Ethics*, 9 (1), in Bosanquet (1917) *Social and International Ideals*, London: The Macmillan Company, p. 267.

[19] J.S. Mackenzie (1907) *Lectures on Humanism*, London: Swan Sonnenschein & Co., Lim.

[20] Mackenzie, *Lectures on Humanism*, p. v.

international as to make the precise form of earlier accounts almost entirely inapplicable'.[21] Mackenzie contended that the modern outlook was so international that it was possible to perceive all European nations as a single unity; and as distant and unique a country as Japan was also becoming an intrinsic part of the international community.[22]

Mackenzie's approach to humanity was decisively different from what Comte called the 'religion of humanity'. While Comte's humanitarianism necessitated individuals' complete reverence for humanity, it was not realistic to expect such love towards a concept, which was not a real unity.[23] Instead, the object of love and devotion was to be to a humanity of the future that could only be achieved through human endeavour. Mackenzie's definition of humanity did not constitute a fallacious antagonism between humanitarianism and nationalism. He argued it was erroneous 'to think of a real humanism as obliterating the significance of national distinctions'.[24] Instead humanity was to be understood as a brotherhood of nations, which were intertwined through their social, economic, intellectual, and sentimental relations. Mackenzie noted in his lectures: 'the nation cannot properly be regarded, any more than the individual, either as an independent atom or as something that may be mechanically moulded by external forces.'[25] The overall emphasis of Mackenzie's discussion of humanity was on the brotherhood of nations and their participation in a larger unity. But he also recognized the possibility of 'help' for the development of a nation from the 'larger life of the world' even with an element of compulsion.[26] His reasoning largely depended on his understanding of democracy. For him, understanding democracy as the requirement that each individual should

---

[21] Mackenzie, *Lectures on Humanism*, p.89.
[22] Mackenzie, *Lectures on Humanism*, p. 89.
[23] Mackenzie, *Lectures on Humanism*, p. 181.
[24] Mackenzie, *Lectures on Humanism*, p. 103.
[25] Mackenzie, *Lectures on Humanism*, pp. 103–04.
[26] Mackenzie, *Lectures on Humanism*, p. 104.

have an equal voice in the ruling of his country was deficient. He argued in this work that the essential nature of democracy was that 'each may be at once sovereign and subject...'[27] According to Mackenzie, a political order was to be considered democratic so far as everyone found 'a place as an organic member in the progressive life of humanity' and became sovereign 'in those things in which he has insight, subject in those in which he is dependent on the insight of others'.[28] Such a conception of democracy required not subjection of races to other races, or classes to other classes, but 'of the inferior elements in all to the superior'.[29] But if a whole nation or race was to be perceived as inferior in the ladder of civilization, it might have been possible to form a defence of 'democratic imperialism' based on Mackenzie's approach to humanity.

Muirhead embraced a similar mission to reconcile the democratic ideal with imperialism in his 1908 book *The Service of the State*. Following an imperialist interpretation of Green's political philosophy, Muirhead concluded his book by equating 'the true democratic' faith with 'the true imperialist faith' and argued that if Britain failed to live up to that faith it would not be 'owing to any fault in its theory, but to some defect in ourselves or our instruments, some inability to enter into the common purpose of all civilisation, and to embody the spirit of the best political teaching in our actual administration'.[30] Muirhead's evaluation of the 'true empire' and his assessment of Britain's approximation to it was very similar to the one he put forward in 'What Imperialism Means' eight years earlier. He merely altered the word reconstruction to development in defining the true aim of the Empire and argued that the Empire was to develop what was 'best in the instincts and traditions of these

---

[27] Mackenzie, *Lectures on Humanism*, pp. 98–99.
[28] Mackenzie, *Lectures on Humanism*, pp. 98–99.
[29] Mackenzie, *Lectures on Humanism*, p. 99.
[30] J.H. Muirhead (1908) *The Service of the State: Four Lectures on the Political Teaching of T.H. Green*, London: John Murray, p. 112.

races themselves'.[31] So, instead of planting foreign ideas and values into the subject races, the Empire was to untangle their good values from those that were not so good, and develop those that were beneficial. This principle was based on the belief that 'there is latent in the laws, institutions and ritual observances of even the most backward societies the aspiration after a form of life which, while in its details it is adapted to the particular instincts and experiences of the people who have developed them, yet in its broad features is human and universal'.[32] While he acknowledged the value of these particular expressions of the universal ideas and values in subject races, Muirhead still believed that the British had much to teach them. It was Britain's duty to capture not only the imagination but also the intelligence of the subject races by showing them 'what good government *means*' and that they were dependent on the good government of the British 'for peace and security of person and property, for command of the resources of science in the control of nature, for freedom of thought and speech, for their territorial homes, and for the graves and worship of their ancestors'.[33] From Muirhead's perspective, non-British subjects of the Empire as rational human beings were expected to realize the beneficence of the British rule, if that rule was conducted justly.

At the very end of his discussion of imperialism in *The Service of the State*, Muirhead introduced a new condition for being a 'true empire', which he did not mention in his previous work. Referring to Green's unconditional defence of self-government and active citizenship, Muirhead argued the ideal of the Empire was to bestow self-government on its subject races. By quoting Green's contention that having the 'higher feeling of political duty' was the basic condition of being a loyal and responsible subject, Muirhead argued that any steps taken in including the native races in political deliberation

---

[31] Muirhead, *Service of the State*, p. 106.
[32] Muirhead, *Service of the State*, pp. 106–07.
[33] Muirhead, *Service of the State*, pp. 109–10.

were steps taken towards the realization of the ideal.[34] Although he acknowledged that to 'the distant administrator contending with the superstition, the petty jealousies and the stupidities of communities scarcely emerged from barbarism' such a theory might seem aloof from the situation at hand, he expressed his belief in the moral requirement of gradually including every subject of the Empire in the decision-making processes.[35]

In 1910, it was Henry Jones's turn to deliver the Dunkin Trust Lectures at Manchester College. Jones's lectures were published later under the title *The Working Faith of the Social Reformer* and this volume included a lecture on 'The Moral Aspect of the Fiscal Question' in which he addressed the most contentious aspects of international relations. For Jones, the most pressing issue in regard to Britain's relations with other countries was economic in its nature by 1910. But the economic nature of the problem did not change the necessity of discussing it on the foundation of moral principles. Jones, like all other British Idealists, was a fierce opponent of Chamberlain's tariff reform and his opposition was based on the Idealist contention that any form of conflict between nations' interests was a delusion. According to Jones, the theoretical basis on which a protectionist fiscal policy was advocated was highly erroneous. Protectionists often argued that 'a man cannot, at least so far as concerns material things, be a citizen of the world without neglecting, or at times violating even, his duties to his own country. We are entitled to suspect the patriotism of the humanitarian'.[36] Jones argued, from the perspective of the protectionists, the only moral duty that constrained a state's actions was its obligation to provide larger territories, more powerful military power, and higher material returns for the benefit of its own citizens. Such a perspective naturally resulted in perceiving the international order as a state of

---

[34] Muirhead, *Service of the State*, pp. 111–12.
[35] Muirhead, *Service of the State*, p. 111.
[36] Jones, *Working Faith of the Social Reformer*, p. 141.

perpetual conflict. Jones expressed the inherent contradiction in this position by stating that 'now, as all States have ideally the same obligations to their citizens, and therefore the same unlimited rights, they are natural rivals; and the normal relation between them is that of mechanical strain'.[37] This was a direct application of Hobbesian 'individualism' to states in their relations with each other.[38]

Instead, Jones offered, it was necessary to perceive the international order as a sphere of common good for the benefit of all states. As progress meant moving beyond purely natural concerns, with the use of reason and introduction of moral principles, rivalry and hostility would give place to cooperation and friendly competition. As Mackenzie argued before, Jones noted that humanity was not, as of yet, a concrete unity like the particular states were. States were embodiments of a unity that was 'much more rich, concrete, and strong than that of any private person' and in that capacity they were to be considered as building blocks of the unity of mankind.[39] Actualization of the larger unity of humanity was dependent on particular nations' understanding that 'the good which is exclusive is a false good' and that a strong state is not a threat but a blessing to its neighbours.[40] When such an understanding of the international order was applied to the matter at hand, Jones argued that free trade revealed itself to be an irrevocable principle. He wrote:

> The British Empire, by its political and social progress, by its science and inventions and industrial enterprise, has benefited every country with which it has held intercourse. And other nations have done the same to us. Their good is ours, and ours theirs. Even in international trade, where self-seeking seems to be at the same both evident and most justifiable, our best neighbour is our strongest neighbour; for it

---

37 Jones, *Working Faith of the Social Reformer*, p. 140.
38 Jones, *Working Faith of the Social Reformer*, p. 142.
39 Jones, *Working Faith of the Social Reformer*, p. 145.
40 Jones, *Working Faith of the Social Reformer*, p. 147.

buys from us to supply its own needs and sells most to us so as to supply ours. We cannot profit by its decay, nor it by ours.[41]

According to Jones, acting in contradiction to this moral principle was expressing antagonism to other nations and it was to be considered as a 'wrong against humanity'.[42] It was the British Empire's compliance with this moral law that made it great and that ensured its future contributions to the progress of humanity.

Clearly by 1910 Jones was confident that the British Empire was a beneficiary to humanity. In addition to humanity's progress as an absolute end to which every state should strive towards, a state's moral worth was determined with reference to its service to those peoples it ruled. For Jones, there was a clear-cut formula to determine a state's moral worth: 'Any government is good whose purpose is to serve the permanent interests of the governed.'[43] But, like Mackenzie and Muirhead, Jones did not advocate every single individual's inclusion in the political decision-making processes as a condition for being a legitimate political order. He argued that democracy was the best form 'only because the political wisdom of the many is capable of being much greater than the wisdom of the one'.[44] But his advocacy of democracy was conditioned by the question of whether many actually had political wisdom or not. When the many was ignorant and selfish, democracy was the worst kind of government because 'the political folly of the many brings with it more irretrievable disaster than the folly of one'.[45] Thus, the moral criterion to be applied to determine the legitimacy of a state was not related to the question whether or not it let its citizens take part in politics without considering their capacity to fulfil this role. Rather, the criterion was whether or not a state used its power to

---

41 Jones, *Working Faith of the Social Reformer*, p. 146.
42 Jones, *Working Faith of the Social Reformer*, p. 150.
43 Jones, *Idealism as a Practical Creed*, p. 114.
44 Jones, *Idealism as a Practical Creed*, p. 115.
45 Jones, *Idealism as a Practical Creed*, p. 115.

educate and develop its citizens so that they can realize their full potential and earn the right to have a say about how they are ruled.

On his way to Australia in 1908, Jones visited his eldest son Hal who was an imperial official in Burma. This occasion supplied ample opportunity for Jones to reflect on the moral qualities of the 'savages'. In his biography Hetherington stated: 'what he saw made a deep impression on his mind. He was firmly convinced of the beneficence of British rule in Burma; that there, at least, England sought and secured not her own advantage but the safety and welfare of the native population.'[46] And, in his letters, Jones wrote about the native Burmese with great affection and praise. They were evidently good-natured and their children had an advantage over 'the poor creatures either over-nursed or under-nursed in Glasgow' as the Burmese children were 'fat and free and easy and confident'.[47] Yet they were not to be trusted with the rights of citizenship until they internalized the Western 'genius for statecraft' or a strong 'impulse towards political freedom'.[48] It is remarkable that it was Henry Jones who paid the least attention to the particular values of the subject races among the British Idealists until the Great War broke out. With the war, he became the most explicit critic of the imperialist sentiment that led European civilization to greed, ambition, and a war of unprecedented magnitude.

Lord Haldane's address to the American Bar Association in 1913 was the last extensive reflection by a British Idealist on international order before the outbreak of the Great War. His address was published under the title 'Higher Nationality' in 1914.[49] At the time Haldane delivered his address to an audience composed of

---

46 H.J.W. Hetherington (1924) *The Life and Letters of Sir Henry Jones*, London: Hodder and Stoughton Limited, p. 104.

47 Hetherington, *Life and Letters of Sir Henry Jones*, p. 204.

48 Jones, *Idealism as a Practical Creed*, p. 69.

49 R.B. Haldane (1914) *Higher Nationality: A Study in Law and Ethics*, Washington: United States of America Government Printing Office, reprinted in Haldane (1915) *The Conduct of Life and Other Addresses*, New York: E.P. Dutton & Company.

American and Canadian lawyers, he was the Lord Chancellor of Great Britain. In this address, Haldane did not dwell on the Empire's responsibility towards its 'less-civilised' subjects or the necessity of ensuring the British rule where it was threatened by other European nations. Haldane was interested in the — possible — union among 'the Anglo-Saxon group' which was constituted by the daughter nations of Britain such as Canada and Australia, and the United States of America. According to Haldane, the USA's separation from the British Empire following a war between them was not to prevent the formation of an Anglo-Saxon group with shared ideals and ends.[50] For Haldane, such a unity among the Anglo-Saxon peoples was not only racial but also moral. It was based on what he called 'Sittlichkeit', for the lack of a counterpart in the English language, which meant 'the system of habitual or customary conduct, ethical rather than legal', which embraces all those obligations of the citizen which it is 'bad form' or 'not the thing' to disregard.[51] The USA was a natural part of this unity, as this unity was not based on the administration of a common positive law but on the traditional and voluntary following of a common moral law.

As 'Sittlichkeit' had been hitherto used as the signifier of a moral law within a nation, Haldane asked: 'can nations form a group or community among themselves within which a habit of looking to common ideals may grow up sufficiently strong to develop a General Will, and to make the binding power of these ideals a reliable sanction for the obligations to each other?'[52] According to Haldane, there was nothing in the nature of things that prevented the formation of 'Sittlichkeit' that would apply to multiple nations. Yet it was an ideal to be followed and there was 'a long road to be travelled' until this ideal was realized.[53] For Haldane, the moral unity of the 'Anglo-Saxon group' was significant for the opportunity

---

50   Haldane, *Conduct of Life*, p. 131.
51   Haldane, *Conduct of Life*, p. 115.
52   Haldane, *Conduct of Life*, p. 127.
53   Haldane, *Conduct of Life*, p. 128.

it supplied for constituting a starting point for international cooperation. He observed that almost every nation was starting to realize the
necessity of forming favourable relations with each other. He wrote:

> There are signs that the best people in the best nations are ceasing to
> wish to live in a world of mere claims, and to proclaim on every
> occasion 'Our country, right or wrong.' There is growing up a
> disposition to believe that it is good, not only for all men but for all
> nations, to consider their neighbours' point of view as well as their
> own. There is apparent at least a tendency to seek for a higher
> standard of ideals in international relations.[54]

This tendency to follow a higher moral standard in matters con-
cerning nations' relations with each other was highly observable
among developed nations as they were leaving the ambition of conquest and war behind them. The significance of the 'Anglo-Saxon
group' stemmed from the already existing unity of sentiment among
the members of these several nations. Haldane believed that
development of 'Sittlichkeit' among nations was 'certainly easier and
more hopeful in the case of nations with some special relation, than
it is within a mere aggregate of nations'.[55] Canada, Great Britain, and
the USA were already part of such a group of nations that already
had a special relation. They shared not only a common morality but
also very similar judicial systems.

Possibly due to the special occasion for which Haldane prepared
this address, he did not discuss the nature of Great Britain's relation
with its dependencies with which it did not share a common
morality. He focused on the Anglo-Saxon group, which he perceived
to be a valuable example of international cooperation and a starting
point for larger unity. He called his vision for a peaceful international order 'the group system' in his address. Although he did
not offer a detailed description of this system, he supplied his vision
with examples. According to Haldane, Germany and Austria, and
France and Russia were examples of existing groups that were

---

[54] Haldane, *Conduct of Life*, pp. 128–29.
[55] Haldane, *Conduct of Life*, p. 129.

willing to cooperate with each other although their sentiment was not based on formal conventions. Haldane argued that formation of such groupings was highly desirable for strengthening a mutual acceptance of international obligations. Although such cooperation was 'still young', Haldane was highly optimistic of its future success as European nations were becoming more and more willing to cooperate each other:

> Recent events in Europe and the way in which the Great Powers have worked together to preserve the peace of Europe, as if forming one community, point to the ethical possibility of the group system as deserving of close study by both statesmen and students. The 'Sittlichkeit' which can develop itself between the peoples of even a loosely connected group seems to promise a sanction for International Obligation which has not hitherto, so far as I know, attracted attention in connection with International Law.[56]

Unquestionably, Haldane was unique among the British Idealists in his lack of interest in the question of legitimacy of British rule over its colonies. He was before the war, and remained to be long after it, a believer in Britain's right to have 'a place in the sun'.[57] He seemed to be unaware of the fact that colonies of the Great Powers were already inhabited by native peoples and their rule by foreign powers constituted a dilemma when considered in relation with the European values of freedom and democracy. But Haldane was a pioneer among the British Idealists due to the importance he attributed to the former and current settler colonies of Britain as a precursor for a family of equal nations. His position can be taken as an example of Anglo-American commonwealthism that did not gain much support until 1914.[58] It was not, for instance, until after the Great War that Mackenzie and Muirhead diverted their attention from the dependent colonies and focused on the idea of a British Commonwealth.

Before the Great War, Mackenzie and Muirhead were evidently aware of the moral dilemmas imperialism posed and they

---

[56] Haldane, *Conduct of Life*, p. 130.
[57] Haldane, *Before the War*, p. 102.
[58] Bell, *Reordering the World: Essays on Liberalism and Empire*, p. 196.

endeavoured to reconcile the ideal of democracy with the apparent lack of it in British colonies. Their answer to this problem was that the nations who lived under British rule were not yet ready to rule themselves, and the idea of democracy did not require the rule of an ignorant majority. It was empires', British or otherwise, duty to develop those nations to their full potential before trusting them with the heavy duty of maintaining a state of their own. As the question of legitimacy was answered, Mackenzie, Jones, and Haldane interested themselves in the relations between civilized countries. It was a general contention among the British Idealists that mutual recognition of international obligations and a sentiment of common good was revealing itself in the spirit of the coming era. For them, it was a revelation of the evolving nature of humanity; of the transformation of pure egoism into an 'enlightened egoism, which recognises that the good which is exclusive is a false good'.[59] They maintained that especially European nations were starting to realize that those things that were truly 'good' could be achieved through cooperation rather than through hostility and conflict. Furthermore, the wrong or misfortune of a state was starting to be understood as a problem that affected its neighbours and its solution was transformed into a common responsibility. Overall, there was an emerging sentiment that valued humanity as a whole among the civilized nations. This sentiment was based on the growing recognition of a moral principle that was summarized by Henry Jones as follows:

> The failure or the prosperity of a particular State has always communicated itself to its neighbours precisely in the same way. Every wrong deed on the part of an individual State is a wrong to humanity, and every action that is right and good for itself is in the last resort a contribution to the stability and prosperity of its neighbours.[60]

---

[59] Jones, *Working Faith of the Social Reformer*, p. 147.
[60] Jones, *Working Faith of the Social Reformer*, p. 146.

II. Initial Response to the Great War

The British Idealist optimism regarding the future of the international order as an arena of cooperation and mutual respect among the civilized nations of Europe was proven wrong by the outbreak of the Great War. Mackenzie, in his book published in 1928, expressed the sense of shock experienced by the cultivated men of Europe when the Great War began: 'When the War actually broke out, those who had placed confidence in any of the existing bonds of unity had a rude awakening; and many felt almost as if the foundations of their world had been completely wrecked.'[61] Although he admitted that there were clear signs of preparation for a war of unprecedented scope, the apparent growth of communication and cooperation among nations created a sense of false security. He argued:

> In the early years of the century, although it was well known that preparations for war on a scale of unprecedented magnitude were being made in all the leading European countries, and though its imminence had been emphasised by many competent observers, yet there was in most men's minds an ineradicable disposition to believe that such a calamity was 'unthinkable'... Friendly intercourse between the different peoples was probably more general than it had ever been before. Cultivated men in different parts of Europe appreciated one another's work and were often in relations of cordial friendship with those who shared their special interests in countries that were regarded as their rivals.[62]

Apparently British Idealists were not among those 'competent observers' who warned against the possibility of a Great War. On the contrary, they were quite content with the level of civilization achieved in Europe and they advised only the furtherance of friendly relations on the Continent. Their primary concern in regard to world order was ensuring progress through elevating non-European nations to the level of European civilization. The source of their trust in a peaceful Europe was not only based on the friendly relations

---

[61] J.S. Mackenzie (1928) *Fundamental Problems of Life: An Essay on Citizenship as Pursuit of Values*, London: George Allen & Unwin Ltd, p. 329.

[62] MacKenzie, *Fundamental Problems of Life*, p. 327.

among the cultivated segments of European peoples but also on developing the means of communication among European nations. Muirhead noted, back in 1897, 'we have the growth of international sympathy, industrial cooperation, and a community of intellectual interests, symbolised by such modern phenomena as international boards of arbitration, labour conferences, industrial exhibitions, postal unions, laws of copyright and of extradition'.[63] Similarly, in 1901 Ritchie mentioned 'international postal and telegraph bureaus' as a proof of the emerging union of European nations.[64] Their trust in the new connective powers of technology was not uncommon among British intellectuals at the end of the nineteenth century. Technological advancements, especially in communication and transportation were taken as revolutionary factors that would enable not only a true unity of the British Empire but also more harmonious relations among the European nations.[65]

Based on the good omens of intellectual relations, developing means of communication, and newly emerging fields of cooperation, British Idealists pretty much ruled out the possibility of a war among the Great Powers of Europe. According to Mackenzie, European nations were on a steady path to ensure a unity that approximated to the unity within a nation-state. Thus, he was cautiously hopeful that war among civilized nations would disappear in the future. He wrote in 1901, 'the civilised nations of Europe already form in some respects a unity, even in some respects a more coherent unity than some nations have been able to secure…'[66] A year earlier he wrote in response to those who did not share his optimistic vision of the future of international relations in Europe:

---

63 J.H. Muirhead (1897) *The Elements of Ethics, Revised and Enlarged,* London: John Murray, p. 221.
64 Ritchie, 'War and Peace', p. 109.
65 D. Bell, *Idea of Greater Britain*, p. 63.
66 J.S. Mackenzie (1901) 'The Use of Moral Ideas in Politics', *International Journal of Ethics*, 12 (1), p. 20.

They fear that we are losing our old anchorage before we have found any new moorings, and that a general decay of moral purpose is to be anticipated, giving rise to a recrudescence of barbarism. Some even point to recent events as showing already the beginnings of such a decline both in this country and others... They point to the increase of armaments in Germany, the dominance of militarism in France, and the growth of the imperial spirit in both the great Anglo-Saxon peoples.[67]

For him, those who foresaw the danger of an imminent war among the European nations were 'mistaking the turmoil of the moment for the spirit of the age'.[68]

For the British Idealists, the Great War was not only a source of unprecedented tragedy but also an awakening call to the inconsistencies in their line of thought. Although, as Bosanquet noted, the war did not 'revolutionize' all their ideas, it definitely 'refreshed' their 'view of some things' and forced at least some of them to move away from their imperialist mind-set.[69] The impact of the war on their intellectual endeavours is apparent from their constant reference to the Great War as a landmark that altered the way they approached the subject of international relations. They were aware of the tragedy that was taking place on the battlefields in Europe and elsewhere in the world, and some of them were personally affected by it. Henry Jones had three sons who were fighting in the war, one of whom was killed and another one taken hostage in Turkey. In his letters Bosanquet also mentioned that one of his nephews served during the war, 'an open exhibitioner of Balliol, first in Moderns last year, applied for a commission in the new army... a very fine fellow; would have sat for the Indian Civil next year'.[70] The nephew Bosanquet wrote about, Captain Ralph Dendy, was killed in October

---

[67] Mackenzie, 'Source of Moral Obligation', p. 467.

[68] Mackenzie, 'Source of Moral Obligation', p. 468.

[69] B. Bosanquet (1921) 'Review of *The Group Mind: A Sketch of the Principles of Collective Psychology with Some Attempt to Apply them to the Interpretation of National Life and Character*, by William McDougall', *Mind*, 30 (117), p. 67.

[70] Muirhead, *Bernard Bosanquet and His Friends*, p. 164.

1918. It was the loss of great potential of the youth who died on the battlefields as well as the disillusionment with the European civilization that marked the Great War as a tragedy for British Idealists. Still, they retained their optimism along with some of their contentions regarding the nature of international order. In another letter Bosanquet relayed, 'we shall, I hope, be quite a new people after the war'.[71] For them, the war was an evil that was inescapable at that point, and yet with it came the opportunity to learn from the past mistakes and to prevent recurrence of such evil in the future.

According to Jones, two questions gained unparalleled importance with the beginning of the Great War: 'the first is: How has the present condition of affairs been brought about?... the second question is: What can we do to prevent the recurrence of the present situation?'[72] Other British Idealists, including those who argued for the redundancy of fixating on past mistakes, were also in favour of going to the root of the problems that made the Great War inevitable. British Idealists' willingness to question the ethical misgivings of the European civilization, however, was partly due to their contention that the greater part of the past evils that led to the Great War belonged to Germany and not to Britain. In their condemnation of Germany, British Idealists had to tread a fine line in defending the legitimacy of their philosophical position and yet not appearing to be defenders of German militarism. Both the 'ardent Hegelians from Glasgow' and Green's and Nettleship's students at Balliol College, with their leanings towards Kantianism, were under the suspicion of being secret supporters of Germany in the war against the forces of civilization.[73] Hobhouse had long been the flag-bearer of the attack on British Idealism through his very influential books *Democracy and Reaction* and *The Metaphysical Theory of the State*. While the latter of

---

[71]   Muirhead, *Bernard Bosanquet and His Friends*, p. 171.
[72]   Henry Jones (1914–1915) 'Why We Are Fighting', *Hibbert Journal*, XIII, p. 54.
[73]   J.H. Muirhead (ed.) (1924) *Contemporary British Philosophy: Personal Statements*, London: George Allen & Unwin, p. 310.

the two books was a refutation of Bosanquet's *Philosophical Theory of the State,* the former aimed to reveal idealism's retrograde influence on European humanitarianism. According to Hobhouse, German idealism's introduction into British thought was a direct source of the rising conservatism and irrationality in Britain. As early as 1905, Hobhouse argued that 'for thirty years and more English thought has been subject, not for the first time in its modern history, to powerful influence from abroad... the stream of German idealism has been diffused over the academical world of Great Britain'.[74] With the outbreak of the Great War, Hobhouse's distrust of Germany and German philosophy turned into an outward hostility towards British Idealists and especially to Bosanquet. He perceived his intellectual onslaught towards idealism as a war fought with the 'weapons of the spirit' against German barbarism and its representatives in Britain. His preface of *The Metaphysical Theory of the State* was addressed to his son Oliver who was fighting against the German forces and referred to Bosanquet's *The Philosophical Theory of the State.* He wrote:

> In the bombing of London, I had just witnessed the visible and tangible outcome of a false and wicked doctrine, the foundations of which lay, as I believe, in the book before me. To combat this doctrine effectively is to take such a part in the fight as the physical disabilities of middle age allow. Hegel himself carried the proof-sheets of his first work to the printer through streets crowded with fugitives from the fields of Jena. With that work began the most penetrating and subtle of all the intellectual influences which have sapped the rational humanitarianism of the eighteenth and nineteenth centuries, and in the Hegelian theory of the god-state all that I had witnessed lay implicit.[75]

According to Hobhouse, the founder of the theory of the 'god-state' was Hegel; and Bosanquet was 'his modern and most faithful exponent'.[76] The danger of idealism, Hobhouse argued, was that it cancelled the value of human effort towards the realization of the ideal

---

74 Hobhouse, *Democracy and Reaction*, p. 77.
75 L.T. Hobhouse (1918) *The Metaphysical Theory of the State: A Criticism*, London: George Allen & Unwin; New York: Macmillan, p. 6.
76 Hobhouse, *Metaphysical Theory of the State*, p. 18.

by equating the state with the Absolute. To the extent that the state was represented as an 'incarnation' of the objective mind through 'laws, traditions, customs of the society', the idealist political philosophy required individuals to obey the state regardless of what their reason dictated.[77] There was something intrinsic in the idealist philosophy that gave rise to the Prussian state and legitimized its demands from the individual and from other states. Referring to his years at Oxford, he wrote:

> In older days we passed by the Hegelian exaltation of the state as the rhapsodical utterances of a metaphysical dreamer. It was a mistake. The whole conception is deeply interwoven with the most sinister developments in the history of Europe. It is fashionable to conceive German militarism as a product of the reaction against a beautiful sentiment that reigned in the pre-Bismarckian era. Nothing could be more false. The political reaction began with Hegel, whose school has from first to last provided by far the most serious opposition to the democratic and humanitarian conceptions...[78]

For Hobhouse, the Great War signalled the inevitability of revealing the inherent, if not readily apparent, falsities of idealism as a social and political philosophy. First and foremost, it was necessary to destroy the 'god-state' cult that prioritized states' interests at the expense of the rights of individuals and of humanity. It was essential to combat the 'doctrine of the state as an incarnation of the Absolute, a super-personality which absorbs the real living personality of men and women'.[79] Idealism as Bosanquet represented it was no longer Green's humanitarian social idealism, but a genuine Hegelianism that became an academic orthodoxy in Britain.

But the British Idealists did not perceive their position as an orthodox one in the 1910s. On the contrary, they felt that their position was under attack from various quarters and that they had to defend their theory of the state without appearing to be defenders of German militarism. In this endeavour they formed a unified front

---

[77] Hobhouse, *Metaphysical Theory of the State*, p. 20.

[78] Hobhouse, *Metaphysical Theory of the State*, p. 23.

[79] Hobhouse, *Metaphysical Theory of the State*, p. 24.

and followed a common strategy. First and foremost, they condemned Germany's ideological position as a state and refuted all
their claims to be a 'superior race' or a '*kultur*' without equivalent.
They argued that it was the German state that indoctrinated its
citizens in the belief that they were racially superior and that they
had a natural right to everything on the surface of the Earth. Yet the
German people too were to be held responsible for the atrocities
committed by their state, considering that the German state was an
embodiment of their collective will. Although they were deceived by
their state and by some of their intellectual figures into believing that
Germany's cause was right, it was German society that provided a
suitable incubator for the doctrines of racial superiority and militarism. Thus, it was impossible to make a distinction in terms of the
moral responsibility of the German state and the German people in
the wrongs committed during the Great War. After a clear condemnation of the German state and an indirect condemnation of the
German people, British Idealists offered a defence of German
idealism as it was put forward by Kant and Hegel. They defended
the idealist tradition that was rooted in the works of Plato and
Aristotle but argued that both Hegel's followers and opponents in
Germany distorted this philosophical tradition in the years pre-
ceding the Great War. Thus, the main culprits of the Great War were
identified as German intellectuals such as Treitschke and von
Bernhardi. The culmination of the British Idealists' position on this
matter was complicated, mostly shaped by their dislike of German
militarism and their endeavour to ensure the continuing legitimacy
of their philosophical position. Furthermore, their personal links
with Germany, mostly developed during their research visits to the
Continent, required them to be careful not to be identified as
Prussian supporters. Yet their attempts to tread the fine line did not
always succeed. Lord Haldane, who served as the War Minister
between 1905 and 1912 and as Lord Chancellor from 1912 to 1915,
was not included in the newly founded cabinet of Prime Minister
Asquith after his German affiliations attracted attention in the media.

III. British Idealists on the
German State and Philosophy

In 1918, Haldane started his address under the 'auspices of the workers' educational association' with an acknowledgment of his long-standing admiration for German philosophy. And then he identified the distortion of this great philosophical tradition by military figures as one of the major causes of Germany's immersion in international aggression and argued that this distorted version of German philosophy intoxicated not only the German people but also the German government. The success of the German military caste in influencing public opinion was unexpected, according to Haldane, as he thought that the German nation was not 'so very different' from his own nation. Yet they were very easily convinced to go into a war of domination.[80] Haldane argued that, before the war, both the German Emperor and Chancellor desired to preserve peace among the Great Powers of Europe yet 'to that end they took inadequate means'.[81] They surrendered the reins of the state machinery to the military leaders in 1913 and from then on 'the military party' in Germany 'began to talk of a "preventive" war' against the entente powers who they thought aimed to ring round and crush Germany.[82] Haldane believed that it was due to the dominance of the militaristic mind in Germany at the time that the public succumbed to the unsubstantiated fears of foreign aggression. He argued that the lack of a democratic system in Germany led to the domination of the military caste in politics and resulted in the uncontrolled rule of soldiers.[83] To the extent that the German nation and the German state failed in sustaining a democratic system, the military caste filled the power vacuum and took the initiative in deciding the future of the country. Unfortunately, its decisions affected every country it dealt

---

[80] Haldane, *The Future of Democracy*, p. 4.
[81] Haldane, *Before the War*, p. 149.
[82] Haldane, *Before the War*, p. 56.
[83] Haldane, *Before the War*, p. 90.

with, be they friend or foe. Haldane argued that if it was not for the 'fascinating glitter' of the German army, 'Austria would not have acted as she did, nor would Turkey, nor Bulgaria'.[84]

Haldane insisted that apart from some minor eccentricities there were not many differences between the British and the German peoples. Yet he recognized one vital difference in the German mindset which allowed the military to easily seize control of the country prior to the Great War. He described this characteristic with reference to his personal observations from his stays in Germany. About the German people he argued:

> They were very much like our own people except in one thing. This was that they were trained simply to obey, and to carry out whatever they were told by their rulers... What impressed me was the little part they had in directing their own government, and the little they knew about what it was doing.[85]

The German state's power to shape the minds of its citizens was recognized by other British Idealists as well. Henry Jones used it as an example of states' capacity to direct their citizens to collectively adopt certain matters as absolute ends. According to Jones, this capacity in itself was not evil; on the contrary it was impossible for a state to 'avoid educating its citizens'.[86] What mattered was the moral worth of the goal that was designated as the ultimate end. He argued in a speech in 1918: 'Germany has given the world an obvious example, which it would do well never to forget, of the power of the State to form the character of its citizens. That it has turned that power to an evil and most destructive use is in itself no proof that it could not have been turned to a good use.'[87] In the German example, the state evidently encouraged its citizens to take the good of the German Empire as the highest end towards which they were to strive. Such a supreme end naturally required an exaltation of

---

84 Haldane, *Before the War*, p. 75.
85 Haldane, *Before the War*, p. 25.
86 Jones, 'Obligations and Privileges of Citizenship', p. 122.
87 Jones, 'Obligations and Privileges of Citizenship', p. 122.

'military force and aggressive domination' to subdue other states. According to Jones, designating the good of the German Empire as the ultimate goal of a nation was immoral as it automatically implicated hostility between the German Empire and other states so far as international relations were perceived as a zero-sum game. Such a perception did not only make the gain of the German Empire dependent on the loss of other nations but also precluded the possibility of collective effort towards the common good of humanity.

Based on his evaluation of the sources of German aggression, Jones argued that 'a state which is itself inspired by nobler, that is, by moral ends, or ends which are as universal as rational life, broad and deep as humanity, could lead its citizens to adopt these ends as their dominant motives'.[88] Jones added that a state's responsibility to direct its citizens towards wider and nobler ends did not remove its citizens' duty to use their own reason and question the state's guidance regarding the most vital matters of life. The German people were guilty of their 'passivity and slight love of internal freedom for the present carnage'.[89] They had been ruled for some time according to the distorted ideology of a military caste in a political system that lacked democratic procedures of decision-making. Still, all these adverse conditions were not enough to absolve them of their duty towards humanity and the highest moral values of this larger unity, as these duties were a direct result of the fact that they were rational human beings. They were aware, thanks to their knowledge of history and the works of their great philosophers, that wars of aggression were morally wrong and unacceptable. Jones's condemnation of the German people was harsh and, in a way, reflective of his disappointment in one of the most advanced members of the European civilization:

> The Germans have deserved their Emperor and their Nietzsche... It is the nation that has willed the war; and we must expect that the

---

[88] Jones, 'Obligations and Privileges of Citizenship', p. 122.
[89] Jones, 'Why We Are Fighting', p. 60.

strength of the nation in every fibre will be strained to make it successful. Thorough in this as in other matters, the German people as a whole—statesmen and generals, scientific men and philosophers, merchants and working men—have little by little but year by year educated one another into the belief that while Slavs are barbarous, and the French are shallow and frivolous, and the British people effete, they, themselves, in the heyday of their national strength, stand for the highest civilisation yet attained by the human race, and have not only the right but the duty of imposing it, if necessary by force, upon mankind.[90]

Bosanquet also shared the view that the German people were not exempt from the moral responsibility of the war no matter how much they were misguided by their state. After all, they adopted the militaristic mind-set without any real resistance. In a letter in which he reflected on the chances of further collaboration with Germany following the end of the war, he wrote: '*if* the German people would take a disgust to their military system, and erect a true democracy, I think we should fraternise; but of course that can't be "octroyé" by strangers, to them.'[91] For Bosanquet, the German people were to blame as they let their state 'intoxicate' them with a false ideology of racial superiority and the immoral end of world domination. Yet the greater responsibility was on the state and the intellectual circles that produced and disseminated that false ideology. Furthermore, the harm they inflicted was doubled by their distortion and defamation of the great tradition of German idealism, which taught the world the moral worth of perpetual peace with Kant and the centrality of the state in its realization by Hegel.

Most of the British Idealists during the Great War were reluctant to recognizse several central differences between Hegel's and Green's perceptions of international relations. Even when Hegel was referred to as 'the philosopher of war', they traced back their genealogical roots from Green to Hegel and Kant; and sometimes to

---

[90] Jones, 'Why We Are Fighting', p. 60.
[91] Muirhead, *Bernard Bosanquet and His Friends*, p. 166.

Aristotle and Plato.[92] Before the Great War, the British Idealist defence of Hegel was focused on two central matters: the limits of state power and the prospects for social and political progress in Hegelian philosophy. While the question of state power became inflamed from time to time, the accusation of an inherent conservatism in Hegelian idealism was a constant one to which British Idealists answered briefly yet continually in their works. With the outbreak of the Great War, the focus of criticism towards Hegel and his followers widened its scope. It was no longer only Hegel's political philosophy that was under attack but also his reflections on the nature of international order. He was now called the philosopher of militarism and the main inspiration for German aggression towards other states. British Idealists were aware of this new wave of criticism towards Hegel and their response was to show that it was not Hegel's work but its distortion by his followers in Germany that constituted a philosophical justification of German militarism. In his autobiography, Muirhead recalled the increased interest in anything 'that touched on German mentality and threw light on the depths from which the portent Prussian militarism had sprung...'[93] He also noted the dominantly negative attitude toward German idealism that came with the Great War and wrote that his attempts at 'disposing... of a total misunderstanding of what that whole movement meant' were in vain.[94] Still, in an attempt to prevent the British people from 'doing great injustice to what was in essence a great constructive effort of thought by associating it with the present orgy of violence and ruthless destruction', Muirhead wrote *German Philosophy in Relation to the War*.[95]

---

[92] B. Bosanquet (1917) 'The Function of the State in Promoting the Unity of Mankind', in Bosanquet, *Social and International Ideals*, London: The Macmillan Company, p. 275.

[93] Muirhead, *Reflections of a Journeyman in Philosophy*, p. 172.

[94] Muirhead, *Reflections of a Journeyman in Philosophy*, p. 172.

[95] J.H. Muirhead (1915) *German Philosophy in Relation to the War*, London: John Murray, p. v.

According to Muirhead, the story of German idealism was 'not of a continuous development, but of a reaction — a great rebellion and apostasy'.[96] Muirhead acknowledged that the state constituted a large part in Hegelian political philosophy but emphasized that the state in idealist thought was not an oppressor but the provider of justice to its citizens. He argued that Hegel attributed great importance to a central state, as he was witness to 'the enthusiasm of the French Revolution, and, like Burke, had come to realise the element of individualism and anarchy it contained'.[97] But for Hegel the state was neither an authority based on the rule of force, nor was its end to employ force against other states. The state was the exact opposite of a brute force so far as it was the embodiment of the will of the people and the highest expression of that will in its totality. Thus, Muirhead argued: 'there is no ground to ally this political teaching with militarism as we are learning to know it today. The keynote to militarism is the doctrine that the State rests upon force. But this is precisely the view against which Hegel contends in the *Philosophy of Right*.'[98]

Bosanquet, who was accused of being 'the most modern and the most faithful exponent' of Hegel in Britain, also wrote a book chapter in which he defended the Hegelian roots of British Idealism. He started the chapter with the following statement: 'we shall see how the splendid political philosophy of Germany a hundred years ago has passed on the one hand into her intoxication of today, while on the other hand, elsewhere, in face of a more liberal experience, it has found a decisive completion in a human and democratic sense.'[99] Bosanquet argued that the true inheritance of Hegel was received and praised in Britain by philosophers and intellectuals but the

---

[96] Muirhead, *German Philosophy in Relation to the War*, p. 3.
[97] Muirhead, *German Philosophy in Relation to the War*, p. 35.
[98] Muirhead, *German Philosophy in Relation to the War*, pp. 35–36.
[99] B. Bosanquet (1915) 'Patriotism in the Perfect State', in *The International Crisis in Its Ethical and Psychological Aspects*, London: Oxford University Press, p. 132.

situation in Germany was drastically different. Hegel's works 'degenerated into the creed of violence and self-interest' in Germany due to the 'passage of a large and many-sided philosophical doctrine into the hands of ignorant and biased amateurs, soldiers, historians, politicians'.[100] A very basic yet vital concept's miscomprehension was mainly responsible for the distortion of the whole Hegelian system: the good. According to Bosanquet, the military and political elites of Germany understood the good of the state as a merely material self-interest that totally excluded its moral aspect. When the concept of 'the good' was reduced to a selfish interest in material wealth, 'a great idea' was turned 'into the meanest of worldly maxims'.[101] The good, from this distorted perspective, no longer referred to a state's role in constituting a moral order in which individuals and families had the means of working towards their particular betterment and the common good of the community. As this central concept in Hegelian philosophy was distorted by 'mere omission and exaggeration', the German mind-set was 'brought to the point that what a man desires for his country is military supremacy to be used without scruple in the promotion of its exclusive interest'.[102] Such an ideology did not only exalt the state for the military power it accumulated but it also equated the good of a state with its capacity to expand its territories. Its justification was an unsubstantiated belief in racial superiority and its driving force was a crude materialism.

British Idealists, being true heirs of German Idealism, held in contempt the German intellectuals who distorted Hegel's work into shallow materialism. Heinrich von Treitschke and Friedrich von Bernhardi were the main culprits from their perspective. In his examination of German philosophy after Hegel, Muirhead argued that there was a single and very basic similarity between Hegel and

---

[100] Bosanquet, 'Patriotism in the Perfect State', p. 140.
[101] Bosanquet, 'Patriotism in the Perfect State', p. 141.
[102] Bosanquet, 'Patriotism in the Perfect State', p. 143.

von Treitschke's approach to the concept of the state: both believed that the state was 'primeval and necessary'.[103] But apart from this very basic agreement, von Treitschke set out to challenge the totality of Hegelian philosophy. Muirhead quoted from *Selections from Treitschke's Lectures on Politics* to reveal a very simple yet vital difference between Hegel and Treitschke's conceptualizations of the state:

> The state is in the first instance power, that may maintain itself; it is not the totality of the people itself, as Hegel assumed in his deification of the State—the people is not altogether amalgamated with it; but the State protects and embraces the life of the people, regulating it externally in all directions. On principle it does not ask how the people is disposed; it demands obedience…[104]

From Treitschke's perspective the highest duty of the state was to maintain as much power as necessary to ensure absolute obedience at home and forceful expansion abroad. Treitschke was not concerned about the duties a state had to ensure 'the good life' of its citizens. But, Muirhead argued, this was the exact opposite of the idealistic definition of a state. He wrote: 'with Aristotle, Hegel held that the State came into existence for the sake of life, its abiding purpose was the good life—the life of science and literature, of art and religion.'[105]

In *The Elements of Constructive Philosophy,* Mackenzie also referred to 'the danger' of ignoring the end a state was morally bound to serve in idealist theory and put undue emphasis on the power it yielded. Only a distorted reading of Idealism yielded a conceptualization of a state with the authority and power of a divinity. Whether such a state was organized under the supreme rule of a monarch or the *vox populi,* its power and deeds were bound to remain unchecked by the moral duty of ensuring the good life of its

---

[103] Muirhead, *German Philosophy in Relation to the War*, p. 84.

[104] A.L. Gowans (1914) *Selections from Treitschke's Lectures on Politics*, London; Glasgow: Gowans & Gray Ltd, p. 12.

[105] Muirhead, *German Philosophy in Relation to the War*, p. 85.

citizens. Mackenzie argued that the real problem with such an understanding of the state was that 'such a will would seem to have individuality without responsibility' and 'this way of thinking of it leads naturally to its enthronement as an unaccountable power, after the manner of Treitschke'.[106] When 'the good of the state' was no longer in close connection with the good of its citizens in terms of creating and maintaining a good life in pursuance of the higher ends in science, arts, religion, etc., there emerged the necessity for an 'ultimate end'. The war in itself was not that end for Treitschke. The end was to 'spread the German idea of civilization—German Culture'.[107] Friedrich von Bernhardi's dictum 'world-power or downfall' was a condensed expression of the German ambition to spread German *kultur* and dominance worldwide.

Jones believed that the voice that shouted 'world or downfall' was heard clearly by all the German people and it was this belief in the inescapable necessity of becoming a Great Power along with Britain and France that 'forged the machinery of the war'.[108] The same voice was also heard in England and it was received with a sense of alarm and recognition of an imminent threat from Germany. Yet British Idealists maintained that Germany did not desire to be a Great Power only for the sake of the power it would acquire. Surely, it was a concern on the part of Germany that among the Great Powers of Europe it needed to become an equal if not superior power to ensure its own survival. From the German perspective it was not only the territorial superiority of Britain and France that threatened Germany's success in becoming a world power. Britain's position as a world-empire in the spheres of culture and commerce was received with special disdain in Germany. According to von Bernhardi, the future of the German Empire depended on the successful dissemination of its language and its increased capacity to

---

106 J.S. Mackenzie (1917) *Elements of Constructive Philosophy*, London: George Allen & Unwin Ltd, p. 334.

107 Muirhead, *German Philosophy in Relation to the War*, p. 88.

108 H. Jones, *Principles of Citizenship*, p. 14.

do commerce in new colonies. In his book *Germany and the Next War*, von Bernhardi expressed his concern on this matter very clearly: 'If we count the nations who speak English at the present day, and if we survey the countries which acknowledge the rule of England, we must admit that' the British were justified in claiming that the world was being moulded by them.[109] Von Bernhardi perceived a direct relation between Germany's cultural and political dominance in the world and its future power. He argued: 'in the future... the importance of Germany will depend on two points; firstly, how many millions of men in the world speak German? secondly, how many of them are politically members of the German Empire?'[110] In his lectures, Treitschke made a similar point regarding the importance of increasing the number of German-speaking people in the world.[111] Their recommendation for the future success of the German Empire was the dissemination of German people, language, politics, culture, and commerce to newly acquired colonies as a means of not only 'civilizing the world' but also becoming a rival to Britain in world-domination.

British Idealists were aware of the details of Treitschke and von Bernhardi's work. In *Fundamental Problems of Life* Mackenzie wrote: 'I suppose it is true to say that, in the world as a whole, English is more universally understood than any other language. The diffusion of this somewhat monosyllabic speech, in preference to some of the more finely inflected languages, has been regarded with a certain horror by Treitschke and others.'[112] In another piece, Mackenzie referred to Germany's discontent with the vast territories the British Empire occupied: 'A growing nation that feels the need of "a place in the sun" is naturally jealous of a long-established empire on which

---

[109]   F. von Bernhardi and A.H. Powles (1914) *Germany and the Next War*, New York: Longmans, Green, and Co., p. 79.
[110]   Bernhardi and Powles, *Germany and the Next War*, p. 83.
[111]   Gowans, *Selections from Treitschke's Lectures on Politics*, p. 42.
[112]   J.S Mackenzie, *Fundamental Problems of Life*, p. 247.

"the sun never sets".'[113] Such empathetic remarks on the German 'jealousy' of the British Empire's worldwide influence reflected a belief in the understandability of Germany's imperialistic ambitions. Haldane made a similar remark in his account of the outbreak of the Great War: 'We urged Germany also to enter upon this path with us. We offered to help her in her progress towards the attainment of a "place in the sun".'[114] Clearly, Germany's desire to expand its territories was received, even after the outbreak of the war, as a legitimate claim from a European state to take part in the civilizing mission. What was not received well was the military means Germany was ready to employ against other European powers based on an unsubstantiated claim of racial superiority.

IV. British Idealists and the Real Politik of the Great War

According to British Idealists, German militarism in its hostility towards other European powers amounted to a sanctification of war as a legitimate means for the interests of the German nation. The German state justified war, an absolute violation of the moral order according to British Idealists, so far as it was serving the interests of the highest civilization. Mackenzie argued that Germans were following the lead of the ancient Greeks and Romans in their proclamation of racial superiority and their right to world-dominance.[115] While Germans were superior in certain respects, for instance 'in almost everything that is expressed by the term Organisation' and 'in music and in constructive philosophy', 'their superiority in other respects' was not apparent.[116] Jones also drew attention to the link between German militarism and their conviction of embodying the highest form of civilization. He argued: 'the Germans wished to

---

[113] J.S. Mackenzie (1916) 'Might and Right', in *The International Crisis: The Theory of the State*, London: Oxford University Press, p. 88.
[114] Haldane, *Before the War*, p. 144.
[115] J.S. Mackenzie, *Fundamental Problems of Life*, p. 333.
[116] MacKenzie, 'Might and Right', p. 83.

impose their will on other peoples, and compel them to adopt their way of life, which they call their *Kultur*, because they believed their way of life to be the best. And their ideal led them far in their career of conquest, though without any very obvious benefit to the world...'[117] Their belief in the superiority of their culture required them to achieve complete world dominance and their militaristic ambitions were not to end until they ensured their control over all the peoples of the world. Their vision of a peaceful world order was dependent on the complete dominance of the German *kultur*:

> Once Germany was '*über alles*,' and all the nations had put on the livery of its *Kultur* and learned to rejoice in the service of this Teutonic breed of supermen, there would be no more war — unless it had every now and then to be kindled in order to fan the fighting spirit of heroes into flame, and avert the degenerating effects of a perpetual peace![118]

Thus, the struggle against German aggression was to be understood as a struggle for freedom and democracy. Germany's ambition for world domination was a threat to all nations alike and its cessation required cooperation of states. While France and Russia, being Great Powers themselves, were under direct threat from Germany due to their shared borders, Britain's security as an island was dependent on the strength of its navy. In his reflections on the causes of the Great War, Haldane gave an account of the German military as he had the chance to observe it in 1906 as the War Minister of Britain. He recalled that the German army was more powerful than the French army and it was organized to ensure 'rapid mobilisation'.[119] Furthermore, both Britain and France knew about the process of piling up armaments in Germany, and it constituted a source of great concern for these two Great Powers.[120] Britain's main concern was not the amount of weapons Germany possessed or the vastness of its

---

[117] Jones, *Principles of Citizenship*, p. 25.
[118] Jones, 'Obligations and Privileges of Citizenship', p. 138.
[119] Haldane, *Before the War*, pp. 23–25.
[120] Haldane, *Before the War*, p. 41.

army. Due to the geographical uniqueness of Britain it was free from the imperative of sustaining a large army. But as an island state with dependencies all over the world, Britain was required to have a large navy with the ability to engage in long-range operations. It was a strategic decision on the part of Britain to transfer all the resources it saved from not maintaining a large army into building and sustaining a powerful navy. In 1910, Haldane was confident of the ability of the British Navy in serving its purpose of protecting the 'over-sea outposts'. He wrote, 'it is in point of fact enormously larger than the similar forces of Germany and France put together'.[121]

According to Haldane, the main source of hostility between Britain and Germany was Germany's determination to build a navy that could become a rival to the British naval force. Despite the German Chancellor's desire to maintain friendly relations with Britain, Haldane thought, he was compelled by others to expand the German Navy considerably. A draft of the 'new Fleet Law' that was given to Haldane by the German Emperor himself showed 'very large increases contemplated, of which we had no notion earlier, not only in the battleships... but in small craft and submarines and personnel'.[122] After a careful examination of the contents of the German Navy Bill, the British Cabinet decided to 'counter these increases' by enforcing a similar policy of strengthening the navy. And an additional precaution was taken by Britain to ensure its security by forming alliances with other European powers. An 'entente' was formed among Britain, France, and Russia with the purpose of combining their forces on the occasion of an attack from Germany. The justification for the 'entente' was that neither of these powers had the means to resist the growing military force of Germany on their own, and that it was formed with the sole purpose

---

[121] R.B. Haldane (1910) 'Introduction', in *Compulsory Service: A Study of the Question in the Light of Experience*, London: Hazell, Watson and Viney, Ltd, p. 12.

[122] Haldane, *Before the War*, p. 72.

of defence without any aspirations of launching an offensive against Germany. Haldane argued:

> The last thing wished for was war, and if we had to enter upon it, we should do so only in defence of our own vital interests, as well as those of the other Entente Powers. Our entry, if it was to come, must be immediate and unhesitating. For if we delayed Germany might succeed in occupying the northern coast of France, and in impairing our security by sea.[123]

While the entente was defined as a precaution to ensure a balance of power in Europe by Britain, Germany saw it as an attempt to encircle its territories by hostile powers. According to Haldane, the suspicion that the Franco-Russian Dual Alliance with the support of Britain was preparing to attack Germany was simply a baseless paranoia. He argued: 'The notion of an encirclement of Germany, excepting in defence against aggression by Germany herself, existed only in the minds of nervous Germans.'[124] But, Haldane added, although Germany's fears were baseless, the Great Powers that entered into an entente had a responsibility to prove their good intentions as it was the only way to prevent the outbreak of a great war in Europe. Thus, Britain was determined to build a relationship based on trust between entente powers and Germany. Still, in case of failure in this endeavour, Britain had a secondary policy of preparing the country for a probable war.[125]

Even if Haldane's account of genuine British efforts to build trust among European states is taken to reflect the reality, it was not easy to convince German intellectuals that their country was not under imminent threat from the entente. Treitschke expressed his distrust of Britain in his lectures by saying that 'England, while posing as the defender of Liberalism, egged on the European States against one another, kept Europe in a condition of latent unrest, and conquered

---

[123] Haldane, *Before the War*, p. 151.
[124] Haldane, *Before the War*, p. 36.
[125] Haldane, *Before the War*, pp. 5–6.

half of the world in the meantime'.[126] Von Bernhardi was also convinced that the union of France and Britain was 'cemented by the common hostility to Germany'.[127] He believed that the entente was an aggressive alliance and based on this belief he attributed great importance to the Triple Alliance that was constituted by Germany, Austria, and Italy.[128] In addition to its core members, von Bernhardi had also a vision of including Turkey in the alliance against Britain, France, and Russia. He argued, 'we ought to spare no sacrifices to secure this country as an ally for the eventuality of a war with England or Russia'.[129] He also openly stated that the alliance of countries under the leadership of Germany was not only to aim at negative results, such as deterring a possible attack from the entente, but also to 'actively pursue' the vital interests of their partners with a collaborative effort. For instance, he advised a Turco-Italian partnership in the Mediterranean, which would satisfy the Italian desires for land in this region 'at the cost of France, after the next war'.[130] Evidently, both Treitschke and von Bernhardi believed in the necessity of a war among the European powers. Their belief was based on their suspicions regarding the British intention to hinder German advancement in commerce and territories in the international arena and their strong sense of entitlement to a great German Empire that would have a strong position in the new world order.

What emerged in the first decade of the twentieth century in Europe was an uneasy standoff between two camps of states that had conflicting desires for territorial expansion and commerce. From the German perspective, if Treitschke and von Bernhardi are to be taken as its representatives, the 'balance of power' was a ploy used by Britain 'to stir up enmity between the respective continental

---

126 Gowans, *Selections from Treitschke's Lectures on Politics*, p. 122.
127 Bernhardi and Powles, *Germany and the Next War*, p. 94.
128 Bernhardi and Powles, *Germany and the Next War*, p. 94.
129 Bernhardi and Powles, *Germany and the Next War*, p. 88.
130 Bernhardi and Powles, *Germany and the Next War*, p. 101.

States, and to keep them at approximately the same standard of power, in order herself undisturbed to conquer at once the sovereignty of the seas and the sovereignty of the world'.[131] From the British perspective this volatile balance of power was a dangerous yet unavoidable interim remedy in the current state of affairs. Haldane summarized the British perspective as follows:

> a general friendship between all Great Powers, or, better still, a League of the Nations, is by far preferable. But that consideration does not touch the actual point, which is that we did not seek to set up the principle of balancing that has given rise to so many questions. It was forced on us and was a sheer necessity of the situation.[132]

The situation, in short, was simply a vicious circle in which each state's attempt to gain more territory, to build a stronger military force, or increase its commerce was perceived by their rival states as a threat to their own position and triggered the launch of a similar policy. In this hostile environment those who had compatible interests or shared suspicions towards another country or countries formed alliances. Although those alliances were professedly formed for defensive purposes, their existence gave rise to further agitation in the opposite side of the controversy, resulting in a continent that was divided into two hostile camps continually piling up armaments. By 1914, Green's apprehension that imperialism was bound to give rise to materialism and militarism in Europe was proven right and took his students totally by surprise.

V. Time for Reflection

Evidently, a Europe divided into two hostile camps ready to plunge into a Great War was a far cry from what British Idealists imagined it would be, 'a single unity' and a centre of 'international sympathy' in

---

[131] Bernhardi and Powles, *Germany and the Next War*, p. 110.
[132] Haldane, *Before the War*, p. 10.

an era of civilization and cooperation.[133] It was a true tragedy, according to Jones, as it left 'to an honourable and unselfish people as its highest duty... to put its citizens to the slaughter, and, if it can gain its ends at no lower cost, to "bleed a great country white!"'[134] It was a duty so far as the German state was a threat to humanity overall and it was to be stopped before they gained world dominance in pursuance of a false belief in their racial superiority. But taking the German claim to racial superiority as the singular cause of Europe's destruction in a great war was not adequate. The underlying cause, according to the majority of British Idealists, was the dominance of a materialistic worldview that was embodied in the colonial ambitions of European countries and resulted in the rise of militarism.

In a letter to a friend, Bosanquet wrote: 'I *expect* great catastrophes from time to time as civilisation becomes so intricate and the temptation to materialism so strong', and he added that the Great War served to 'reveal what was there' in Europe in the beginning of the twentieth century.[135] It was an inevitable result of the dominant materialism that urged civilized countries to gain more territories, to have wider areas in which they had exclusive control of commerce. A state organized around the materialistic worldview necessarily engaged in evils such as 'exploitation within or without, class privilege, arbitrary authority, discontent directing ambitions to foreign conquest and to jealousy of other states'.[136] As each country desired simply material gain and not a common good, conflict of

---

[133] Mackenzie, *Lectures on Humanism*, p. 89; Muirhead, *Elements of Ethics*, p. 221.

[134] Jones, 'Why We Are Fighting', p. 53.

[135] Muirhead, *Bernard Bosanquet and His Friends*, p. 210.

[136] B. Bosanquet (1917) 'The Function of the State in Promoting the Unity of Mankind', *Proceedings of the Aristotelian Society*, 17, in Bosanquet (1917) *Social and International Ideals*, p. 276.

interest was inevitable. After all, the doctrine they followed suggested 'one state's gain is ipso facto another's loss'.[137]

It was a common contention among the British Idealists that the dominance of materialism was not peculiar to Germany. In a book co-authored by Muirhead and Hetherington, the overall influence of materialism in Europe was explained as follows:

> Hence among enterprising commercial nations there is a severe competition for 'spheres of influence' — i.e. for tracts of rich and undeveloped country where one nation can establish itself predominantly and secure for itself the major share of the return to this kind of undertaking.
>
> Obviously, in this kind of scramble there are endless possibilities of friction, for the good reason that each group is seeking simply its own interest and seeking it by means which necessarily react against the interests of others.[138]

Though imperialism in itself did not require a pure materialistic interest in undeveloped territories of the world, its execution in the beginning of the twentieth century was mostly devoid of any other concerns. Muirhead and Hetherington argued that as long as the materialistic outlook dominated the imperial policies of the civilized countries, it was 'hard to see what alternative there is to the cold-blooded partitioning of the less developed parts of the world among the more fortunate nations...'[139] In its materialistic execution, imperialism not only meant a total neglect of the needs of the native peoples in the colonies but also was a source of perpetual conflict among the European powers.

Mackenzie also designated materialism as the underlying cause of the Great War. He argued that both the uneasy standoff that preceded the Great War and the war itself was a direct result of 'the

---

[137] Bosanquet, 'The Function of the State in Promoting the Unity of Mankind', p. 276.

[138] H.J.W. Hetherington and J.H. Muirhead (1918) *Social Purpose: A Contribution to a Philosophy of Civic Society*, London: George Allen & Unwin Ltd, p. 277.

[139] Hetherington and Muirhead, *Social Purpose*, p. 279.

materialisation of our Western outlook in recent times'.[140] He argued that the most obvious sign of the materialistic outlook in Europe was 'the worship that was given to riches' with a total ignorance of the moral and spiritual ends they were to serve.[141] With reference to one of Emerson's poems that read, 'things are in the saddle and ride mankind', Mackenzie argued that in this respect Western civilization was weaker than many 'older and more primitive' civilizations.[142] Mackenzie maintained that purely materialistic ends usually resulted in 'a simple struggle for existence' and threatened 'to degrade human life to the level of the brutes'.[143] In this respect there was something Westerners could learn from the Eastern nations that attributed great significance to spiritual values, sometimes with a disregard to their material well-being.

Among the British Idealists who witnessed the Great War, Henry Jones was the most ardent critic of materialism and its culmination in imperialism. Until the outbreak of the Great War, Jones did not perceive imperialism as inherently materialistic. He argued it was possible to adopt a materialistic approach to colonies and dependencies by restricting free trade and perceiving territories overseas as merely sources of raw materials and markets. But there was a higher form of imperialism that prioritized cooperation among civilized nations and served undeveloped peoples. Although he perceived some materialistic tendencies in the way the British Empire was governed, he thought that it was possible to moralize every aspect of public life including the economic sphere and its practice within and among nations.[144] With the outbreak of the Great War, Jones adopted a much more critical approach to imperialism, be it materialistic or

---

[140] J.S. Mackenzie (1923) 'Spiritual Values', *International Journal of Ethics*, 33 (3), p. 258.

[141] Mackenzie, 'Spiritual Values', p. 258.

[142] Mackenzie, 'Spiritual Values', p. 260.

[143] J.S. Mackenzie (1918) *Outlines of Social Philosophy*, London: George Allen & Unwin Ltd, p. 119.

[144] Jones, *Working Faith of the Social Reformer*, pp. 147–49.

otherwise. In his article 'Why We Are Fighting' he described imperialism as 'the reasoned belief in territorial brigandage and in the methods of barbarism' and identified Germany's imperialistic passions as the main cause of the war.[145] It was no longer the native peoples of the conquered territories that were deemed barbaric but the European civilization that 'subjugates and even dedicates the higher, the things of the spirit, to the service of the lower and material'.[146] Furthermore, it was the civilized nations of Europe that constituted the direst impediment to humanity's progress. The imperialistic order was ripe with occasions for armed conflict as it was turned into a sphere of the 'clash of material ambitions'.[147] Later in 1918, Jones wrote that the Great War was, or at least was supposed to be, a wake-up call for the European nations:

> for the first time in the world's history, it has come to seem possible that by their very inventions the civilised peoples of the earth may bring upon themselves universal ruin: *possible* in the eyes of everyone, *probable* in the eyes of the many men versed in man's history, *certain* in the eyes of those who reflect on the motives that make history, *unless the spirit of envy, greed, and ruthless self-assertion perishes and the nations learn the meaning of mutual reverence and regard.*[148]

The Great War showed that the materialistic mind-set had prevailed over the idealistic one in Europe and materialism was an inevitable consequence of the hostile world order it created. In Germany, the materialist ambition and its translation into a militaristic rage was acute and quite easy to perceive. Yet British Idealists, and especially Jones, argued that Germany was not an isolated case in its pursuance of material gain at the expense of higher moral values; it was singular mostly due to its late involvement in the empire-building practice of the European nations and its haste in becoming a Great Power through an accelerated process of militarization. But other European nations, including Britain, were also to be blamed for

---

[145] Jones, 'Why We Are Fighting', p. 61.
[146] Jones, 'Why We Are Fighting', p. 61.
[147] Jones, 'Why We Are Fighting', p. 55.
[148] Jones, 'Obligations and Privileges of Citizenship', p. 135.

making a Great War inevitable. Jones's condemnation of the British Empire along with Germany's imperialistic ambitions is worth quoting at length:

> If, therefore, in attempting to find the cause of the present war we are driven to turn the light of inquiry mainly upon another people, it is not because our own hands are spotless. It was not by converting the heathen that we acquired their lands, nor for the sake of 'the ends of civilisation' that we drove the savages out of their hunting-grounds. We may say, with much truth, that our conquests have followed our trade, and that what we now possess has come 'in the way of business.' But at what time in our history were our business ways with crude peoples honourable; or how often has the right of the savage to his wigwam been respected? We have been as ruthless, and we have been as ready to plead 'the rights of a higher civilisation over a lower,' as the German people are to-day.[149]

According to Jones, accusing Germany of sacrificing moral values for the sake of material wealth, yet sustaining an empire based on the exploitation of conquered territories, was hypocrisy. He argued that what Germany did was reduce 'our own ways to a theory, in disregard of ordinary views of morals, and to seek to apply it in their thorough way to ourselves'.[150] Jones maintained that all the European powers including Britain brought down this great catastrophe upon the world:

> I do not think we can claim that, while other nations were entangling one another's ways through conflict of low aims and the clash of their material ambitions, doing and suffering great wrong, our own nation stood aloof in the 'splendid isolation' of innocence. On the contrary, it has taken all the nations of Europe in the past to make the war inevitable, and it will take them all in the future to make it impossible.[151]

VI. After the Empire

Without denying the moral responsibility of Britain along with other European powers, Jones argued that the side that fought against

---

149 Jones, 'Why We Are Fighting', p. 56.
150 Jones, 'Why We Are Fighting', p. 56.
151 Jones, 'Why We Are Fighting', p. 56.

Germany held the higher moral ground in the Great War. Although Britain itself was complicit in the moral wrongs committed that resulted in the Great War, it was justified to fight against Germany because it was growing out of the immoral practices of imperialism. Jones wrote: 'our right [to condemn the German nation], such as it is, springs from the fact that we are emerging' from imperialism.[152] The evidence of Britain's emergence from imperialism was evident in its willingness to 'respect the rights of small nations and seeking, little by little, to nurse into liberty all the peoples over whom we rule'.[153] Jones seemed to be convinced that the desirable world order was no longer inhibited by a better or ethical version of empires, but by a moral order of independent and cooperative nation-states. In the way forward, the Great Powers were required to recognize that every nation had a legitimate and overriding interest in maintaining its own state and moving away from the materialistic passions that led to and in turn were strengthened by imperialism.[154]

Mackenzie too offered a critique of the imperialistic mind-set that had been morally justified with a reference to the 'white man's burden' in his book *Outlines of Social Philosophy,* published in 1918.[155] According to Mackenzie, maintaining a belief in the existence of 'a country with so high and unique a civilisation that it would be to the obvious advantage of the world to have it universally imposed...' meant ignoring 'the actual conditions of human life'.[156] Although he did not offer a direct criticism of imperialism, evidently he was arguing against the moral legitimacy of maintaining colonies regardless of the end it was argued to serve. In his next book, published in 1920, Mackenzie referred to the Great War as a turning point that revealed the central importance of 'a vigorous development of moral life' through the contribution of free citizens who live in a

---

[152] Jones, 'Why We Are Fighting', p. 56.
[153] Jones, 'Why We Are Fighting', p. 56.
[154] Jones, 'Why We Are Fighting', p. 56.
[155] Mackenzie, *Outlines of Social Philosophy*, p. 192.
[156] Mackenzie, *Outlines of Social Philosophy*, pp. 193–94.

democratic order.[157] His preference was no longer with a world of colonies and dependencies schooled by the European nations but with a world inhabited by free and cooperating nation-states. He expressed his conviction on the importance of national self-determination as follows:

> Now, it might be thought that the best way to secure that human beings shall march side by side would be to tie them together. But this obviously is not true of bodily marching. They can keep step better when each has complete control of his own movements. The same would seem to be true of spiritual advancement in individuals and of social development in nations. When they interfere with one another, they provoke antagonism; when they leave each other alone, they tend gradually to arrive at the same results. It is one of the essences of every important human achievement that it must be gained by voluntary effort. This is the real ground for national self-determination.[158]

In 1923, Mackenzie published an article that marked a change in his strategy of defending nations' right to independence. In this article, Mackenzie maintained that in the modern world the importance of spiritual values finally received the attention it deserved, and it was translated into all spheres of life including the political and the international. In its specific application to politics, those spiritual values led people 'to see that commonwealths exist for the sake of the good life, and not merely for the protection of bodily life and property'.[159] He argued that what was first organized as the British Empire was now on its way to being transformed into a common-wealth thanks to the recognition of independence and democracy as essential values that serve humanity's spiritual development. Mackenzie argued it was

> important now to lay stress on the federation of the world, not in the sense of creating a sort of super-state, but rather as the recognition of what is already perceived in what used to be known as the British

---

157 J.S. Mackenzie (1920) *Arrows of Desire*, London: George Allen & Unwin Ltd, p. 209.

158 Mackenzie, *Arrows of Desire*, p. 195.

159 Mackenzie, 'Spiritual Values', p. 257.

Empire, that the countries of the world, though having distinct methods of organisation and different national characteristics, are essentially parts of a single Commonwealth, with great human interests that far outweigh their separate rivalries and apparent antagonisms.[160]

What Mackenzie called a commonwealth was 'a community of a more comprehensive kind than most nations and including some diversity of races'.[161] Its significance was due to its ability to provide a sense of communal unity without requiring a 'uniform system of law and organisation'.[162] According to Mackenzie, in the first quarter of the twentieth century Britain was the most developed commonwealth, although it still maintained some of the characteristics of an empire. This was to be expected so far as the Commonwealth had 'grown out of the conception of Empire' but it was increasingly basing itself 'less and less upon a uniform system of law and organization, and more and more upon ties of a less palpable kind – partly upon the recognition of community in race, language, and traditions, and partly, perhaps very slowly, upon a growing consciousness of the unity of mankind as involving a Common Good'.[163] Thus, Mackenzie concluded, 'this particular conception [of commonwealth is] a specially British contribution to the solution of the problem of World Citizenship' and was to be developed and widened in time.[164]

Muirhead also moved away from the idea of reforming the British Empire into a moral unity by 1918 and, like Mackenzie, he also adopted the language of the 'commonwealth' and paid increased attention to the values it indicated: democracy, nation-state, and world-citizenship. In the introduction of the book he co-authored with Hetherington, Muirhead wrote: 'In the idea of a "commonwealth" we are seeking to realise a wider citizenship...

---

160 Mackenzie, 'Spiritual Values', p. 261.
161 Mackenzie, *Fundamental Problems of Life*, p. 188.
162 Mackenzie, *Fundamental Problems of Life*, p. 190.
163 Mackenzie, *Fundamental Problems of Life*, p. 191.
164 Mackenzie, *Fundamental Problems of Life*, p. 350.

Looked at from within the nation, it is demanded by all modern conditions that government shall be strong and efficient... But it is also demanded... that it shall be democratic'.[165] As the idea of a 'true empire' no longer seemed to be a viable option to ensure world peace, both Muirhead and Hetherington advised a gradual process of granting independence to existing colonies.[166] In an article in which he answered the 'recent criticisms of the Idealist theory', Muirhead argued the British Commonwealth constituted a moral community that was 'at least a partial embodiment of the will to a common human good greater and more compelling than that embodied in their own national State'.[167] As he used the examples of Canada and Britain in his evaluation of the British Commonwealth, it seems reasonable that his account of the Commonwealth referred to the union of Britain with its territories that were largely inhabited by British immigrants. Seemingly, both Mackenzie and Muirhead replaced the idea of forming a 'true empire' with a mission to civilize the savages with what Haldane called a 'Sittlichkeit' of the Anglo-Saxon people in the post Great War period. They referred to it as a commonwealth and maintained the belief that it constituted an example for the unity of mankind within a commonwealth of nation-states. Jones remained an exception on that specific issue, as he moved away decisively from the idea that the British Empire would serve the common good of humanity either in its pre-Great war form or in its transformation into a commonwealth.

VII. Conclusion

Although the philosophical basis of British Idealists' approach to international relations remained unchanged, following the outbreak of the Great War the vocabulary they used shifted in this period. As they tried to distinguish themselves from German intellectuals that

---

[165] Hetherington and Muirhead, *Social Purpose*, p. 24.
[166] Hetherington and Muirhead, *Social Purpose*, p. 282.
[167] J.H. Muirhead (1924) 'Recent Criticism of the Idealist Theory of the General Will', *Mind*, 33 (132), p. 365.

defended German militarism by claiming national superiority, they abandoned their imperialistic arguments and emphasized nations' equal worth. Furthermore, the political developments that ended in the Great War showed that European Great Powers were prone to unite in ententes against opposing groups in pursuance of their material interest. Thus, by the end of the Great War, British Idealists were quite aware of the interconnectedness of imperialism and militarism. This shift in their understanding of imperialism brought with it two interrelated concerns. Firstly, they lost their confidence in the moral legitimacy of the British Empire. They became aware of the impossibility of condemning German militarism without recognizing the British responsibility in the rise of an imperialistic world order. Secondly, in recognition that defending the British Empire in the post Great War period became untenable, they advocated its transformation into a commonwealth of free and equal nations. They started to define Britain more as a commonwealth than as an empire, and attributed considerable importance to nations' right to self-government. This did not mean that they no longer believed in the superiority of European civilization. On the contrary the 'Neo-Darwinian belief in a hierarchy of peoples' persisted long after the Great War among British intellectuals including the British Idealists.[168] The main difference was that colonization was no longer perceived as a legitimate or sustainable way of civilizing the world. This shift in their position can be placed in a wider movement from imperialist sentiment to liberal political values in British intellectuals' approach to international relations.

In *The Oxford History of the British Empire,* Brown argued that at the end of the Great War, 'in establishing liberal goals for the Commonwealth, imperialists lessened their dependence upon dubious claims of racial superiority and forced their critics into the uncomfortable position of arguing that Britain lacked the capacity to

---

[168] Tinker, *Race, Conflict and the International Order*, p. 130.

promote good government'.[169] According to Brown, this move from the vocabulary of empire to that of commonwealth was a tactical one as it 'offered an attractive vision of Empire as a kind of training academy in liberal democracy', and 'the gap between "imperium" and "libertas" that had provided the point of leverage for pre-war anti-imperialists was now welded tightly shut'.[170] From a rival position, Porter argued that the rebranding of the Empire into a commonwealth was indicative of intellectuals' devotion to 'liberal values' rather than to the project of an eternal British Empire. When the contradiction between liberalism and imperialism became manifest, the British liberals shed their imperialistic title and upheld liberal values at the expense of the Empire.[171] Evidently, British Idealists were not an exception among British intellectuals in their shift from favouring the British Empire as a civilizing force to advocating its transformation into a commonwealth of equal and independent nation-states. Like the rest of British intellectuals, in the years following the Great War they paid increased attention to the project of uniting self-governing nation-states within the Commonwealth or, sometimes preferably, within a League of Nations as a means of ensuring world peace and humanity's rights.

---

[169] Cacoullos, *Thomas Hill Green*, p. 193.
[170] Brown, *Dictionary of Twentieth-Century British Philosophers*, p. 193.
[171] Porter, *The Absent-Minded Imperialists*, p. 312.

Chapter 4

A New Hope
The League of Nations

British intellectuals did not wait for the end of the war to start their advocacy for the immediate establishment of a League of Nations. Especially the last couple of years of the Great War witnessed an almost all-encompassing call for the establishment of such a League. Alfred Zimmern, in *The League of Nations and the Rule of Law*, expressed the extent of devotion to the idea of a League of Nations by stating that 'it became almost a religious duty to "believe in" it and to "support it"' for a section of the British population.[1] Starting from 1915, several individuals and groups published books, reports, and booklets in which they offered a detailed account of why they supported the idea of a League of Nations, and what such a League would entail. One of the first such works was J.A. Hobson's *Towards International Government*. As an early example of its kind, it mostly dealt with the catastrophe-prone nature of the pre-Great War world order that relied on 'secret diplomacy of Powers'.[2] For Hobson, the mood in Europe in 1915 was one of scepticism as all the links that were believed to be holding the European states together through commerce and communication broke down under the weight of militarism.[3] Hobson was convinced that the only force that could

---

[1] A. Zimmern (1936) *The League of Nations and The Rule of Law, 1918–1935*, London: Macmillan and Co., p. 327.
[2] Hobson, *Towards International Government*, p. 7.
[3] Hobson, *Towards International Government*, p. 177.

ensure a lasting peace among nations was the establishment of a reign of law at the international level. A year later, the Fabian Society published *International Government* in which Bernard Shaw supplied a justificatory account of their dedication to the League of Nations project and L.S. Woolf contributed a lengthy narration of European history of international treaties, concerts, and conferences and why they failed to protect the peace among the Great Powers of Europe.[4] The following year, the Fabian Society had Woolf write a tentative framework for a League of Nations, which was published under the title of *The Framework of a Lasting Peace*.[5] *Proposals for Prevention of Future Wars*, which was drafted by Viscount Bryce's group a couple years earlier, was published in 1917.[6] These reports supplied by the Fabian Society and the Bryce Group are judged highly influential both in the public perception of a League of Nations and its initial reception by the British government.[7]

Other well-known intellectuals published their perceptions of a League of Nations and put forward detailed accounts of how such a League was to be organized. Among them were H.G. Wells, Gilbert Murray, Viscount Grey, Henry Noel Brailsford, and J.C. Smuts.[8] Although these writers were located at various and sometimes opposing sides of the political spectrum, they all advocated the cause of establishing a League of Nations in their works. These works did

---

4	L.S. Woolf (1916) *International Government*, New York: Brentano's.

5	L.S. Woolf (1917) *The Framework of a Lasting Peace*, London: George Allen & Unwin Ltd.

6	J. Bryce (1917) *Proposals for the Prevention of Future Wars*, London: George Allen & Unwin Ltd.

7	H.R. Winkler (1948) 'The Development of the League of Nations Idea in Great Britain, 1914–1919', *The Journal of Modern History*, 20 (2), p. 99.

8	H.G. Wells (1919) *The Idea of a League of Nations*, Boston: The Atlantic Monthly Press; G. Murray (1918) *The League of Nations and the Democratic Idea*, London: Oxford University Press; E. Grey (1918) *The League of Nations*, New York: George H. Doran Company; J.C. Smuts (1918) *The League of Nations: A Practical Suggestion*, London: Hodder and Stoughton; H.N. Brailsford (1917) *A League of Nations*, New York: The Macmillan Company.

not only dwell on the moral and political necessity of a League's establishment but also dealt with the technical details that emerged from such a broad project. Reflecting on a satisfactory peace treaty, designating the limits of the League's responsibilities, and its member states, designing the legislative, executive, and judiciary branches of the League, and ensuring its long-lasting functionality were among the favourite subject matters of British intellectuals. This newly emerging literature on the League was dominated by highly technical discussions on the possible sanctions that would ensure reduction of armaments among the Great Powers and oblige these Powers to go to courts of arbitration in the case of future conflicts. On the matter of reduction of armaments, options ranging from a gradual and voluntary process of disarmament to a forced hand over of arms to an international authority were suggested.[9] The matter of arbitration was mostly considered with reference to the Second Hague Conference, and the League was expected to oblige all 'the signatory Powers to agree to refer to the Court of Arbitral Justice'.[10]

Curiously, the future of British colonies and dependencies received limited attention in the Bryce Group and Fabian Society's evaluation of the future of international order. Actually, the British Empire was sometimes pointed out as an archetype of a League of Nations and as a functioning example of international unity.[11] The harsh criticism imperialism received from several British intellectuals with the outbreak of the Great War did not find a reflection in prominent League of Nations schemes that were pro-moted at the time. In Hobson's *Towards International Government*, for example, imperialism was mentioned as a primary reason for the rise of militarism in Europe, but his recommendations for a future inter-national government did not propose any solution to the problem of imperial rule. Although the question of who would have the

---

9   Hobson, *Towards International Government*, p. 21.
10 Woolf, *Framework of a Lasting Peace*, p. 18.
11 Woolf, *International Government*, p. 367.

ownership of the former German colonies and the lands previously held by the Ottoman Empire constituted an important subject matter in these discussions, the existence of colonialism itself did not emerge as a central issue.

But following the declaration of President Wilson's Fourteen Points, imperialism itself started to receive consideration from British intellectuals, and the future of the British as well as the German colonies was assessed in relation to the doctrine of self-determination. As President Wilson emerged during the Great War as 'the unquestioned leader of mankind' and as an ardent critic of colonialism, British intellectuals distanced themselves from the idea of acquiring new territories for the Empire in the form of reparation from Germany.[12] Wilson's scheme for a League of Nations whose details were pointed out in his Fourteen Points was accepted as the blueprint for the future peace and well-being of Europe and the world. In his *The League of Nations,* Viscount Grey, the British Ambassador to the United States at the time, wrote that 'the establishment and maintenance of a League of Nations, such as President Wilson has advocated, is more important and essential to a secure peace than any of the actual terms of peace that may conclude the war: it will transcend them all'.[13] Mostly, due to the importance attributed to president Wilson's moral leadership, the matter of colonies was avoided as an unpleasant discussion topic. Still, the intellectuals of the time 'were not anti-imperial in the sense of wanting to liquidate the Empire, at least not immediately. They wanted to reform it and to make it more accountable'.[14] To that end, British intellectuals received the Mandate System that was designated to be a solution for the problem of colonialism very

---

[12] D. Drake (1919) 'Will the League of Nations Work?', *The International Journal of Ethics,* 29 (3), p. 339.

[13] E. Grey, *The League of Nations,* pp. 14–15.

[14] J.M. Brown and R. Louis (eds.) (2001) *The Oxford History of the British Empire: Volume IV: The Twentieth Century,* Oxford: Oxford University Press, p. 20.

positively.[15] Lord Robert Cecil, who was President Wilson's main British ally in his endeavour towards the establishment of the League, was confident that the British Empire had already met the standards required by the Mandate System. Thus, he welcomed the Mandate System programme, as it 'would force reform on "the badly governed colonies of France and Portugal"'.[16] Such confidence in British ability and experience in ruling 'savage peoples' in colonial territories supplied British intellectuals with an understanding that a well-functioning Mandate System would naturally place new territories under British rule.

The fate of the colonies was not among the most important points of consideration in designing a League of Nations. British intellectuals were mainly interested in ensuring that a functioning and long-lasting League was founded, and there were two equally important components to that mission. Firstly, as discussed above, it was mandatory to come up with a fail-proof design of the judicial, legislative, and executive capacities and duties of the League. Secondly, creating and maintaining a general will towards the establishment and conservation of such a League was perceived to be essential. To that end several societies were established which held public meetings, lobbied MPs from both Liberal and Labour Parties, and published pamphlets.[17] It was a common assertion that ensuring

---

[15] For a detailed account of the Mandate System under the League of Nations see: A. Antony (2004) 'Colonialism and the Birth of International Institutions: The Mandate System of the League of Nations', in *Imperialism, Sovereignty and the Making of International Law*, Cambridge: Cambridge University Press, pp. 115–94.

[16] Pedersen, *The Guardians: The League of Nations and The Crisis of Empire*, p. 28.

[17] Winkler, 'The Development of the League of Nations Idea in Great Britain, 1914–1919'; C. Sylvest (2004) 'Interwar Internationalism, the British Labour Party, and the Historiography of International Relations', *International Studies Quarterly*, 48 (2), pp. 409–32; J.C. Heim (1995) 'Liberalism and the Establishment of Collective Security in British Foreign Policy: The Alexander Prize Essay', *Transactions of the Royal Historical Society*, 5, pp. 91–110.

a sense of loyalty in individuals to the League in addition to their respective nation-states was a precondition for the success of the League project. Such loyalty was to be encouraged at schools and churches and societies, and newspapers were to contribute towards creating an international sentiment. To that end Wells noted: 'it is clear that if a world-league is to be living and enduring, the idea of it, and the need and righteousness of its service, must be taught by every educational system in the world.'[18] Creating a will to remain within the League even when its dictates seemed to contradict national interests was understood to be vital for the success of the project and it was realized it would be an even harder task than managing the technical details of international law and administration. Viscount Grey argued that it was an essential condition for 'the foundation and maintenance of a League of Nations' that 'the Governments and Peoples of the States willing to found it understand clearly that it will impose some limitation upon the national action of each, and may entail some inconvenient obligation'.[19] The only remedy to overcome such inconvenience was for people to know that the real interest of each and every people was international in its nature and maintaining peace was the primary condition of ensuring the realization of that common interest.

I. The League of Nations Project and British Idealists

Although the tone of intellectual discussion on international relations had shifted from a philosophical discussion of human morality to that of technicality of international law from 1916 onwards, British Idealists demonstrated little to no interest in adjusting their tone. Rather, they remained content with applying their philosophical tools to newly emerging problems at a highly abstract level. On rare occasions some of them actively participated

---

[18] Wells, *Idea of a League of Nations*, p. 44.
[19] E. Grey, *League of Nations*, pp. 7–8.

in the League of Nations Society activities or took official duties in the workings of the League. In 1918, for instance, Henry Jones wrote a pamphlet for the League of Nations Union titled 'Form the League of Peace Now: An Appeal to my Fellow Citizens', whose main purpose was to increase public awareness regarding the matter; and in 1919, Hetherington served in the secretariat of the International Labour Organization's Washington Conference. Additionally, Haldane is credited in several sources as the person who made the plans for the establishment of a League of Nations known to the government through a memorandum in 1915.[20] Apart from that the names of British Idealists are hard to find in published works on the League of Nations, 1915 onwards. Even the lack of criticism implies that the British Idealists were no longer considered to be central figures in British intellectual circles. Thus, from 1915 onwards, their publications appeared mostly in the form of books instead of journal articles possibly with a narrower appeal to those who were not already sympathetic to the Idealist school of thought.

Their approach to international relations also remained distinct in its tone and scope from the mostly practical and technical discussions on international law and organization. As they had been before the outbreak of the Great War, British Idealists were mostly concerned with the teleological basis of morality that was present in all human societies. But they were not totally unaffected by the new atmosphere of hope for a new and better international order. Thus, their works from this period were marked by a renewed interest in the moral basis of international cooperation and moral unity of mankind and Green's influence on their thinking became more apparent. Mackenzie described the most central question that needed to be answered in this period as the one that was first raised by the Sophists: was morality based on the nature of things or was it a mere

---

[20] Winkler, 'The Development of the League of Nations Idea in Great Britain, 1914–1919', p. 109.

arbitrary convention.[21] In other words, in a period of increased interest in international relations, British Idealists returned to the question of whether morality was universal or particular in its nature. In an attempt to combine the universal and the particular characteristics of morality with the help of Green's theory of the common good and individual self-perfection, they tried to make sense of variations between particular manifestations of morality in different societies and the universality of human nature. Their return to the matters of the common good and individual self-perfection, when coupled with the rising liberal sentiment in Britain, led them to move away from the language of civilization and back to the language of rights. Furthermore, their discussion of individual rights, especially in Bosanquet's writings, was closely linked with the maintenance of a peaceful international order. Although the relation was pointed out in Green's work before, Bosanquet placed the matter at the heart of his reflections on the establishment of a League of Nations and the limitations such a project entailed.

Another theme that resonated through British Idealists' post Great War writings was the significance of liberty at the national, and fraternity at the international, level. The distance they placed between themselves and the imperialist sentiment grew through the years—except some occasional lapses—to the extent that they condemned foreign intervention and advised freedom to all self-sufficient nations. Although they were not totally beyond making distinctions between the 'civilized and the barbarous' peoples—as no one was at the time—for the most part they acknowledged nations' right to their own sovereign states so that every human being would be endowed with the rights and duties that are due to him/her. The end to be reached was clearly designated as the 'moral welfare of citizens' all over the world, and the progress of civilization was ascribed only an instrumental value. Furthermore, in their considerations of the British Empire they put great emphasis on its

---

[21]   Mackenzie, *Outlines of Social Philosophy*, p. 20.

transformation from an empire to a commonwealth and perceived the voluntary cooperation among the members of the British Commonwealth as an encouraging sign for the development of further international collaboration.

In this period, it was common among British intellectuals to designate the British Commonwealth as an embryonic stage of a more inclusive international organization. The idea itself gained momentum in the Edwardian era as a transformative approach to the role and constitution of the British Empire.[22] According to Duncan Bell, the Commonwealth was constituted as a rival system of civic rule opposed to France's oppressive imperialism. Yet an important point to bear in mind is that, for many British liberals, the 'commonwealth' signified the 'settler colonies', which they perceived to be 'more legitimate and more durable'.[23] Thus possession of imperial dependencies in Africa, Asia, and the Caribbean were not accounted for in many liberal thinkers' evaluation of the British Commonwealth and what it signified in a rapidly changing world order.[24] When the conditions in the dependencies of the British Empire were excluded from the rationale of the Commonwealth, what remained was a hope for the further improvement of a cooperative order of liberal states. From such a point of view, the pioneering scholar of international politics, Alfred Zimmern, defined the British Commonwealth as a 'smaller and more intimate league'.[25] Similarly, Bosanquet — who was sceptical of both the idea of commonwealth and the League of Nations — contended in the introduction to the third edition of his *The Philosophical Theory of the State* that 'to belong to the British Commonwealth will mean belonging to the League of Humanity; the great values and qualities are to display themselves and to show their full bearing for mankind'.[26] Muirhead

---

[22] Bell, *Idea of Greater Britain*, p. 118.
[23] Bell, *Reordering the World*, p. 33.
[24] Bell, *Reordering the World*, p. 33.
[25] Zimmern, *League of Nations and The Rule of Law*, p. 495.
[26] Bosanquet (1920) *Philosophical Theory of the State*, p. lxi.

also pointed to the British Commonwealth as a precursor to the future League of Nations as it was 'at least a partial embodiment of the will to a common human good greater and more compelling than that embodied in their own national State'.[27]

From a different perspective, Mackenzie argued that the organically growing sense of unity among the English-speaking peoples constituted the most significant opportunity for the establishment of an 'ultimate federation of the world'.[28] Written in 1924, Mackenzie's reflection resonated with what Haldane argued in 1913 in his speech 'Higher Nationality'. The difference of tone among these authors is indicative of the varying degrees of faith they had in the possibility of establishing a functional League of Nations, although they all believed in the necessity of increased international cooperation. While Muirhead, Hetherington, and Jones believed that the time was ripe for the realization of such a League that would include and benefit all the (independent) nations of the world, Bosanquet remained sceptical of the project until the 1920s as he was highly cautious about any unity beyond the nation-state.[29] Mackenzie's position on the matter fluctuated greatly and his belief in the effectiveness of the League seems to dwindle in time. In 1924 he seemed to believe that strengthening the unity within the Commonwealth seemed to 'hold out a more genuine prospect of an ultimate federation of the world than any number of leagues could

---

27   Muirhead, 'Recent Criticism of the Idealist Theory of the General Will', p. 366.

28   J.S. Mackenzie (1953) 'Constructive Philosophy', in *Contemporary British Philosophy*, second impression, London: George Allen & Unwin Ltd, p. 245.

29   For an account of Bosanquet's approach to international organizations see: M. Dimova-Cookson (2014) 'Do We Owe More to Fellow Nationals? The Particular and Universal Ethics of Bosanquet's General Will and Miller's Public Culture', in Brooks (ed.) *Ethical Citizenship: British Idealism and the Politics of Recognition*, London: Palgrave Macmillan, pp. 200–23.

yield' because 'the ultimate basis of community must be spiritual rather than legal'.[30]

For Henry Jones, establishment of a League was an urgent necessity in 1918. In his pamphlet published by the League of Nations Union, Jones defined the League as a monument of nations' will to peace that 'must embody itself amongst other state institutions'.[31] In a series of lectures he delivered the same year, he repeated his belief in the value and necessity of the League but he also expressed his disappointment with the prevailing plans of a League that gave only the restrictive duties of 'the policeman, judge, and executioner' to the organization in restricting armaments and punishing aggressive behaviour.[32] According to Jones, a League that would genuinely serve humanity would also have 'multiform positive services which constitute the main activities and all the virtues of good citizenship *within* a state'.[33] In the existing plans the League 'can only say "Don'ts" and frown — the method of the mother to the child when it is too small to understand the doing of anything'.[34] Still, Jones was hopeful for the service the League would provide even in a highly limited form, as it would signify ' a change of mind on the part of the nations'.[35]

Mackenzie's fluctuating approach to the League can be understood as a reflection of his day-to-day evaluations of the League's endeavours. In *Outlines of Social Philosophy*, published in 1918, Mackenzie appeared to be quite supportive of the idea of a League of Nations. He argued that establishing and maintaining a League was possible as it would not pose any challenge to states' sovereignty and that it would guarantee a 'good that is essentially the same for

---

[30] Mackenzie, 'Constructive Philosophy', p. 245.
[31] H. Jones (1918) *Form the League of Peace Now: An Appeal to My Fellow Citizens*, London: The League of Peace Union, p. 2.
[32] Jones, 'Obligations and Privileges of Citizenship', p. 140.
[33] Jones, 'Obligations and Privileges of Citizenship', p. 139.
[34] Jones, 'Obligations and Privileges of Citizenship', p. 139.
[35] Jones, 'Obligations and Privileges of Citizenship', p. 139.

all—viz. the freedom to maintain its own civilization'.[36] As 'peace and freedom' were 'closely related goods that are common to all nations', all nations would reasonably be expected to unite in their defence.[37] In 1920, Mackenzie again supported the project of the League and wrote 'the future well-being of the world depends upon the establishment of a genuine League or Society of Nations' and added that 'without this, it seems clear that there cannot be such a sense of security as would empower us to put our hearts thoroughly into the work of reconstruction within any particular State'.[38] But in the following years, Mackenzie returned to the idea of common-wealth as a more reliable basis of international unity and coopera-tion. In 1924, contradicting his earlier writings, he bluntly wrote: 'I have never been able to believe that any mere machinery, such as that of a League of Nations could serve as a substitute for the conception of human brotherhood…'[39] Mackenzie's position on the question of the importance of the League seemed to change again by 1928. In his book *Fundamental Problems of Life*, he noted that 'the institution of the League of Nations, even in its present imperfect form has gone a considerable way' in strengthening international sentiment.[40] In the following pages he contradicted his earlier assertion that international unity was about spiritual instead of legal union and argued, 'the chief desideratum for a genuine international unity is a common system of international law… it is the problem with which the League of Nations is concerned'.[41] By then, Mackenzie saw a potential in the League of Nations that would make its seat as the World Capital of 'enlightenment on all the aspects of human life'.[42]

---

36   Mackenzie, *Outlines of Social Philosophy*, p. 207.
37   Mackenzie, *Outlines of Social Philosophy*, p. 207.
38   Mackenzie, *Arrows of Desire*, p. 220.
39   Mackenzie, 'Constructive Philosophy', p. 245.
40   Mackenzie, *Fundamental Problems of Life*, p. 330.
41   Mackenzie, *Fundamental Problems of Life*, pp. 330–43.
42   Mackenzie, *Fundamental Problems of Life*, p. 343.

Though Muirhead did not write much about the League of Nations in the inter-war period, he commented on Bosanquet's scepticism towards the League. In 1924, without naming him, Muirhead criticized Bosanquet's lack of conformity with the over-riding ambition for the League of Nations. He wrote: 'I find myself in entire agreement with much that has been said in criticism of the scepticism with which some Idealists continue to regard the idea and such attempts to realise it as are represented by the League of Nations.'[43] Muirhead argued that the League would greatly help each state in its work only if 'they could be delivered from the fear of external aggression and from the paralysing burden of armaments' through the services of the League.[44] Mackenzie directed a similar criticism at Bosanquet as well in 1917. From a perspective similar to that of Hobhouse, Mackenzie wrote: 'Hegel did emphasize the importance of the State in such a way as to discredit attempts to secure any larger mode of unity, and, on the whole, to represent war as being necessarily a permanent institution. Dr. Bosanquet does not follow him entirely in this, but he appears to do so to a considerable extent.'[45] But in retrospect, Muirhead questioned the fairness of his criticism of Bosanquet. Being one of the few Idealists who lived long enough to see the dissolution of the League of Nations and the outbreak of the Second World War, he wrote in his autobiography that 'most of us at the time were caught up by the enthusiasm for world peace' and did not see that Bosanquet's fear 'was almost too literally doomed to be verified'.[46]

Bosanquet was indeed the single one of these Idealists who continuingly criticized the attempt to establish a League of Nations, which he deemed to be premature. Bosanquet's lack of faith in the

---

[43] Muirhead, 'Recent Criticism of the Idealist Theory of the General Will', p. 366.

[44] Muirhead, 'Recent Criticism of the Idealist Theory of the General Will', p. 366.

[45] Mackenzie, *Outlines of Social Philosophy*, p. 150.

[46] Muirhead, *Reflections by a Journeyman in Philosophy*, pp. 180–81.

possibility of maintaining an international unity was based on his conviction that there was not a general will at the international level that can sustain a political organization at the time. He collected his reflections on international relations in *Social and International Ideals,* published in 1917. In one of the articles he included in this volume, he argued: 'you may find several communities desiring peace. And they may make a league to enforce it. But their "general wills" taken together are not one will, that is, they have not in common the same principal objects...'[47] So, when the conditions presented states with conflicting interests, the bond between them would not be strong enough to unite them around their common good. Such a unity would be completely dependent on the use of force, which is neither a moral nor a dependable source of political legitimacy. Such a league that was maintained only by force due to its very nature would be prone to fall prey to discord.[48] Furthermore, the probability of discord within such a league posed a risk that may not have been present in its absence. Bosanquet maintained that every league that was not based on the general will of its members 'must sooner or later (being a mere convention of separate wills) arouse a counter league' and such an order would be a fertile ground for war.[49] Overall, Bosanquet argued, the world was not ready for an international 'praetor'; and already existing 'international laws, treaties, and usages' were 'at bottom, only agreements of a number of particular wills, the wills of absolute independent bodies'.[50] Evidently, Bosanquet was not against the establishment of a League of Nations even when he was critical of those who advocated its immediate realization. Rather, he was suspicious of the existence of a moral basis upon which it could be built at the time. Instead of focusing on the legal and technical details of a League, he believed in the

---

47 B. Bosanquet (1917) 'The Wisdom of Naaman's Servants', in *Social and International Ideals,* London: The Macmillan Company, p. 314.

48 Bosanquet, 'Wisdom of Naaman's Servants', p. 314.

49 Bosanquet, 'Patriotism in the Perfect State', p. 281.

50 Bosanquet, 'Patriotism in the Perfect State', p. 273.

necessity of building the moral capacity of each and every nation on Earth so that they could partake in a general will to international unity in the future.

All other British Idealists agreed on the necessity to build an internationalist general will among peoples, but they also believed that the League of Nations was going to be successful in maintaining world peace. They held the opinion that the League of Nations, though necessarily based on legal formalities in the beginning, had the potential to evolve organically into a moral unity of humanity. Furthermore, they perceived it as a potential source of influence on the internal affairs of states. It can be argued, yet again, that the optimism of the minor figures among British Idealists was getting ahead of their reason by bestowing a newly formed League of Nations with the capacity and the duty of ensuring the well-being of each and every individual on Earth. Although their optimism was not philosophically unsupported, it lacked a certain degree of caution that was present in the arguments of a more seasoned Idealist.

II. The Will towards International Unity and Cooperation

The Great War marked the end of an era that was doomed by the lurking dangers of materialism and militarism to which the British Idealists were mostly oblivious. Thus, their writings—especially 1916 onwards—centred around the question of how materialism gained such a strong foothold in nineteenth-century Europe and how this could be prevented from recurring in the future. Although the war itself brought inexpressible sorrow and anguish to millions of people, it was also an eye-opener for the Great Powers of Europe. In 1918, Haldane wrote:

> This war has been like a fire that has burned up chaff and stubble. It has swept away many prejudices, toned down many passions. It has got rid of much slackness and indifference, and it has opened the

eyes of men and women to great duties, not only to themselves, but to their fellow men and women... It has raised our ideals.[51]

It was a common contention among the idealists at the time that the trauma of the war gave rise to new ideas that required mutual service among peoples beyond the borders of nation-states.[52] An increased amount of interest in the possibility of international cooperation within the wider intellectual circles of Britain was evident from the sheer number of publications that focused on the necessity of establishing an international organization of nations. Through these publications, 'most people have become familiar with the general conception of a League of Nations, and many have been led to think seriously about problems that are at least international, if not even cosmopolitan'.[53] Dissemination of interest in international matters from the intellectual circles to the wider public was significant in terms of giving rise to a general sentiment towards international cooperation. While the technical reflections on the limits and structure of the League were focused on the intricacies of international jurisdiction, British Idealists were predominantly concerned with identifying the means for creating such a general sentiment for international unity.

In the pamphlet Jones wrote for the League of Nations Union, he argued that the 'War Aims' of the Allied world were reflective of the principles that were to be followed in the new world order once the war was over. These principles were 'freedom, independence, and the right of every nation, great or small, to live its own life and to develop its own best powers while respecting and being respected by its neighbours'.[54] These were the principles that were upheld when the Allied countries took up arms in defence of Belgium, to

---

51 Haldane, *The Future of Democracy*, p. 5.
52 Mackenzie, *Fundamental Problems of Life*, pp. 327–31; Jones, 'Obligations and Privileges of Citizenship', p. 157; Hetherington and Muirhead, *Social Purpose*, p. 96.
53 Mackenzie, *Fundamental Problems of Life*, p. 327.
54 Jones, *Form the League of Peace Now*, p. 4.

make sure that it would continue to be 'an equal among equals, possessing and enjoying the right to make use of the world's resources and to develop its powers in doing so'.[55] Clearly, Belgium was not one of the Great Powers of Europe; still it was a European country whose occupation by a foreign nation seemed to be unacceptable to the British government and to British Idealists alike. Furthermore, the official justification of Britain's involvement in the war—as it was not directly attacked—was 'defence of the rights of small states and the principles of international law'.[56] But this justification revealed the Euro-centric biases that were inherent in international law at the time. When it was coupled with the anti-imperialist principles that were advocated by the United States of America, a move from defending the moral duty of civilizing the world to defending the moral right of every society to sustain and develop its own civilization became inescapable.

British Idealists adopted this change in tone by revisiting Green's moral and political philosophy. The interdependency of the good of each individual and the common good of the society constituted one of the cornerstones of Green's moral theory.[57] In the works of younger idealists, the individual was replaced with nations and the society was replaced with the universal unity of mankind, and the same reciprocal understanding of the good was applied to the international sphere. What was truly good for a nation was necessarily good for the whole of mankind and contributed to its advancement. They designated each ethical system that is embodied in each particular society as an indispensable part of the whole that is called morality. As it was the case in relations between the particular and the universal, existence and development of ethical systems in line with each country's unique experiences and material conditions was vital for the revelation of the many-sided nature of human morality.

---

[55] Jones, *Principles of Citizenship*, p. 65.
[56] Pedersen, *The Guardians: The League of Nations and The Crisis of Empire*, p. 24.
[57] Green, *Lectures*, p. 54.

Furthermore, a ranking among the ethical systems of societies that marked the moral thinking of the Idealists a couple decades previously was mostly abandoned in the post Great War period. By that time, they perceived each ethical system as a unique and invaluable expression of the moral law that resonated through all human interaction. For British Idealists, the unity of humanity was a given that could not be denied or destroyed. Yet the awareness of this unity and human beings' will to act in accordance with it was something that developed through time and conscious effort.

As Green put forward in his *Prolegomena to Ethics*, the natural limits of human community could only be drawn around 'all who have dealings with each other and who can communicate as "I" and "Thou"'.[58] Thanks to the progressive nature of mankind, realization of greater unities was an underlying pattern in the history of human life. The transitions from the family to tribe, and from city-states to nation-states were to be understood as extensions of 'the area of the common good'.[59] By the end of the Great War, most British Idealists were convinced that the time was ripe to go beyond the borders of nation-states in considerations of the common good. They put unequalled emphasis on the importance of a consciousness of a common good inclusive of all mankind as a precondition of legal and political cooperation. Following Green's argument that 'no development of morality can be conceived, nor can any history of it be traced... which does not presuppose some idea of a common good...' the younger Idealists argued that the 'good' achieved through international cooperation must be common to all humanity. In regards to the extension of common good to whole humanity, Mackenzie argued that nations from then on were to serve as 'cooperative groups' within the larger unity of the 'Commonwealth of Nations' as families do within villages.[60] He maintained that the

---

[58]   Green, *Prolegomena*, p. 242.
[59]   Green, *Prolegomena*, p. 237.
[60]   Mackenzie, *Fundamental Problems of Life*, p. 103.

'common good' and not the 'general will' was to be taken as the fundamental moral determinant in international relations so far as 'the only kind of General Will that is of much value is that which is the expression of a cooperative purpose directed towards the Common Good'.[61] Pursuance of the common good was possible by every member of humanity in cooperation with others as they were all endowed with reason and they were naturally associative.[62] Peace and freedom, for instance, were common goods in pursuit of which all nations could be united. Mackenzie wrote in *Outlines of Social Philosophy*: 'peace and freedom are two closely related goods that are common to all nations alike; and all might very well combine to defend them.'[63]

In *Social Purpose*, Muirhead gave a similar account of the good that was common to all the peoples of the world. He argued that, at the present time, the common good was the 'peaceful development' of human potential all over the world and the greatest threat to its realization was 'the overgrown power of particular States'.[64] In other words, militarism, which was considered to be in the self-interest of certain states, constituted the most important obstacle to the development of international interests. Yet Muirhead was convinced that 'if the will and conscience of a nation is pledged, not merely to an abstract ideal of perfection, but to a condition of the world which makes its realisation possible, the creation of other guarantees can only be a matter of time'.[65] Thus, he argued, especially after the Great War, the outlook of men was to go beyond the limits of the nation-state. Each individual from his particular position within a nation was to take part in the 'corporate will to good'.[66] When such will

---

61 Mackenzie, *Fundamental Problems of Life*, p. 101.
62 Mackenzie, *Outlines of Social Philosophy*, p. 37.
63 Mackenzie, *Outlines of Social Philosophy*, p. 207.
64 Hetherington and Muirhead, *Social Purpose*, p. 95.
65 Hetherington and Muirhead, *Social Purpose*, p. 94.
66 Muirhead, 'Recent Criticism of the Idealist Theory of the General Will', p. 366.

found expression in the official dealings of states—as it was starting to do—some of the most demanding duties of the states would be met collectively, leaving individual states free to focus their resources on higher purposes. The most concrete example of this was visible in the work of the League of Nations:

> If the League of Nations succeeds in its central aim of guaranteeing security to its members, it is only relieving them by their own free consent of one of the more elementary functions of States, so as to leave them free for their real work of developing their own material and spiritual sources. The corporate will to good remains the same... What will have happened is merely that for one of the primary needs of society the forces of civilisation as a whole will have become available to replace those of the individual State.[67]

When states were 'delivered from the fear of external aggression and from the paralysing burden of armaments', a good common to all humanity was to be realized, revealing the existence of further interests that mark the opportunity for progress.[68] In short, Muirhead's argument amounted to the designation of peace itself as a moral good common to all humanity.

While Mackenzie and Muirhead perceived the unity of mankind as a progressive sphere of influence in which individuals perceived a common good and accepted certain rights and obligations in its pursuance, Henry Jones argued that the unity of humanity was 'possibly more real than the unity of the parts of a physical thing'.[69] Although this variation in approach was not significant in terms of its practical implications, it necessarily put more emphasis on the unifying attributes of societies in comparison with their distinct characteristics. Jones, while recognizing that all societies were 'individual' in terms of their distinctive characteristics, argued that they

---

[67] Muirhead, 'Recent Criticism of the Idealist Theory of the General Will', p. 367.

[68] Hetherington and Muirhead, *Social Purpose*, p. 366.

[69] H. Jones (1919) 'Some Unexamined Assumptions that Hinder the Study of the Conditions of Social Well-Being', *Rice Institute Pamphlet – Rice University Studies*, 6 (3), p. 143.

were not in any sense 'isolated'.[70] Thus, he maintained that the good common to all peoples was always present; what needed to be realized was how to pursue it collectively. According to Jones, in all endeavours where individuals or states paid regard to the 'principle of mutual help' and acted in accordance with the dictates of moral rights and duties, there existed a common good. It necessitated not only refrain from causing harm but a 'positive care of one another'.[71] Thus, according to Jones, beyond the moral duties of maintaining peace among nations and respecting other nations' freedom, the pursuance of the universal common good of humanity required individuals and states to take positive steps for humanity's progress.

The unity of humanity, although natural in its moral capacity, faced considerable problems when it was translated into a political one. Maintaining the sovereignty of states while ensuring their cooperation was a major concern in the schemes for the establishment of the League of Nations. The critics of the League were mainly concerned with the League's capacity to enforce international legislation that would intervene in the spheres that had been traditionally considered to be in the sovereign power of states. For instance, as the primary aim of the League was to prevent armed conflict among states in the future, it had to utilize certain preventive and punitive measures and 'it was hard to be done without compromising national sovereignty'.[72] Especially the matter of reduction of armaments was perceived by some as a threat to national security and sovereignty. In his reflections on the International Labour Organisation Conference, Hetherington identified such a tendency towards the 'resurgence of the spirit of nationalism, jealous of every restraint on national sovereignty' as a counter force to the rise of international

---

[70] Jones, 'Some Unexamined Assumptions that Hinder the Study of the Conditions ff Social Well-Being', p. 143.
[71] Jones, 'Some Unexamined Assumptions that Hinder the Study of the Conditions ff Social Well-Being', p. 165.
[72] P.J. Yearwood (2009) *Guarantee of Peace: The League of Nations in British Policy 1914–1925*, Oxford: Oxford University Press, p. 16.

spirit.[73] Other British Idealists also gave consideration to these suspicions and argued that the League had a moral justification for its duties and powers, although they were not very clear on the limits of the League's sphere of influence.

Jones, Muirhead, and Mackenzie all agreed that delegation of certain powers from states to an international organization did not necessarily mean a breach of individual states' sovereignty. And even when they considered the possibility that some aspects of states' sovereign powers were to be surrendered, they did not perceive it as a necessarily negative occurrence. The main reason behind their dismissive attitude towards apprehensions about state sovereignty was that they viewed the move from national to international cooperation as a natural step in human development. They were convinced that, as families did not vanish within nations, nations would not vanish within an international organization. Furthermore, they contended that especially under modern circumstances, absolute sovereignty was a sham; states were already dependent on each other for commerce, finance, science, and politics. In *Principles of Citizenship,* Jones argued that 'the sovereignty of states, like the liberty of individuals, depends, not upon being free *from* the world, but upon finding the world to be bone of their bone and flesh of their flesh'.[74] As the world was already an interdependent whole that consists of nation-states, '"exclusion" or "privacy"' was 'a miserable half-truth, and gives to them no claim to respect nor any right or power'.[75] Muirhead too was convinced that international organizations were not a threat to states' sovereignty. He was confident that states' inclusion within international organizations would strengthen their position, as they would be able to fulfil their duties towards their own citizens and to humanity in their fullest capacity without being obstructed by fear of external threats

---

[73] H.J.W. Hetherington (1920) *International Labour Legislation,* London: Methuen & Co. Ltd, p. 2.

[74] Jones, *Principles of Citizenship,* p. 64.

[75] Jones, *Principles of Citizenship,* p. 65.

and the burden of armaments. Muirhead argued: 'the abiding result of the Hohenzollern-Hapsburg war will be the rise of a greater State as the organ of the "Great Society" of mankind which will endow the national State with... freedom and renewal.'[76] Such freedom and renewal was guaranteed as the state was and would continue to be 'the particular embodiment or (if it be preferred) the particular organ of the general will' of a society.[77]

From a similar perspective Mackenzie argued that, under prevailing conditions, establishment of an international organization for ensuring peace was a necessity for states' sovereignty. As peace was a common good to all nations, an organization that worked towards its maintenance did not necessitate 'in reality to sacrifice sovereignty, but... to secure the necessary conditions upon which... the essentials of sovereignty can be maintained'.[78] What appeared to be a restriction on a state's sovereignty was in reality contributive to a fuller understanding of its independence. Mackenzie argued: 'a sovereign state... is one that has complete independence. This does not mean that it possesses a government that is authorised to do whatever it pleases.'[79] This was in line with the Idealist understanding of freedom that denied the possibility or morality of freedom without rational or social constraints. Individuals within a society were to be free 'for the attainment of rational ends' which did not warrant a freedom to do whatever one pleases.[80] Similarly states were to be free in pursuance of their moral and rational ends, while being restricted, for instance, in being aggressive towards other states or curtailing their citizens' rights. Thus, Mackenzie argued that 'no sovereignty can be absolute' and so far as states acted in

---

[76] Hetherington and Muirhead, *Social Purpose*, p. 96.
[77] Muirhead, 'Recent Criticism of the Idealist Theory of the General Will', p. 241.
[78] Mackenzie, *Outlines of Social Philosophy*, p. 207.
[79] Mackenzie, *Outlines of Social Philosophy*, p. 129.
[80] J.S. Mackenzie (1901) *A Manual of Ethics, Fourth Edition*, New York: Hinds, Hayden & Eldredge, p. 316.

accordance with the dictates of an international authority with their free will in pursuance of the common good, such dictates would not restrict but only expand states' freedom.[81]

While absolute sovereignty was understood to be an unrealistic 'sham' by the British Idealists in the post Great War period, the ideal of national independence and the right to national self-dependence gained unprecedented importance in their writings in this period. In 1920, Mackenzie argued that for nations to arrive at the dictates of the universal moral order, they were to be free in its pursuance, without being distracted by the antagonistic feelings that were raised due to external interference. As it was the nature of morality that it could not be enforced on a person or a people but could only be achieved voluntarily, national self-determination was to be taken as a 'human right'.[82] He added that national self-determination 'when it is thus sought as a simple human right, it is not claimed for one people in the spirit of opposition to others, but rather in a spirit that is essentially cosmopolitan'.[83] As he put emphasis on the impossibility of moralizing an individual or a society by force, he condemned every external intervention except in a very limited number of situations. In 1918, he wrote:

> any nation that seeks to impose its civilization on others, without restraint or scruple, cannot be regarded as benefactor, but rather as the enemy of the human race, even if it be true (of which, at any rate, it can hardly be entitled to be the sole judge) that its civilization is, on the whole, superior to that of others. Indeed, a claim of this kind is in pretty manifest contradiction to the general principle from which it sets out — viz. that *every* state has the right to maintain and defend its own civilization.[84]

Perhaps more importantly, freedom of nations at the international level was deemed to be essential for the healthy functioning of the whole humanity. With the use of a bodily analogy, Mackenzie

---

81 Mackenzie, *Outlines of Social Philosophy*, p. 206.
82 Mackenzie, *Arrows of Desire*, p. 195.
83 Mackenzie, *Arrows of Desire*, p. 195.
84 Mackenzie, *Outlines of Social Philosophy*, p. 194.

explained that, as tying human beings together did not result in a harmonious march, the forward movement of societies was also not possible when they were forced into uniformity. Instead, when societies were left to their own devices, they tended to arrive at what morality dictated through their own reasoning.[85] For the world to 'become a more completely united system' it was necessary to ensure that it had 'an intenser life and a more ample freedom throughout its parts'.[86] From Mackenzie's perspective humanity's progress was not to be a march of individuals in identical uniforms but a harmonious gathering of peoples that were unique and valuable in their particularities. Mackenzie defined this ideal in 1928 as 'to make the World more and more into a "fellowship," a fellowship where free men and women help each other to achieve what beauty and purpose they can in their lives'.[87]

This younger generation of British Idealists' attempts to apply Green's moral theory to the international arena revealed a problem with which Green himself was not concerned: there were variations and even contradictions among ethical orders that developed in different societies. The possibility of their consolidation within a universal moral whole was questionable. Thus, this generation of British Idealists was set the task of proving that the particular ethical orders of different societies were not 'purely arbitrary or conventional' though they were variable.[88] It was Jones's and Mackenzie's common contention that while material conditions and historical background of a society led to certain variations in their ethical systems, the common attributes of human beings, namely their reason and their will to self-perfection, united them in the pursuit of the highest moral good. While no single ethical order was perfect in its approximation to the moral 'law', they all had the potential to evolve into better and more comprehensive realizations

---

85 Mackenzie, *Arrows of Desire*, p. 194.
86 Mackenzie, *Arrows of Desire*, p. 221.
87 Mackenzie, *Fundamental Problems of Life*, pp. 349–50.
88 Mackenzie, *Outlines of Social Philosophy*, p. 25.

of morality. This was actually the basis of states' right to maintain and develop their own form of civilization from Jones's and Mackenzie's perspective.

Mackenzie's self-ascribed purpose in his *Outlines of Social Philosophy* was to reveal the underlying unifying characteristics of mankind that were not always so apparent under the veil of evident cultural and political differences. With reference to Sophists of ancient Greece, he put forward the contention that ethics and its legal reflections in the laws of particular states could be seen as the outcomes of 'human agreements or contracts, or... arbitrary choices of particular rulers' without any universal or 'natural' basis.[89] The Sophists' position assumed a sharp distinction between what was natural and what was arbitrary or man-made. But, Mackenzie argued, the great works of Plato and Aristotle went beyond that binary distinction and revealed that the ethics that ruled any social unity were 'growing out of a particular fact in the nature of man'.[90] According to him, these great philosophers revealed the basis of human society as men's social nature and the role of ethics as the source of the most favourable principles that gave rise to 'the form of human organisation in which the need for cooperation would be most perfectly supplied'.[91] In a similar pursuit, Mackenzie tried to reveal the sources of variation among ethical systems and the underlying 'natural' unity in his work.

Mackenzie argued that the most significant reason for the emergence of various ethical systems was the material conditions under whose influence societies evolved. Using the examples of Great Britain and India, Mackenzie argued the material conditions that were mostly due to the considerable differences between these two geographies' climates led to the development of two distinct modes of valuation. According to Mackenzie, the Indian civilization,

---

[89] Mackenzie, *Outlines of Social Philosophy*, p. 20.
[90] Mackenzie, *Outlines of Social Philosophy*, p. 21.
[91] Mackenzie, *Outlines of Social Philosophy*, pp. 21–25.

which was quite foreign to the natives of Great Britain, was shaped in accordance with the favourable climate of that region.[92] As their material necessities such as food, clothing, and housing were met quite easily, this encouraged 'leisurely and contemplative habits and the belief in beneficent powers behind the workings of nature'.[93] Clearly, this was in contrast with the valuation of the Western civilization that attributed great importance to material possessions and the endeavour for their acquisition in the way of discipline and hard work. As these differences could not be explained with reference to race—Mackenzie noted both the British and Indian peoples were descendants of the Aryan race—greater importance was to be attributed to the 'geographical and social conditions' that shaped the characters of these societies.[94]

Mackenzie contended that differences in the outlook of societies were not sufficient grounds for strife among peoples. They were after all outcomes of material conditions that were quite arbitrary. Furthermore, he argued, claiming superiority to other civilizations was baseless so far as the international mind-set was gaining ground in all societies. Although differences of language, manners, laws, as well as thought and action existed, it was no longer possible to designate a single civilization as superior to others. The belief in the superiority of a single civilization was mostly the result of a failure to understand different cultures and the ethical codes they pursued. In accordance with this international sentiment that was becoming dominant among all societies, Mackenzie argued 'it would not be easy to arrange an order of merit' among various peoples, and if such an order was to be made he 'should be inclined to say that the best race or mixture of races is the one that is best able to appreciate others'.[95] Overall, Mackenzie was content that 'things that distinguish men from one another' were 'insignificant in comparison

[92] Mackenzie, *Fundamental Problems of Life*, p. 231.
[93] Mackenzie, *Fundamental Problems of Life*, p. 231.
[94] Mackenzie, *Fundamental Problems of Life*, p. 187.
[95] Mackenzie, *Fundamental Problems of Life*, p. 107.

with the things that unite them'.[96] He thought that the right way to overcome the illusion of contradiction among various ethical systems was through use of communication and free exchange of ideas. In 1934 he wrote: 'though the supreme values are the same for both [Britain and India], the subordinate values are in many respects different. All that can fairly be expected is that Eastern philosophers should pay attention to the best thought of the West and that Western philosophers should return the compliment in kind.'[97]

If ethical orders of societies were full of particularities, what was the relation of moral law that is deemed to be universal to human conduct at national and international levels? In the *Principles of Citizenship,* after defending the universality of moral order and its separateness from human contingencies, Jones argued that its realization was totally dependent on the will of humanity. According to Jones, the moral order, due to its ideal nature as something that is present not in the material but in the contemplative form, was in a constant process of reconstruction.[98] Furthermore, as it was constantly being reconstructed in the actual world, it was impossible for an individual or a society to know its dictates in full. Based on these two contentions, Jones argued, 'it is a prolific error to hypostatise the moral world, in the sense of giving it an existence *apart* from the imperfect forms of social order within which men live their ordinary lives'.[99] Morality was realized through an ongoing—and potentially endless—process in which men strove to live up to their capacity as human beings and the moral world was not 'a world aloof from the real' but an idea that was realized through mankind's constant effort for self-actualization.[100] Both Jones and Mackenzie argued that all human beings had the capacities for reason and will.

---

96 Mackenzie, *Outlines of Social Philosophy*, p. 177.
97 J.S. Mackenzie (1934) 'Counter Attack from the East', *Mind*, 43 (120), p. 121.
98 Jones, *Principles of Citizenship*, p. 71.
99 Jones, *Principles of Citizenship*, p. 71.
100 Jones, *Principles of Citizenship*, p. 72.

While reason bestowed individuals and the communities they formed with the ability of evaluating facts and coming up with the best possible conduct in pursuance of the common good, their will gave them the power to pursue it in their endeavours. While these two capacities were universal, their application showed variances due to the material conditions that changed the best course of realizing their human potential.

The relation between universal morality and particular ethical orders from the perspectives of Jones and Mackenzie is significant in terms of supplying the principle of national self-determination with a moral theoretical justification. As they perceived each ethical order as a unique approximation to universal morality, they defended nations' right to develop their own civilization independent from foreign intervention. From this perspective, the most important duty of an international organization was to ensure that free nation-states would work in harmony with each other for the common good of humanity.

III. Bosanquet and 'The Function of the State in Promoting the Unity of Mankind'

Bosanquet's outlook on international order is best gathered from a book of collected essays published in 1917 under the title of *Social and International Ideals*. Unlike many books published in those years on international relations, it was not concerned with the legal and technical difficulties that faced a future League of Nations. Bosanquet, in the preface of the book, clearly stated that his work was 'about the enduring conditions of peace', but it was not concerned with 'the ending of the present war, or about diplomatic arrangements for providing directly against its recurrence'.[101] Like other British Idealists who witnessed the Great War and reflected on the conditions that led to it, Bosanquet was concerned with the moral basis of international cooperation. Yet, unlike them, he

---

[101] Bosanquet, *Social and International Ideals*, p. v.

focused on the internal structures of states and the nature of 'patriotism' that was maintained by the general will of particular societies. He argued that 'the warlike atmosphere means disease within the State; the healthy State, however strong, is non-militant in temper'.[102] The disease itself was a flawed form of patriotism and its most visible and destructive symptom was a desire for 'the things which diminish by sharing'.[103] True patriotism, on the contrary, was marked by the pursuance of those goods that were universal, such as 'beauty, truth, kindness'.[104] Bosanquet argued that pursuit of these supreme values could only be guaranteed by a satisfactory organization of rights and duties within each political community. In other words, without organizing each state for the pursuance of universal values that are available to all, it was impossible to guarantee peace and prosperity at the international level by merely establishing a league. Thus by 1917 Bosanquet was sceptical of the chances of success of a League of Nations. Instead, he advocated further efforts for the education and better organization of particular societies. He summarized this position as follows:

> My point is throughout, then, that the really important thing is also the thing open to all of us; the amelioration of the social spirit and social detail here where we live; and that this is the principal ground on which the victory of all humanity is to be won, because it alone can furnish a solid foundation on which extended unities of will can be built up... I repeat here that the essential thing in all international agreements is the quality and real aim of the will that sustains them; and that throughout great communities and systems of these, this will can only be in stable harmony in so far as it possesses that outlook on life which takes the supreme values as its criterion and embodies them in a well-ordered community.[105]

Social and International Ideals was not significant in terms of the originality of its arguments, as all the articles in the book except one were published before. The book was significant as it showed that

---

102 Bosanquet, *Social and International Ideals*, p. v.
103 Bosanquet, *Social and International Ideals*, p. v.
104 Bosanquet, *Social and International Ideals*, p. vi.
105 Bosanquet, *Social and International Ideals*, p. vii.

Bosanquet's approach to international relations—which was very much influenced by Green's teaching—was still defendable in 1917. In that regard, Bosanquet diverged from the rest of the Idealists who witnessed the Great War. Arguably, it was because Bosanquet was never an enthusiastic supporter of imperialism although his works revealed he was not free from some of the basic contentions of an imperialist mind-set. Although he was not totally oblivious to the practice of ranking civilizations, he did not necessarily believe in the effectiveness of maintaining colonies to 'civilize' foreign peoples. For him the best service to humanity was to create and maintain the best possible system of rights and duties at home. Although he was often criticized, even by his fellow Idealists, for his unwillingness to support the League of Nations, his reluctance on the matter was actually quite consistent with his overall theoretical position. He believed in the gradual development of mankind and advocated the view that without each state creating an adequate moral order at home it was impossible to create a moral international order. This, for sure, was not an argument in favour of abandoning the goal of striving towards the higher moral unity of mankind; it was simply a reminder that skipping steps would most probably hinder realization of this goal and might even lead to greater disasters in the future. As Maria Dimova-Cookson wrote: 'The Bosanquetian moral horizon is outwardly expanding: its limitation by particular parameters of the general will is contingent, not necessary.'[106]

In *Social and International Ideals,* Bosanquet's approach to international relations revolved around Green's contention that the more each state 'attains its proper object of giving free scope to the capacities of all persons living on a certain range of territory, the easier it is for others to do so'.[107] By applying Green's argument to the post Great War world, Bosanquet recognized that the state was

---

[106] Dimova-Cookson, 'Do We Owe More to Fellow Nationals? The Particular and Universal Ethics of Bosanquet's General Will and Miller's Public Culture', p. 220.

[107] Green, *Lectures*, pp. 170–71.

not the ultimate end of life but it was an essential form of social and political unity, contributive to the realization of the unity of mankind. Bosanquet argued that as humanity was not—for the time being—a real unity, a singular devotion to it, at the expense of one's own country, would possibly end in hypocrisy. Instead, individuals as constitutive parts of their own political unions were to work towards the betterment of the system of rights and duties recognized by their own states. From this perspective, each state was the 'guardian of one type of humanity', and it was in the service of the whole by 'maintaining the particular contribution of its community to the total of human life and human mind'.[108] And regardless of national peculiarities, Bosanquet expected every satisfactory political system to be organized around the principles of justice and public welfare. When the parts acted in pursuance of the common good and the supreme values of humanity within their own political systems, the ground for war was expected to disappear at the international level.

As early as 1891, Bosanquet was willing to acknowledge one's duty to humanity to be higher and more general than his duty to his own country.[109] What he rejected was an unqualified devotion to humanity that is marked by a false belief 'that humanity is a real corporate being, an object of devotion and a guide to moral duty'.[110] This was a position he associated with Comtism and found highly erroneous. By supporting humanity as if it was a concrete whole with shared characteristics, this approach was capable of uniting mankind only at the lowest level possible. Instead, Bosanquet argued, humanity was to be understood as an 'ideal unity'; a unity that existed only 'in the medium of the thought... made up of certain

---

108 Bosanquet, 'Function of the State in Promoting the Unity of Mankind', in *Social and International Ideals*, p. 277.

109 B. Bosanquet (1891) 'Some Socialistic Features of Ancient Societies', in *Essays and Addresses*, London: Swan Sonnenschein & Co., p. 53.

110 Bosanquet, 'Function of the State in Promoting the Unity of Mankind', in *Social and International Ideals*, p. 292.

sentiments, purposes, and ideas'.[111] From Bosanquet's perspective, the sentiments, purposes, and ideas that were implied in the unity of mankind were not necessarily realized in every human society, let alone in the mind of every single individual. Actually, these ideals were rather to be found in the 'national culture and kindness' of the 'great civilised nations, with all their faults, than in what is common to the life of all men'.[112]

If the apparent arrogance of being a member of a civilized nation is overlooked, Bosanquet's main point was to look for the unity of mankind not in the mere quantity of human beings, but in their quality *as* human beings. In other words, mankind's value was apparent in the ends they pursued, the social and political perfection of their communities, and the advances they achieved in arts, science, and technology. Bosanquet made a clear distinction between approaching humanity with reference to quantity or quality. He argued that taking all existing human beings as an aggregate would only lead to a crowd with 'no common character in which the values to which we are devoted as the qualitative essence of humanity are adequately represented'.[113] And from a sober and non-romanticized perspective, devotion to such a crowd meant equating the value of humanity with 'all human beings, past, present, and future, with their wicked and wasted lives'.[114] According to Bosanquet, the unity of mankind did not signify the unity of actual human beings, the majority of which pursued lives where they did not or could not realize any of the qualities that marked them as human beings. Against the contention that humanity as a whole should be valued regardless of the specifics that constituted it, Bosanquet argued:

---

[111] Bosanquet, *Essays and Addresses*, p. 97.
[112] B. Bosanquet (1917) 'The Teaching of Patriotism', in *Social and International Ideals*, London: The Macmillan Company, p. 15.
[113] Bosanquet, 'Function of the State in Promoting the Unity of Mankind', p. 291.
[114] Bosanquet, *Civilization of Christendom*, p. 66.

> The idea to be got rid of is the idea that specialised circumstances are a fetter upon individuality and genius. Homer and Shakespeare, for instance, are characteristic individual voices each of his country, race, and climate. Do we wish that it were not so? Do we think that they would be more themselves if they were not? What is the world there for if it is not, with all its rich individuality, to come to utterance in mind?[115]

Yet it was not his contention that those individuals who lacked the opportunity to pursue truly human lives should be left to their own devices or that they should be eliminated or taken advantage of. Rather they were to be supported with the powers necessary to realize their potentials within their own social and political community.

Still, each particular social and political community was to abide by certain universal qualities that are common to all well-ordered societies. One of these qualities, according to Bosanquet, was the existence of a sense of patriotism within the community. He believed that keeping a sense of patriotism was vital so as not to fall into 'coldness and pessimism' or lose the will to strive for the advancement of the social whole.[116] What Bosanquet advocated as a safeguard against international strife was 'the purest kind of patriotism' that took pride in the achievements of the nation so far as they were in the pursuance of supreme values, and those goods that were not 'diminished by sharing'.[117] But there was another kind of patriotism that was not a desirable attribute of nations. Bosanquet defined it as a 'source of brainless and often fraudulent clamour, or at best a dangerous fanaticism'.[118] From Bosanquet's perspective, the true patriot was not to take pride in the military power of his state, the vastness of territories it occupied, or the material advancement of it at the expense of other peoples. Rather, a true patriot was to cherish

---

[115] B. Bosanquet, 'A Moral from Athenian History', in *Social and International Ideals*, p. 262.

[116] Bosanquet, 'Teaching of Patriotism', p. 3.

[117] Bosanquet, 'Teaching of Patriotism', p. 15.

[118] Bosanquet, 'Teaching of Patriotism', p. 3.

its state due to the political order it established within which the principles of justice and communal welfare were realized, as well as due to its contributions to overall human advancement. While the militant form of patriotism was 'the spirit of romantic and occasional glorification of the group', true patriotism was most visible in 'the daily spirit of communal labour and duty'.[119] Clearly, a true and intelligent patriot was not militant but noble in purpose and zealous in his work in pursuance of the supreme values within his own community and in accordance with his powers.

It was a logical outcome for Bosanquet that when peoples were devoted to the true form of patriotism, they would work for the establishment and maintenance of a satisfactory system of rights and duties within a justly ruled community. After all, these were the conditions that strengthened their devotion to their state and encouraged them for further service to their community. The internal organization of a community in the above specified manner was also vital for the manner in which its state engaged with external affairs. Bosanquet argued that the determining factor in the international arena was specifically the kind of patriotism that was upheld within specific communities. And from his perspective 'the way to peace and security' was simple enough; it was 'to do right at home, and banish sinister interests and class privileges from the commonwealth'.[120] While this was an end to be pursued privately by each community, it was also a universal end for whose realization every community must comply with the shared values of humanity. In other words, for the establishment of the ideal of 'non-interference' as a universal rule of conduct in international relations it was mandatory that each state maintained a satisfactory order of rights and duties within its own borders. Bosanquet was thoroughly confident that when each community established a just social and political order, the grounds for international strife would disappear.

---

[119] Bosanquet, 'Review of *The Group Mind*, by William McDougall', p. 66.
[120] Bosanquet, 'Wisdom of Naaman's Servants', p. 309.

He wrote in 1917: 'There is not the smallest reason why, under such a policy as is here outlined, every individual and society should not find communication and co-operation with every other on the earth's surface as easy and convenient as within his own country.'[121]

Bosanquet was convinced that the necessary conditions for peace could only be realized within nation-states, and external institutions to enforce peace would be totally ineffective in the absence of a general will towards their maintenance within national communities. From this perspective, instead of pinning his faith upon the foundation of the League of Nations, he recommended that everyone should focus on the betterment of their own state's internal organization. He argued: 'a system of nation-states or of commonwealths… each internally well organised, would not perhaps give us all that a world-state might give us, but it would place the world in a wholly different ethical position from that which it occupies to-day.'[122] Bosanquet grew to trust the League of Nations through time. In the 1920 edition of his *The Philosophical Theory of the State*, for instance, he wrote, 'I believe in the League of Nations as the hope and refuge of mankind'.[123] Still, he retained a level of caution and added that even when such a League fulfilled its promise, it would not 'divest' any individual or state from its obligation to act morally. Even when he acknowledged the potential of the League as a means for humanity's progress his emphasis was on individuals' and states' duty to serve humanity through fulfilling their particular moral potential.

Bosanquet was sure that, even if a real unity of mankind was never established in the world, 'reciprocal good will, with understanding and appreciation, even intensified by the sense of forgiveness and mystery' would tie nations together and ensure their

---

[121] Bosanquet, 'Wisdom of Naaman's Servants', p. 317.

[122] Bosanquet, 'Function of the State in Promoting the Unity of Mankind', p. 295.

[123] Bosanquet (1920) *Philosophical Theory of the State*, p. 1.

cooperation in the future.[124] Although he did not deny the possibility of having a successful League of Nations, he was convinced that without a general will within the communities towards peace and pursuance of supreme values, any attempt was bound to fail. The existence of a general will towards peace and cooperation within each community was a precondition for the healthy functioning of a League and not vice versa. A League as a mere 'machinery' was insufficient to protect peace, but 'if... there were to exist, in one or more communities, a prevailing general will... in favour of peace, for example; then there would so far be a solid foundation for practical steps towards international or cosmopolitan unity'.[125] Ensuring that each community upheld a general will toward peace and coopera-tion was the most basic and the most vital step towards ensuring further unity of mankind; without it, all attempts to establish leagues and federations were in vain.

IV. Patriotism, Cosmopolitanism, and Service to Humanity

British Idealists shared the conviction that patriotism and cosmo-politanism—contrary to commonly held suppositions—were not contradictory but interdependent aspirations. Their dedication to this position was most evident in their repeated references to a quote from Green's work: 'there is no other genuine "enthusiasm of humanity" than one which has travelled the common highway of reason—the life of the good neighbour and honest citizen—and can never forget that it is still only on a further stage of the same journey.'[126] Bosanquet was the one who was most interested in the relation between the existence of a general will towards the pursuance of supreme values, i.e. a true kind of patriotism at the

---

[124] Bosanquet, 'Function of the State in Promoting the Unity of Mankind', p. 297.

[125] Bosanquet, 'Wisdom of Naaman's Servants', p. 314.

[126] T.H. Green (1885) *Works of Thomas Hill Green*, Vol. 1, R.L. Nettleship (ed.), London: Longmans, Green, and Co., p. 371.

national level, and its consequences for international relations. He consistently maintained in his works that a people who were satisfied at home with the internal organization of their community would not pursue adventures abroad.[127] Thus, according to Bosanquet, one's duty to humanity was not something that was distinct from his duty to his country. On the contrary, these two duties were one and the same thing in actuality, and when they appeared to be in contradiction it was either one's patriotism or one's humanitarianism that was ill defined. Based on this perspective, he wrote:

> in our best humanitarianism we do not really discover a duty to mankind that is beyond, much less in conflict with, our patriotism. Our nation, after all, remains our instrument for doing service to humanity and our main source of the ideal of humanity itself... Therefore, it is our nation which is our clue and ideal, even in the service of man, and therefore again it is doubly important here that our patriotism should be of the purest kind.[128]

In that sense, individuals' duty to work towards the betterment of their own community was a way of indirectly fulfilling their duty towards the whole of mankind.

This was an argument often repeated by other British Idealists in the post Great War period. Jones, for instance, was of the same mind with Bosanquet on the matter of humanitarianism and patriotism. Like Bosanquet, Jones perceived individuals' duty to humanity to be of a higher moral order than their duty to their own community, as the ideal was in its nature universal and any limitations on its scope were arbitrary.[129] Once the individual and the state acquired a moral character by designating the supreme purposes as their ultimate ends, they sought 'a good which is Absolute, and therefore all comprehensive'.[130] Thus, Jones argued, 'both the State and the Individual are in truth, if they only knew it, in the service of humanity,

---

127 Bosanquet, 'Patriotism in the Perfect State', p. 145.
128 Bosanquet, 'Teaching of Patriotism', p. 15.
129 Jones, *Principles of Citizenship*, p. 56.
130 Jones, *Principles of Citizenship*, p. 111.

and they are loyal to their own good in the degree in which they are faithful to its well-being'.[131] The service to humanity was not an unmitigated effort; humanity without reference to its constitutive components was a non-existent entity. While the universal that is called humanity was a mere fiction without the particularities that came together to constitute it, these particularities lost their value without a reference to the universal. Referring to the underlying idealist metaphysics, Jones argued that 'universal and particular exist only as elements in a system, and disappear when separated'.[132] When this principle was applied to the matter at hand, it revealed that 'the true good of the State is at the same time the true good of humanity and of the individual'.[133]

Jones's expectations from the individual in his contribution to the betterment of mankind were modest in nature. He argued that although 'the station which the good man fills may be small and his duties may have a narrow range' — his contribution to the world's good may be 'a widow's mite', he was still a partaker in the pursuit of supreme values.[134] It can be discerned by keeping Green's quote in mind that being a good neighbour and honest citizen was a step in the service to humanity as a whole. In that sense, even before the Great War, Jones was convinced that it was the outcome of an individualistic mind-set to perceive the interests of the state and humanity as antagonistic to each other. He wrote in 1910: 'to represent the good of a State as antagonistic to that of humanity, or to set patriotism and cosmopolitanism against each other, is as wrong in theory and as mischievous in practice as it is to oppose the good of the individual citizen to that of his State'.[135]

Like Bosanquet and Jones, Muirhead argued in *Social Purpose* that an international outlook was an essential quality both for individuals

---

131 Jones, *Principles of Citizenship*, p. 111.
132 Jones, *Working Faith of the Social Reformer*, p. 70.
133 Jones, *Principles of Citizenship*, p. 70.
134 Jones, *Principles of Citizenship*, p. 70.
135 Jones, *Working Faith of the Social Reformer*, p. 146.

and states although it was often obstructed by the pursuance of false ideals or by a fixation on materialistic self-interests.[136] Convinced that the state was not the highest or final organization of humanity, he argued that an unconditional loyalty to the state was prone to turn into an erroneous form of patriotism and become obstructive to the realization of the true purpose of the state.[137] According to Muirhead, the main purpose of a state was ensuring 'the moral welfare of its individual citizens', and due to the universal nature of morality, its full realization necessitated 'an outlook beyond the nation'.[138] In the same volume, and in compliance with Green's contention that the moral unities created by men were bound to become wider through time, Muirhead and Hetherington argued that 'looking beyond the nation, our citizenship must be a national one, but it must also have an outlook beyond the nation. It must be European, ultimately a citizenship of the world'.[139] From this perspective, they maintained that the 'truthfulness' of patriotism was to be evaluated with reference to the international outlook it endorsed. To the extent that patriotism constituted a barrier to 'devotion to the remoter interests of humanity' it was deemed to be false, an equivalent of the kind of patriotism that was adopted by Germany and resulted in the Great War.[140] Such false patriotism was marked by a narrow and uncritical devotion to the state and a lack of 'proper concern for the general welfare of mankind'.[141] Real patriotism on the other hand meant a free interest in the service of one's country and fellow men so far as such service was perceived to be not only a fulfilment of his duty to the state but also to the 'whole community of mankind'.[142]

---

[136] Hetherington and Muirhead, *Social Purpose*, p. 95.
[137] Hetherington and Muirhead, *Social Purpose*, p. 227.
[138] Hetherington and Muirhead, *Social Purpose*, p. 253.
[139] Hetherington and Muirhead, *Social Purpose*, p. 25.
[140] Hetherington and Muirhead, *Social Purpose*, p. 26.
[141] Hetherington and Muirhead, *Social Purpose*, p. 221.
[142] Hetherington and Muirhead, *Social Purpose*, p. 266.

For Muirhead, the most significant result of such an outlook was present in the countries that attained a democratic form of rule. He argued that while democracy was possible only through a conscious effort that required 'discipline, self-sacrifice, and devotion to the best it can find', its realization constituted the basis of hope as 'those conditions will achieve an organisation of the common will and aspiration of the world'.[143] That was the basis for Muirhead's optimism in regards to the possibility of a higher level of unity that was to be realized beyond the limits of particular states. He believed that the consciousness towards the fulfilment of moral duties beyond national communities was taking hold among the civilized peoples and such consciousness created the conditions for international unity and cooperation. Mackenzie too perceived humanity as a wider form of human community. He argued that its realization was not contradictory to narrower forms of union but necessarily dependent on their healthy functioning. In his *Fundamental Problems of Life*, he almost paraphrased Green's argument:

> Just as the good father or son is naturally prior to the good neighbour, the good neighbour to the good citizen, and the good citizen to the patriotic worker; so, perhaps even more emphatically, it is still essential that one should be a good patriot before he can be a 'good European' and a good European before he can hope to be, in any effective sense, a good citizen of the world.[144]

V. A Just Social Order

As it has been argued above, British Idealists' reflections on the nature of humanity continually pointed to an underlying unity of human morality that is often overshadowed by the differences among the particular ethical systems that are adopted by various communities. While the differences were explained through the impact of material conditions such as geography and climate, the unity was taken to be the result of universal human nature as social

---

[143] Hetherington and Muirhead, *Social Purpose*, p. 290.
[144] Mackenzie, *Fundamental Problems of Life*, p. 332.

and reasonable. This social and reasonable nature of man was used by Green to explain the basis of human society. In the post Great War period, British Idealists used it to explain the underlying similar qualities on which apparently distinct communities were founded. Based on this contention, Bosanquet argued that the conditions of social function constituted the root of individual morality and that 'these ideas furnish matter for social ideals, and extended social ideals may certainly appear applicable to the welfare of all conceivable members of humanity'.[145] The supreme goods of truth, beauty, and goodness supplied the ends towards which all human communities worked in their own particular ways. In this sense, the basis and end of all human societies were 'universal' but not 'general'.[146] Mackenzie made the same point when he wrote that '…what is natural is not necessarily invariable, and that the special features of human nature give rise to special kinds of order which, though not uniform, are not without law and reason'.[147]

According to Bosanquet, the British Idealist approach to morality was an improved version of Kant's work on the 'law universal'. In a chapter published in *Contemporary British Philosophy*, Bosanquet wrote:

> It appears to me absolutely plain that by developing the conception of 'law universal' into that of a concrete system, embodied in the actual whole of existing institutions, and yet furnishing through its particulars a content in which the universal end lives and grows within the individual will, a meaning is given to the Kantian ethical idea which Kant very likely would have disowned, but which really satisfies the theoretical demand which his system recognized but failed to meet.[148]

To apply this philosophical position to the matter of international relations, both an interpretative and critical approach was necessary.

---

[145] Bosanquet, *Some Suggestions in Ethics*, p. 32.

[146] Bosanquet, *Some Suggestions in Ethics*, p. 33.

[147] Mackenzie, *Outlines of Social Philosophy*, p. 25.

[148] B. Bosanquet (1924) 'Life and Philosophy', in *Contemporary British Philosophy*, London: Brandford & Dickens, p. 58.

While British Idealists tried to make sense of the reasons that created so much difference among the ethical systems of societies, they also sought to reveal the basic conditions any morally organized community was expected to meet. These basic conditions and the extent to which particular communities met these conditions were to be judged with reference to the 'good that is being aimed at in a human society'.[149]

With reference to the most basic premise of British Idealist philosophy, the good that was to be aimed at within any human society was each individual's ability to reach his/her full potential that was often called self-development, self-realization, or self-perfection; and individual self-realization was expected to culminate in the common good of particular societies, and then in the good of mankind in general. From this perspective, certain conditions had to be met for the pursuance of the moral good. First and foremost, each individual was to be a part of a community; he/she had to be a partaker within a moral system of coexistence. Second, each community was to meet certain conditions so as to supply the necessary grounds for each individual's physical and spiritual development in accordance with his/her own capacities. While many British Idealists perceived certain forms of justice and equality to be essential attributes of every moral community, the most common indicator they used in judging the morality of a community was the nature of the system of rights and duties they maintained.

Being a part of a community was equated with being a citizen by British Idealists, which indicated the centrality of the state in ensuring the functioning of the social system in accordance with existing ethical rules. This was a point most apparent in Bosanquet's work, but it was not absent in the writings of younger British Idealists. Haldane, for instance, argued in *The Future of Democracy* that in an ethical community 'every man, woman, and child ought to have the opportunity of developing what is in them' and ensuring

---

[149] Mackenzie, *Fundamental Problems of Life*, p. 105.

the necessary conditions was the duty of the state.[150] Similarly, Muirhead maintained that the state was and would continue to be a condition 'of the integrity of human life' despite the possibility that new organs beyond the nation-state would be established for the maintenance of wider human interests.[151] As the good of a human being was perceived to be dependent on the conditions the state ensured for its citizens, Muirhead and Hetherington claimed that 'to deny one's citizenship is to deny one's humanity'.[152] And Jones, while criticizing the contention that every human being had rights solely because he was a human being, wrote, 'a citizen of no state, member of no community, and enjoying none of the rights of a state or community, he could not find a place to sit or stand except in some island over which no flag has ever flown'.[153] As this was neither a realistic nor a desirable position for a human being, he designated membership within a political community as an indispensable condition for man to have rights, i.e. to have the conditions necessary for the realization of his human potential.

For British Idealists, a society was not an unspecified crowd. To be able to fulfil its moral purpose, a society, and the state as its political embodiment, was bound to be organized around the principle of justice. The principle of justice, according to Mackenzie, qualified a state as a moral power at the national level. A state that solely relied on power to rule its citizens without ensuring the existence of a just social and political system would be inadequate in its moral capacity.[154] In defining justice, Mackenzie followed Plato's conception of 'distributive justice' with some modifications.[155] He argued 'distributive justice' meant placing everyone 'in the position

---

150 Haldane, *Future of Democracy*, pp. 7–8.
151 Muirhead, 'Recent Criticism of the Idealist Theory of the General Will (II)', p. 362.
152 Hetherington and Muirhead, *Social Purpose*, p. 97.
153 Jones, 'Obligations and Privileges of Citizenship', p. 168.
154 Mackenzie, *Outlines of Social Philosophy*, pp. 138–39.
155 Mackenzie, *Outlines of Social Philosophy*, p. 156.

for which he is best fitted, adequately prepared to fulfil his function in that place, and supplied with the materials and instruments that are necessary for its proper discharge'.[156] Admitting that this principle was not applicable in the modern world as it would mean subordination of 'the individual life too completely to the service of the State', Mackenzie suggested that the State was to ensure justice by making sure that 'no unnecessary obstacles are placed in the way of each one discovering for himself what is the position for which he is best fitted, and eventually gaining that position'.[157] In *Social Purpose*, Muirhead and Hetherington also defined the moral duty of the state with reference to the principle of justice. They perceived that while the primary tool used by the state to ensure justice was the courts, more 'positive attempts' for its promotion were possible through 'control and regulation of many relationships of life, and the provision of safeguards to secure that the enterprise of individuals and groups should not bring injury to others'.[158] Such restrictions were necessary to ensure that, as Mackenzie also argued, each individual within the society had the opportunity to strive towards the realization of his potential. As self-development was a universal attribute of each and every individual, every state had the duty to maintain a just social and political order in which human beings had the opportunity to fulfil their potentials.

It was Bosanquet who most articulately related states' moral duty with reference to its organization around the principle of justice and related it to the organization of a system of rights and duties. According to Bosanquet, justice was an ideal that was both universal and social in its nature. It was universal as it was 'in a sense the lowest of social claims', the basic condition for the moral existence of individuals.[159] It was social because its realization was only possible

---

[156] Mackenzie, *Outlines of Social Philosophy*, p. 156.

[157] Mackenzie, *Outlines of Social Philosophy*, pp. 159 and 157.

[158] Hetherington and Muirhead, *Social Purpose*, pp. 229–31, quotation 231.

[159] B. Bosanquet (1917) 'Three Lectures on Social Ideals', in *Social and International Ideals*, London: The Macmillan Company, p. 198.

when human beings came together and developed a social unity in which they all recognized certain rules whose observance was essential for their individual good and the good of the community. In that sense, in 'any social system, which is to be satisfactory', its participants' claims for justice were to be recognized. Such recognition was possible through two factors, 'one constant, the other variable'.[160] The first factor required the state to uphold the law it professed to keep under any circumstances without making exceptions for individuals or groups. The second factor, on the other hand, depended on the question whether or not the rules upheld by the state were compatible with the good of the individuals under its rule.[161] Maintenance of justice at these two levels was an indispensable quality of a satisfactory social system as it was a condition for 'making possible an impartial development of human capacity' within each and every social unity.[162] The clearest indicator of the extent to which the principle of justice was upheld in a particular community was the system of rights and duties that was maintained by the state.[163] So far as a satisfactory level of justice prevailed in a political community, individuals were expected to have a satisfactory set of rights and duties for realizing their best possible selves.

VI. Conclusion

In the post Great War period, the question British Idealists focused on the most was an old one that Mackenzie traced back to the ancient Greek philosophy. He wrote in 1918:

> That problem is still, on the whole, the one that was raised at its first beginning — viz. in what sense, and to what extent, can human society be properly described as natural? If it is purely arbitrary or conventional, its study can be little more than an attempt to trace the external, variable, and, in a sense, accidental circumstances by which its forms have been, from time to time, determined. If, on the other

---

160 Bosanquet, 'Three Lectures on Social Ideals', p. 196.
161 Bosanquet, 'Three Lectures on Social Ideals', p. 196.
162 Bosanquet, Three lectures on social ideals, p. 196.
163 Bosanquet, 'Three Lectures on Social Ideals', p. 195.

hand, it is in its essence natural, we have to try to explain in what sense it is natural, and what are the particular forms to which its fundamental nature gives rise.[164]

Being confident in the universal moral nature of humanity, British Idealists argued that under the apparent multiplicity of human experience there was an underlying consistency. Each and every functioning society and every civilization worthy of the name complied with the most basic tenets of human morality. In every ethical society dishonesty was frowned upon, for instance, while a sense of justice was observed. While no society was a perfect embodiment of human morality, none was completely disconnected from it either. The apparent contradictions among laws and customs of specific peoples were mostly due to the material and geographical differences under which specific ethical orders and political institutions evolved. So far as every society tapped into the same universal morality, it was not impossible to find a set of moral values that can be utilized as a common denominator for all nations for their internal and external conduct.

One significant variance between the younger generation of British Idealists and Bosanquet in their post Great War writings was in regard to the appropriate way of ensuring compliance with the basic premises of universal morality. While Mackenzie, Muirhead, Jones, and Hetherington favoured a more direct form of cooperation among nations through international institutions for the articulation and maintenance of universal moral standards of conduct, Bosanquet was highly sceptical of such an approach. Instead he argued each nation had to be responsible for its own moral development through a better and more just organization of its laws and institutions, before they could develop a general will to become a part of a larger international unity. A premature attempt to form a universal league, according to Bosanquet, would fail inevitably, possibly giving rise to leagues and counter-leagues in conflict with

---

[164] Mackenzie, *Outlines of Social Philosophy*, p. 25.

each other. Still, this difference of opinion between Bosanquet and other Idealists did not signify a fundamental divide in their approach to humanity. On the contrary, they agreed on the most basic premises that morality, in itself, necessitated larger circles of community in pursuance of a common good that could only be complete when it comprised the whole of humanity. The apparent obstacles to such unity were mostly variations of human experience that did not necessarily mean a fundamental contradiction of norms but variations in application. So far as each nation followed the most basic dictates of morality in pursuit of justice and individual self-realization, these variations in particular ethical norms were to be celebrated as embodiments of unique realizations of the human potential. Furthermore, they all maintained that the national and international sentiments were not contradictory in their nature; on the contrary, they were the expression of the same sentiment—pursuance of a common good—at different levels of social unity. Thus, development of an international sentiment, as well as international organizations, was not a threat to nation-states. Rather, it was a necessary step in the moral development of humanity.

Chapter 5

An Internationalist Approach to Human Rights

Although British Idealism lost its central position in the British intellectual arena after the Great War, British Idealists' focus on rights in maintaining a peaceful and cooperative international order constituted a unique position at the time. While technical matters of concern such as arbitration and disarmament dominated the intellectual discussions from 1918 onwards, British Idealists' emphasis on the moral nature of international relations enabled them to come up with an internationalist scheme of human rights. The ingenuity of their theory of human rights was based on their unique adaptation of Green's theory of rights with an increasingly internationalist mind-set. The most significant contribution to these Idealists' perceptions of internationalist human rights came from Green's emphasis on the universal moral basis of any conception of rights.

In contemporary accounts of the British Idealist theory of rights, Green's 'recognition thesis' attracts much more interest than the metaphysical basis of his political philosophy. While the metaphysical roots of Green's ethical and political theory constitute a point of interest for several thinkers, its centrality to a British Idealist theory of rights has not been acknowledged by everyone. These two aspects are sometimes argued to be self-sufficient theoretical constructs that can be separated from each other. Furthermore, the distrust towards metaphysics in contemporary political theory that is most adequately exemplified by Rawls's claim to develop a 'political' theory without falling into discussions regarding 'metaphysical' argumentations has been echoed in attempts to transform Green's theory of rights into a theory of human rights.[1] In *The Limits of Ethics,* David Boucher drew attention to this tendency in contemporary literature, arguing: 'Modern philosophers have retained the conventionalism, or communitarianism, sometimes called constitutive theory and jettisoned the metaphysics.'[2] But apart from the apparent lack of consensus in the literature regarding what does or does not count as metaphysics, attempts to divide British Idealist theory into clear compartments poses the risk of glossing over one of the most interesting aspects of Green's theory of rights. When Green's perception of the universe as a consistent whole is left out of the equation, his claims regarding the compatibility of personal well-being and the common good of society loses its support point. Although very commonly in contemporary human rights literature 'the deeper philosophical questions about what human rights are and how we come to have them… are avoided', this attitude is not necessarily beneficial, especially in the case of a British Idealist theory of human rights.[3] Arguably, the disproportionate attention given to Green's rights recognition thesis in comparison with his metaphysics leads to human rights theories that emphasize particularities of societies in contrast to the universal moral character of humanity. This, in turn, gives rise to the criticism that a British Idealist theory of human rights is a relativist one, a criticism contemporary literature on British Idealism seems to be at pains to disprove.[4]

Admittedly the lack of interest or trust in metaphysics is not a new tendency in political philosophy. It is quite telling that Hobhouse chose the title *The Metaphysical Theory of the State* for his

---

1   J. Rawls (1993) *Political Liberalism,* New York: Columbia University Press, p. 10.
2   Boucher, *The Limits of Ethics in International Relations,* p. 13.
3   Boucher, *The Limits of Ethics in International Relations,* p. 246.
4   R. Martin (1997) *A System of Rights,* Oxford: Clarendon Press, p. 74.

book that was devoted to discrediting Bosanquet's *The Philosophical Theory of the State*. But from the British Idealist perspective metaphysics was an integral part of their work without which their moral and political theory lost their ground. In his *A Manual of Ethics*, Mackenzie defended the centrality of metaphysics to their philosophical work:

> The truth is that the theory of Ethics which seems most satisfactory has a metaphysical basis, and without the consideration of that basis there can be no thorough understanding of it. If we could have satisfied ourselves with a Hedonistic theory, a psychological basis might perhaps have sufficed. On the other hand, if one of the current evolution theories could be accepted, we might look for our basis in the study of biology. But if we rest our view of Ethics on the idea of the development of the ideal of self or of the rational universe, the significance of this cannot be made fully apparent without a metaphysical examination of the nature of the self; nor can its validity be established except by a discussion of the reality of the rational universe.[5]

Although younger Idealists' perceptions of the international order changed considerably in the first twenty years of the twentieth century, their dedication to idealistic ethics and metaphysics remained unaltered. When, after the Great War, they distanced themselves from imperialism and instead embraced an internationalist mind-set, their dedication to the metaphysical suppositions of self-realization and the common good enabled them to devise a genuine theory of human rights. As it is traced in the following pages, Green's theory of rights was transformed by these Idealists into a human rights theory that was based on the universal ideal of individual self-realization. This transformation was possible only when these Idealists left behind their paternalistic belief in the 'white man's duty to civilize the savages' and recognized that human progress was possible only when its parts were independent social and political communities in free pursuit of the universal common good. The emerging internationalist sentiment in Britain

---

5   Mackenzie, *Manual of Ethics*, p. 431.

that was also adopted by British Idealists in the post Great War period proved to be a very fertile ground for developing Green's work into an internationalist theory of human rights.

I. Green's Ethical Theory as
a Basis for His Theory of Rights

In the secondary literature it is commonly contended that Green's ethical theory is an unprecedented combination of Kantian deontology and Aristotelian eudemonic ethics.[6] Colin Tyler, for instance, notes that 'Green corrected Aristotle with the idealist tradition and not least with Kant, putting particular weight on the latter's metaphysics and ethics (especially the "good will", "categorical imperative" and "kingdom of ends")'.[7] While the Kantian/deontological aspect of his work dealt with the ethical norms that regulate individuals' other-regarding actions, the Aristotelian legacy of eudaemonist ethics substantiated Green's emphasis on the 'good' by designating self-realization as a universal end whose pursuance is intrinsic to human nature.[8] Unquestionably, Green's perception of human nature was intrinsically linked to his metaphysics that presupposed the existence of an eternal consciousness that cloaked the moral end of self-realization with a transcendent justification. He argued that, although human beings were limited due to their 'animality', human reason was the vessel through which eternal consciousness was coming to its own realization. In the *Prolegomena*, he argued: 'it will be found, we believe... in the growth of our experience, in the process of our learning to know the world, an animal organism, which has its history in time, gradually becomes

---

6   W.J. Mander (2016) 'Idealism and the True Self', in W.J. Mander & S. Panagakou (eds.) *British Idealism and the Concept of the Self*, London: Palgrave Macmillan, p. 289.

7   C. Tyler (2010) *The Metaphysics of Self-Realisation and Freedom*, Exeter: Imprint Academic, p. 28.

8   Tyler, *Metaphysics of Self-Realisation and Freedom*, p. 140.

the vehicle of an eternally complete consciousness.'[9] For Green, the most apparent indication of man's capacity to realize the eternal consciousness in himself was the quality that separated him from all the lower orders of animals: his capacity to envision himself as something that he is not, i.e. an ideal self, and his will to act with the intention of becoming that self. He explained this truly human quality as follows:

> The reason and will of man have their common ground in that characteristic of being an object to himself which... belongs to him in so far as the eternal mind, through the medium of an animal organism and under limitations arising from the employment of such a medium, reproduces itself in him. It is in virtue of this self-objectifying principle that he is determined, not simply by natural wants according to natural laws, but by the thought of himself as existing under certain conditions, and as having ends that may be attained and capabilities that may be realised under those conditions. *It is thus, again, that he has the impulse to make himself what he has the possibility of becoming but actually is not, and hence not merely, like the plant or animal, undergoes a process of development, but seeks to, and does, develop himself.*[10]

Thus, Green identified the moral end to be pursued by any human being as self-realization in a truly Aristotelian manner. In comparison with the hedonistic end of gaining pleasure and avoiding pain, Green argued, the end of self-realization served as a source of a higher order of satisfaction for the individual as well as a guiding principle in his endeavours to act morally.[11] But for Green the ideal of self-realization did not entail a readily identified conception of the best possible human being. On the contrary, Green acknowledged that each individual had a unique potential for an individualized form of self-realization. As Rex Martin explained, when Green used the concept of self-realization as a justificatory human quality for ethical life what he meant was not the 'sameness of the ends themselves' but the 'sameness of the means' that were necessary for its

---

9   Green, *Prolegomena*, p. 77.
10 Green, *Prolegomena*, p. 199, emphasis added.
11 Tyler, *Metaphysics of Self-Realisation and Freedom*, p. 157.

actualization.[12] The unifying characteristic for being human was not the type of person they became in the end but their potential to envision a better version of themselves and strive towards its actualization. The centrality and importance of the idea of self-realization in Green's ethical—and following from it social and political—theory was most clearly explained by Dimova-Cookson and Mander:

> Green goes on to argue that the motive determining an agent's will is always an idealized future of his own self, a conception of himself as satisfied—whatever it may be that he seeks. For this reason, argues Green, moral action is 'the process of self-realization, i.e. of making a possible self real.' In historical terms, Green's arrival at the formula of self-realization represents an important shift in ethical thinking. Instead of asking with the utilitarian, intuitionist, and even the Kantian philosophers of the day, 'What ought I to do?', Green and the many Idealists who followed him re-construed ethical inquiry in the mould of an older question, 'What kind of person ought I to be?'[13]

While Green's appropriation of Aristotle's eudaemonist ethics focused his ethical inquiry into the subject of self-realization at the individual level, his perception of an ethical society was decisively different from Aristotle's. In acknowledging the discrepancy between Aristotle's and his own understanding of an ethical society, Green himself noted that the difference was not a fundamental one in effect, it was only in regards to 'the range of persons' who can claim to be participants in an ethical society.[14] While 'the Greek of Aristotle's age' 'could only conceive the self-devotion in some form in which it had actually appeared... in the citizen-soldier', Green argued that Christian thought enabled men to recognize a higher

---

[12] R. Martin (2014) 'T.H. Green's Idea of Persons and Citizens', in T. Brooks (ed.) *Ethical Citizenship: British Idealism and the Politics of Recognition*, London: Palgrave Macmillan, p. 22.

[13] M. Dimova-Cookson and W.J. Mander (2006) 'Introduction', in *T.H. Green: Ethics, Metaphysics and Political Philosophy*, Oxford: Clarendon Press, p. 9.

[14] Green, *Prolegomena*, p. 237.

moral standard in which all human beings were partakers.[15] The ethical society envisioned by the Greeks was shaped around virtually identical ethical values and their application was limited to only a select group of citizens; large numbers of aliens and slaves were excluded from the ethical society.[16] In short the ancient Greek perception of ethical society embodied the ideals of equality and fraternity among citizens but it lacked universalizability. Green maintained that the lack of universality in Aristotle's description of an ethical society was a trait of his time. Ancient Greeks did not know such a conception of universality. Thus, when Aristotelian ethics were to be applied to modern societies, it was to be modified with an all-inclusive conception of the common good.

Green believed that, especially with the rise of Christian thought, humanity was moving beyond the arbitrary classifications of human beings and recognizing the true unity of humanity. According to Green, signs of this continuing movement towards a truly universal understanding of human community were present in different philosophical schools of thought. While the hedonistic line of thought formulated the universal principle as '"everyone should count for one and no one for more than one," Kantian ethics expressed the same sentiment through the categorical imperative of "act so as to treat humanity, whether in your own person or in that of others, always as an end, never merely as a means"'.[17] Green argued that the hedonistic interpretation of the universal principle was neither theoretically nor practically capable of offering a sustainable guideline for ethical action. On the contrary, the hedonistic principle was open to exploitation by a superior race or class, so far as the equality prescribed by the hedonists was not an equality of persons but an equality of pleasures.[18] Green argued that so far as there was a surplus of pleasure in 'hedonistic calculus', it was not concerned

---

15 Green, *Prolegomena*, pp. 300, 305.
16 Green, *Prolegomena*, pp. 315–16.
17 Green, *Prolegomena*, p. 247.
18 Green, *Prolegomena*, p. 248.

with which individual or group of individuals were barred from participating in its enjoyment. Thus, Green designated the Kantian imperative as a superior expression of the universal ideal. He restated it as follows:

> That every human person has an absolute value; the humanity in the person of every one is always to be treated as an end, never merely as a means; that in the estimate of that well-being which forms the true good everyone is to count for one and no one for more than one; that everyone has a 'suum' which everyone else is bound to render him.[19]

Green maintained that inclusion within a community was a pre-condition for individuals' ability to pursue an ethical life. While at the individual level the ideal of self-realization offered a tentative guide to the ways of maintaining an ethical life, individuals' inclusion within a society required a further consideration in regard to the nature of their interaction with other human beings. To deal with this secondary layer of ethical concerns Green incorporated Kantian deontology into his assessment of moral action. In doing so he designated the conditions for maintaining a society that in effect enabled individuals' pursuance of self-realization as the primary criteria. In that sense, the eudemonic concept of self-realization that guided individuals in their pursuance of an ethical life was incorporated in the categorical approach to ethics that aimed to regulate individuals' interactions with each other within an ethical social whole. This additional criterion for ethical action required individuals to pursue their own self-realization while being mindful of the existence of a common good in which they were to participate both as contributors and as benefactors. Green perceived a categorical duty for every individual not only to strive for their own self-realization but also to strive for creating and maintaining the necessary conditions for the realization of a common good.

Yet again, the good that was common to all individuals within a designated society was explained with reference to the ideal of self-

---

19　Green, *Prolegomena*, p. 253.

realization. According to Green, the ideal of a common good, just like the ideal of self-realization, was a precondition for the possibility of a moral life, as human beings were social in nature and their self-realization was possible only in cooperation with their fellow human beings. As man was a finite creature who was aware of his own mortality, his innate capacity to realize himself required him to search for ways that could carry him beyond his spatial and temporal limitations. Green argued, in his attempt to go beyond his own death, man 'associates his kindred with himself' and through this association he 'neutralises the effect which the anticipation of death must otherwise have on the demand for permanent good'.[20] Green believed that humans' sociability was one of the earliest and most intrinsic aspects of his nature as far as 'in the earliest stages of human consciousness in which the idea of a true permanent good could lead any one to call in question the good of an immediately attractive pleasure, it was already an idea of a social good—of a good not private to the man himself, but good for him as a member of a community'.[21] According to Dimova-Cookson, this line of thinking which she calls 'the salvation argument' comprises the basis of Green's belief in the social nature of man.[22] This idea that individuals' enjoyment of their personal good understood as the realization of their innate capacities was dependent on their inclusion in a social whole creates the basis on which Green establishes an interdependence between the ideal of self-realization and the ideal of the common good.[23]

---

[20] Green, *Prolegomena*, p. 271.
[21] Green, *Prolegomena*, p. 271.
[22] M. Dimova-Cookson (2001) *T.H. Green's Moral and Political Philosophy: A Phenomenological Perspective*, Basingstoke: Palgrave Macmillan, p. 87.
[23] For alternative readings of Green's 'social man' see: C. Tyler (2017) 'Contesting the Common Good: T.H. Green and Contemporary Republicanism', in *Common Good Politics: British Idealism and Social Justice in the Contemporary World*, Switzerland: Palgrave Macmillan, pp. 61–101; D.O. Brink (2003) *Perfectionism and the Common Good: Themes in the Philosophy of T.H. Green*, Oxford : Oxford University Press.

While the basis of the idea of common good is easy to find in Green's writings, the exact content of the term proves to be more elusive. Green himself recognized the impossibility of designating a 'constant' common good or unalterable law that must be complied with. Instead, he defined the common good as an ideal which does not exist yet but is in the process of realization.[24] So far as it was impossible to know what the ideal was until its full realization, the duties of its pursuance also remained more or less undefined.[25] Still, Green expected that the desires that came from the animal part of human nature would be in conflict with the pursuit of an ethical life. So, he argued that it was a categorical imperative for every individual to ignore these animal impulses and strive for their self-realization and the common good of the society. Yet Green's designation of self-realization and common good as universal moral ends did not specify any clear guidelines for ethical action. He wrote that individuals were to observe all established traditional duties until such a time that these duties proved to be insufficient or contradictory.[26] While acknowledging the impossibility of coming up with ethical instructions based on his ethical theory, he wrote that although the categorical imperative appeared to 'have no particular content' or that it appeared to have too much, the duties that should be met by individuals in specific circumstances were clear enough.[27]

In a more precise manner, Green gave examples of the common good, which was built and enjoyed by the seemingly mundane actions of individuals within a community. He wrote that the common good was continually created by 'the craftsman or writer, set upon making his work as good as he can without reference to his own glorification; by the father devoted to the education of his

---

[24] Green, *Prolegomena*, p. 226.
[25] W.J. Mander (2014) 'British Idealism and Education for Citizenship', in T. Brooks (ed.) *Ethical Citizenship*, London: Palgrave Macmillan, p. 151.
[26] Green, *Prolegomena*, p. 227.
[27] Green, *Prolegomena*, p. 227.

family, or the citizen devoted to the service of his state'.[28] The daily pursuits of these individuals were means to their personal end of self-realization as well as contributions to the overall good of the society. While these individuals pursued their own ends by their endeavours, they were also conscious of their contributions to a common good from which other individuals also benefited. Yet their contribution to others' lives was not understood by Green as an act of benevolence. By rejecting a simplistic dichotomy between actions born out of self-love and actions born out of a concern for others' well-being, Green recognized an interdependence between the goods of all human beings who acknowledge each other as partakers in the pursuance of an ethical life. At a very basic level individuals were aware that the possibility of their personal good was dependent on their ability to be partakers of a common good with others, which implied that their concern for others' good was, to a certain extent, 'derivative' from their concern for their own good. But the categorical imperative of treating every individual as an end precluded the possibility of an instrumental approach to the ideal of the common good.[29] Instead, Green argued, individuals were to recognize that the common good was the outcome of the collective endeavours of individuals within a society and each individual within it was both a contributor and a benefactor.

Green's seminal work on political theory, *Lectures on the Principles of Political Obligation*, located the concept of rights at the heart of his discussion of the basis of an ethical political community. Green described rights as guarantees that ensured the 'individual [has] certain powers secured to him by society'.[30] These rights, Green argued, were not innate in the sense that individuals were born with them or contractual in the sense that each and every individual consciously entered into a contract with each other to respect these

---

28 Green, *Prolegomena*, pp. 335–36.
29 Green, *Prolegomena*, p. 253.
30 Green, *Lectures*, p. 41.

powers. On the contrary, these rights were recognized and observed due to the moral nature of man; because man needed these rights to realize his human potential. Green argued that the justification for the recognition of these powers lay in the 'fact that these powers are necessary to the fulfilment of man's vocation as a moral being, to an effectual self-devotion to the work of developing the perfect character in himself and others'.[31] Green maintained that actual recognized rights within every society were ethical as well as historical and traditional. The imperatives to be followed by each and every individual within ethical communities had been established and developed throughout history, giving rise to the laws and norms that regulated individuals' relations with each other. From such a perspective Green noted that the most basic rights in every ethical society were derived from the same moral source while 'the form in which these claims are admitted and acted on by men in their dealings with each other varies with the form of society'.[32]

In his *Lectures,* Green examined the moral sources of those rights that he expected to be present in every well-ordered society despite the variations in their codification/observance. According to Green, those rights that 'naturally' arose in every society in which individuals recognized each other as equal participants in the pursuance of a common good were the right to free life, property, and family. While Green perceived these rights to be the bare minimum for an individual to pursue his self-realization without undue restraint, this list was by no means exhaustive of the powers that may be necessary for individuals' self-realization under all conditions. Rather, these rights were recognized as powers without which it would have been impossible to talk about the existence of an ethical community. The right to free life—a combination of the right to life and the right to liberty—was understood by Green as the foundation for the 'capacity on the part of the subject for membership of a society, for

31   Green, *Lectures*, p. 41.
32   Green, *Lectures*, p. 154.

determination of the will, and through it of the bodily organisation, by the conception of a well-being as common to self with others'.[33] Green perceived only two potentially legitimate conditions for the violation of the right to free life in a well-organized community. The first condition applied to times of war in which the community might legitimately demand an individual to give up his right to life for the protection of the social whole.[34] The second condition applied to the case of legal punishment within a well-organized community. In this case, Green argued, the individual punished was understood to be in violation of the moral end so far as he caused harm to his fellow men, and thus lost the right to free action 'for the moral good of the community'.[35] Green also noted that morally legitimate punishment took for its end not vindictiveness but the 'moral new birth' of the individual punished so that he can pursue an ethical life thereafter.[36]

The second basic right Green expected to be present in well-organized societies, i.e. the right to property, was also substantiated with reference to the moral end individuals sought. Green argued that a right to property was to be judged legitimate so far as the property acquired served as 'realised will', a 'sort of extension of the man's organs, the constant apparatus through which he gives reality to his ideas and wishes'.[37] In other words, Green recognized the appropriation of material things that enabled men to pursue his own self-realization as a right. But the right to property was not an unconditional power according to Green. He maintained that the right to property did not condone a system in which 'one set of men are secured in the power of getting and keeping the means of realising their will, in such a way that others are practically denied

---

[33]   Green, *Lectures*, pp. 155–56.
[34]   Green, *Lectures*, pp. 160–70.
[35]   Green, *Lectures*, p. 204.
[36]   Green, *Lectures*, p. 205.
[37]   Green, *Lectures*, pp. 217, 214.

the power'.[38] Thus, Green argued, in a society where property was disproportionally owned by an individual or a group of individuals, it was equal to theft. For the legitimate use of the right to property, society was to be organized in such a way that every individual had a reasonable chance to acquire the necessary materials for his self-realization. Lastly, Green viewed family rights as indispensable powers for men and women to pursue a moral life. If the underlying patriarchal tone of Green's argument is disregarded, in consideration of the prevailing social structure in which his ideas were formed, it can be seen that his main concern was with establishing for both men and women the power to pursue their self-realization within a family setting. He argued that family rights were especially vital for ensuring that children had access to powers that were indispensable for their physical and moral development.

Green recognized these three rights to be universal in character and maintained that in every ethically organized society recognition of these rights preceded the establishment of a proper state. Due to the universal nature of men as social, reasonable, and moral beings, all human societies, even the most primitive, had an understanding of the vitality of these rights for the pursuit of the ideal of the common good. Furthermore, Green argued, so far as each individual had a natural affinity with the 'common language of right' within their own society, it was possible to extend the sphere of these rights beyond the nations and to the whole of humanity.[39] He believed that Christian nations were further ahead in recognizing and maintaining satisfactory systems of rights within their own borders as well as securing friendly relations with their counterparts.[40] With time, ethical relations based on an understanding of rights and duties that existed within nations or among the members of Christian peoples were expected to apply to all relations among man. Such movement

---

[38]   Green, *Lectures*, p. 220.
[39]   Green, *Prolegomena*, p. 252.
[40]   Green, *Prolegomena*, p. 243.

was evident in the 'conscience of those citizens of the modern world who are most responsive to the higher influences of their time', and it was to be accelerated through increased means of communication and cooperation among members of different states.[41] Green maintained that the spread of the ideal of human fraternity was the basis on which individuals from different nations would acquire the capacity to realize the rights and duties they owed to each other simply because they were human and regardless of their 'race or religion or states'.[42]

As has been noted before, Green did not have much to say on the possibility of founding international institutions. While he recognized that establishing an international authority with the capacity to oversee the rightful conduct of states with their citizens and with other states was a distant dream, he did not see this as an insurmountable obstacle to the observance of rights among individuals from different nations. On the contrary, he maintained that the very familiarity of the 'claims of a common humanity' was proof that the idea was already affecting 'laws and institutions'.[43] Green thought that the main driving force behind the newly appreciated ideal of the unity of mankind was the increased opportunities of intercourse among individuals from different nations. Furtherance of this mind-set was possible only through strengthening 'the habit' of observing rights and duties among individuals from different nationalities through increased intercourse.[44] His focus on the relations among individuals rather than states carried strong undertones of a cosmopolitanism, which was more moral than political in its wording. Although it is sometimes assumed that Green's cosmopolitanism left the possibility of a world state open from a British Idealist perspective, Green himself clearly believed that 'the love of mankind, no doubt, needs to be particularised in order to have any

---

[41] Green, *Prolegomena*, p. 239; Green, *Lectures*, p. 178.
[42] Green, *Prolegomena*, p. 239.
[43] Green, *Lectures*, p. 249.
[44] Green, *Lectures*, p. 241.

power over life and action'.[45] Additionally, states were defined as the
efficient means of organizing the rights and duties of individuals in
Green's political theory. Green made his position on this matter quite
clear when he wrote that 'the man whose desire to serve his kind is
not centred primarily in some home, radiating from it to a commune,
a municipality, and a nation, presumably has no effectual desire to
serve his kind at all'.[46]

Green's moral cosmopolitanism did not necessarily get translated
into his political theory. He did not foresee elimination of state
borders or eradication of national identities by the realization of a
universal human community. Instead, Green argued for a better
organization of states themselves so that their citizens would freely
cooperate with each other. His approach to international relations
was echoed by Bosanquet, and after the Great War by a younger
generation of British Idealists. British Idealists' reflections on the
issue of international relations in the post Great War era amounted
to a more detailed — and clearer — restatement of Green's following
argument:

> though a nation, with national feeling of its own, must everywhere
> underlie a state, properly so called, yet still, just so far as the perfect
> organisation of rights within each nation, which entitles it to be called
> a state, is attained, the occasions of conflict between nations dis-
> appear; and again,... by the same process, just so far as it is satis-
> factorily carried out, an organ of expression and action is established
> for each nation in dealing with other nations, which is not really
> liable to be influenced by the same egoistic passions in dealing with
> the government of another nation as embroil individuals with each
> other.[47]

---

[45] Hann, *Egalitarian Rights Recognition*, p. 149.
[46] Green, *Lectures*, p. 175.
[47] Green, *Lectures*, p. 175.

II. British Idealism, Internationalism, and
Human Rights in the Post Great War Period

British Idealists' approach to human rights in the post-1914 era was quite uniform in its basic premises and in its pursuance of the basic tenets of Green's rights theory. They all considered rights as teleological instead of deontological concepts in their nature. They thought these rights were applicable only within well-defined social orders whose members formed a general will. Lastly, they all avoided putting forward definite lists of rights that would be universally applicable; although the rights they perceived to be necessary within all well-ordered communities carried a universal quality. As their understanding of rights differed considerably from theories of 'natural rights', the British Idealist understanding of human rights turned out to be quite different as well. While their arguments on the matter supplied a theoretical basis in defence of the universal application of certain rights as human rights, their outlook was not strictly cosmopolitan. Instead, they combined the moral cosmopolitanism of Green with his emphasis on the social and historical aspects of communal rights and arrived at an 'internationalist' approach to human rights. Although the tone of their argument was not in accordance with the 'institutionalist' turn the British intelligentsia took after the Great War, the internationalist position they defended was in keeping with the overall sentiment that prevailed in Britain at the time.

As is discussed above in detail, a central attribute of Green's rights theory in distinction from theories of natural rights was the emphasis he put on the 'moral end' for which rights were essential.[48] Rights were perceived to be 'sacred' so far as they were understood as necessary powers for the pursuance of the moral end. Green wrote in his *Lectures*:

> The claim or right of the individual to have certain powers secured to him by society, and the counter-claim of society to exercise certain

---

[48] Green, *Lectures*, p. 40.

powers over the individual, alike rest on the fact that these powers
are necessary to the fulfilment of man's vocation as a moral being, to
an effectual self-devotion to the work of developing the perfect
character in himself and others.[49]

In his *Rule and End in Morals*, published in 1932, Muirhead argued
that Green's theory of rights was set apart from other right theories
because he perceived rights as teleological rather than deontological
and this established an essential link between individuals' rights and
the universal moral end. According to Muirhead, the appeal to
'natural rights' was marked by vagueness in regard to the moral
basis of rights and led the discussion to more technical matters such
as the correlativity of rights and duties. Muirhead argued the matter
of rights should be discussed instead with reference to the ends they
served; i.e. 'self-development of individuals'.[50] In his discussion of
rights, Mackenzie too emphasized the relation between rights and
the moral and progressive nature of human beings. As the moral end
was the self-realization of individuals, the rights an individual had
were to be instrumentalized for this purpose, although it was
impossible for the community or the state to assess in which
direction an individual was to develop himself or in which exact
way he/she would use their rights.[51] Jones expressed the same conviction in 1920 when he wrote: 'Neither State, nor individual, nor
"humanity" (whose good is taken to be higher as well as wider, and
whose rights are held to be supreme) has any authority or right "*in
itself*" so long as its "self" is regarded as something merely separate
from other selves and its individuality as exclusive.'[52] Rights of individuals as well as rights of states could only be perceived as sacred
or inalienable insofar as they were thought in relation with the moral
end they served. In other words, rights were to be 'thought as

---

[49]   Green, *Lectures*, p. 41.
[50]   J.H. Muirhead (1932) *Rule and End in Morals*, London: Oxford University
       Press, p. 104.
[51]   Mackenzie, *Outlines of Social Philosophy*, p. 168.
[52]   Jones, *Principles of Citizenship*, p. 69.

something instrumental to my purposes' and not as 'anything primary'.[53] They were simply powers 'by reason of their relation to the end of the whole as manifested in me,… imperative alike for me and for others'.[54]

Rights in and of themselves were not to be considered 'primary' or 'sacred', as nothing in separation from the whole had a claim to such attributes according to British Idealists. But this did not mean that rights were not vital for the well-being of the individual, of the community, and of humanity. On the contrary, rights were of crucial importance when they were organized 'in accordance with universal reason' and when they were one 'with the nature of things'.[55] While natural rights theories deemed rights sacred and inalienable with reference to what man was, British Idealists attributed importance to rights in regards to what man had in him to become. From this perspective, rights were perceived to be 'natural' only because man was moral and progressive in his nature. As the moral and progressive nature of man was universal, a satisfactory system of rights and duties was an indispensable attribute of every human community.

A second and equally important attribute of rights on which all British Idealists agreed was their communal nature. The Rights of Man in its singularity was a fiction because moral action was only possible when two or more people came together. On the impossibility of man having rights in a non-social setting, Green wrote:

> 'Natural right,' as = right in a state of nature, which is not a state of society, is a contradiction. There can be no right without a consciousness of common interest on the part of members of a society. Without this there might be certain powers on the part of individuals, but no recognition of these powers by others as powers of which they allow the exercise, nor any claim to such recognition; and without this recognition or claim to recognition there can be no right.[56]

---

53 Bosanquet (1920) *Philosophical Theory of the State*, p. 192.
54 Bosanquet (1920) *Philosophical Theory of the State*, p. 192.
55 Jones, *Principles of Citizenship*, p. 140.
56 Green, *Lectures*, p. 48.

The communal nature of rights was evident from its role in the life of man. Muirhead and Hetherington explained this role by arguing: 'Within every institution there is a system of rights and duties; that is, each institution defines a certain set of relations between its members, and, imposing on them the obligations consonant with these obligations, it also confers on them the corresponding rights.'[57] From this perspective a system of rights and duties was understood to be the regulative principle in a community in which each and every individual had the necessary powers to pursue the moral end. The communal character of rights was also central to the distinction British Idealists made between right claims and right recognition. While individuals continually put forward new right claims, only a general recognition of these claims' legitimacy turned them into proper rights. Jones explained this point by arguing that without social recognition there would not be any rights: 'my rights *are* mine because they are accorded to me by the society of which I am a member. Yours are yours not in virtue of your assertion of them, but because the social system to which you belong grants and sustains them.'[58] Thus the Idealists understood a system of rights as a traditional social pact, which constituted the basis on which each and every 'free society' maintained its life. This system was also understood to be in constant development in relation with the changing needs of its members.

Due to this perception of an organic relationship between a community and the system of rights and duties it developed, British Idealists did not propose an unalterable list of universal human rights. Instead, their reflections on human rights in the post Great War period focused on revealing the necessary political organization that should be maintained by states so that each individual had the necessary powers to reach his/her full potential. Instead of adopting a top-down approach to rights by requiring every state to recognize

---

[57] Hetherington and Muirhead, *Social Purpose*, p. 129.
[58] Jones, 'Obligations and Privileges of Citizenship', p. 171.

certain basic rights, Idealists argued for the establishment of a just political system so that communities can develop their organic adaptations of universal rights. As rights and duties were claimed and recognized with reference to a universal moral end, certain basic rights were expected to be recognized by every state with a just form of government. The process of right claims and recognition was to be an organic one in which states recognized and legalized the right claims of their citizens when those claims were in compliance with the necessities of a moral life. As the rights and obligations recognized in a community were closely related with the ends that were pursued by its members, these systems were believed to be reflective of the community from which they emerged. Muirhead and Hetherington argued, for instance: 'a right differs from a mere demand, or a threat, just in that it belongs to a different world. It rests, not on force, but on a view of the nature and ends of a given Society.'[59] As no external power would know better the necessities of individuals within particular communities than its members, the recognition, reform, and enforcement of a system of rights and duties were considered to be the responsibility of each community and their government.

British Idealists' insistence on the communities' responsibility to shape their own system of rights and duties was related to their preference for the principle of non-intervention in the international arena in the post Great War era. Thus Muirhead and Hetherington argued that when a general sense of injustice ensued within a particular community, it was 'always better that wrong-doing by any community should be overcome by the outraged sense of justice of that community itself'.[60] Similarly, Mackenzie maintained that each government 'acting on behalf of its people' was to be left free in its pursuit of the moral good through its own means as the moral good could only be achieved by voluntary effort. He maintained that

---

[59] Hetherington and Muirhead, *Social Purpose*, pp. 129–30.
[60] Hetherington and Muirhead, *Social Purpose*, p. 282.

foreign interference was only acceptable when the government of a people was 'so flagrantly unjust that it could not properly be regarded as a state at all'.[61]

Evidently British Idealists in this period expected that when a just government ruled a community, the rights and duties maintained would form a 'tolerable' system. This contention was based on their perception of rights and duties as organic growths of a community's general will which was always in motion, preferably towards better organization of the community. In this scheme, the state was expected to be responsive to the changing demands of the community. Mackenzie and Muirhead defined such a state as a republic in the Kantian sense. While Mackenzie noted that in each community a republic 'must be constituted as to enable a genuine national will to become effective', Muirhead argued that each community was to be ruled by 'a state in which the idea of the common good permeated all public action'.[62] When a state was not a Kantian republic or a true state, British Idealists thought that resistance became a duty for its citizens. This was again based on Green's argument that 'when the authority from which the objectionable command proceeds is so easily separable from that on which the maintenance of social order and the fabric of settled rights depends', such a sovereign can be resisted without disturbing the ethical order of the society.[63] Following Green, Jones argued that when the rule of a state was not based on the general will of a people but on mere force, it was considered to be failing in its duty of ensuring the conditions under which its citizens can strive towards their individual and communal good.[64] Similarly, Mackenzie argued that when the legal rights that are recognized by the state did not 'coincide with the moral rights, it is incumbent on people to use any

---

[61]　Mackenzie, *Outlines of Social Philosophy*, p. 194.

[62]　Mackenzie, *Fundamental Problems of Life*, pp. 288–89; Muirhead, *German Philosophy in Relation to the War*, p. 16.

[63]　Green, *Lectures*, p. 111.

[64]　Jones, *Principles of Citizenship*, p. 141.

legitimate means that may be at their disposal to bring about reform'.[65] The legitimacy of 'active resistance' was to be decided through a comparison of the evils suffered under the existent system of rights and duties and the probable 'evils of anarchy, civil war, or general insecurity'.[66] Although it was a very high bar met very rarely, the use of resistance against a *de facto* state was not overruled as a means of ensuring the recognition of moral rights by a state. It was only when a state formed such a tyranny that it became impossible for its citizens to resist its dictates, that foreign intervention was seen to be legitimate by the British Idealists in the post Great War era.

III. Mackenzie's Preliminary List of Human Rights

Although British Idealists rejected the idea that a universal list of human rights can be forcefully imposed upon every society, they did not think that rights were dispensable. On the contrary, rights were given a central position in their political theory as powers that enabled individuals to realize their moral ends within a political community. Although the form and content of rights were expected to vary from community to community, their reference was to a universal ideal. While British Idealists did not believe in a single unalterable set of human rights, they also did not condone moral relativism. So far as rights operated with reference to a universal truth, beneath their apparent divergences, they were to comply with a universal standard of morality. A certain minimum of rights that enabled individuals to live healthily and ethically in pursuance of their self-realization was to be ensured in every well organized society. Those rights were vital not only for the well-being of individuals but also for the healthy functioning of societies and the maintenance of peaceful and cooperative relations among states. In

---

[65] Mackenzie, *Outlines of Social Philosophy*, p. 167.
[66] Mackenzie, *Outlines of Social Philosophy*, p. 167.

the post Great War years, British Idealists occasionally dealt with questions in regard to the nature and scope of human rights. In addition to the political rights that were listed by Green as those rights that were to develop 'naturally' in every society, they also recognized the necessity of certain social and economic rights for individuals to pursue their self-realization. Among them, Mackenzie offered the most comprehensive account of human rights in *Fundamental Problems of Life* that was published in 1928. Other British Idealists were contented with emphasizing the necessity of certain rights such as the right to work or the right to a decent life.

Mackenzie included a section on human rights in his book *A Manual of Ethics* that was published in 1892. In this earlier work Mackenzie discussed the central importance of rights to life, freedom, property, contract, and education in morally organized societies. He argued these rights were 'necessary for the development of our lives in the direction that is best for the highest good of the community of which we are members'.[67] In accordance with Green's teachings, he justified these rights with reference to the moral end of self-realization, and argued that the teleological underpinnings of an idealistic theory of ethics bestowed upon rights an undeniable importance as a means for 'the unfolding of the capabilities of mankind'.[68] Mackenzie justified all the items in this earlier list of human rights with reference to the end of self-realization. He argued that the right to life was the most basic one simply because 'the human good requires the continuance of life for its realization'.[69] The right to freedom was vital for self-realization because only when an individual was 'free to exercise his will' could he act morally.[70] While unconditional freedom was an idea that was counter-intuitive for human beings, the 'desirable' right to freedom was a 'right of having the free development of one's life as little

---

67 Mackenzie, *Manual of Ethics*, p. 319.
68 Mackenzie, *Manual of Ethics*, p. 282.
69 Mackenzie, *Manual of Ethics*, p. 314.
70 Mackenzie, *Manual of Ethics*, p. 315.

interfered with as is possible, consistently with the maintenance of social order'.[71] The third right in his list, the right to property, was justified by its vital importance for individuals in pursuing their self-realization. Mackenzie argued that 'nearly all the ends at which a man can aim require instruments; and if a man has not the right to use these instruments, his liberty of pursuing the ends is practically rendered void'.[72] He suggested that in an ideal system the right to property would be supported by a practice of educating property owners in the ways to use their goods for the common good of the society.[73] Mackenzie maintained that education in itself too should be considered as a human right but also as a duty of every human individual since it was a precondition 'for the realization of the rational self'.[74] Although, Mackenzie argued, the right to education was the precondition for the exercise of all truly human endeavours, it 'has been but tardily recognized even in some highly-civilized countries'.[75] In this earlier list of human rights, the right to contract was the least developed in terms of its importance and justification. Mackenzie argued that the right to contract signified an improvement from a social order based on status to a society based on free engagement of individuals. Not surprisingly, the right to contract was dropped out of his list of human rights in its improved version in 1928.

Mackenzie's list of human rights was more comprehensive than the rights Green endorsed in his *Lectures*. The inclusion of a right to education in this list of human rights was especially significant due to its relevance to the moral end of self-realization. But Mackenzie's earlier list of human rights was primarily a list of ethical rights that did not deal with the political conditions necessary for their realization. In a footnote at the end of his list of human rights, Mackenzie

---

71   Mackenzie, *Manual of Ethics*, p. 316.
72   Mackenzie, *Manual of Ethics*, p. 316.
73   Mackenzie, *Manual of Ethics*, p. 318.
74   Mackenzie, *Manual of Ethics*, p. 319.
75   Mackenzie, *Manual of Ethics*, p. 319.

acknowledged the primarily ethical nature of his approach to human rights and wrote: 'of course I refer here to rights and obligations in the ethical sense. To what extent, and by what means, these rights and obligations are to be acknowledged and enforced in actual states, are questions for the political philosopher.'[76] Although he noted that 'there are certain definite, though at the same time somewhat elastic and modifiable, rights that come to be gradually recognized in human societies', the possibility of regulating these rights through an international organization of states was beyond his horizon in 1892.[77]

By 1928, not only Mackenzie's list of human rights but also British intellectuals' understanding of the international order significantly changed. The League of Nations as a project of international cooperation attracted considerable attention and support from British intellectuals following the outbreak of the Great War. In spite of British Idealists' inability/unwillingness to engage in highly technical discussions regarding the basis of international law and international organization, they were highly influenced by the internationalist turn in the British mind-set. Their emphasis on the ethical primacy of rights as a means for self-realization that they inherited from Green was incorporated into the internationalist enthusiasm that prevailed in the 1920s. One of the earliest examples of this change was prevalent in the work of Bernard Bosanquet. Bosanquet argued that for the realization of a peaceful and cooperative international order, the most urgent concern was to ensure that in each society 'man has a tolerable set of rights and duties' which naturally would create a community that was 'fair and unbiased towards the outside world'.[78] But due to his long held and well-known distrust towards international organizations, he argued that before states organized themselves in an ethical way by granting their citizens a

---

76   Mackenzie, *Manual of Ethics*, p. 319.
77   Mackenzie, *Manual of Ethics*, p. 333.
78   Bosanquet, 'Wisdom of Naaman's Servants', p. 307.

tolerable set of rights, establishing 'huge federations and alliances' would prove counter-productive.[79]

The younger generation of British Idealists did not necessarily share Bosanquet's distrust of international organizations. They were more optimistic in regard to the League of Nations' potential for creating an arena which would encourage states to maintain peaceful and cooperative relations with each other. Still, in line with Bosanquet, they attributed rights vital importance, as they were sure indicators of a state's disposition towards its own citizens and other states. In his revised version of human rights in *Fundamental Problems of Life*, Mackenzie argued that there was an intrinsic link between the way a state organized the system of rights and duties its citizens were entitled to and its disposition towards other nations.[80] Based on this conviction, Mackenzie argued that to become genuine members of the newly established international community of the League of Nations each state should recognize a tolerable set of rights in a truly 'republican' manner.[81] Clearly, by 1928 Mackenzie was not only interested in the ethical justifications of human rights but in their political and international applications as well. He started his account of human rights in his 1928 book by noting that:

> These rights and obligations are, of course, very largely affected by the special organization of the State within which the citizen happens to live; but it would be a mistake to regard them as being created or entirely determined by that organization. There is a sense in which rights and obligations may properly be described as 'natural' and independent of any kind of political sanction.[82]

What Mackenzie deemed to be 'natural' about these rights was their ethical basis and their assumed recognition in every well-ordered, 'republican' political community. In that sense, Mackenzie's list of human rights did not refer to an ideal set of rights but to 'some of the

---

[79] Bosanquet, 'Wisdom of Naaman's Servants', p. 308.
[80] Mackenzie, *Fundamental Problems of Life*, p. 319.
[81] Mackenzie, *Fundamental Problems of Life*, pp. 315–16.
[82] Mackenzie, *Fundamental Problems of Life*, pp. 304–05.

chief rights that have been commonly claimed for' individuals in well-ordered communities.[83] In that respect it was not definitive but open to improvement and alteration in accordance with the changing needs and claims of individuals, as the circumstances in which they tried to realize their full human potential changed. Arguably, by 1928, Mackenzie realized that basic liberal rights to life, liberty, and property along with the right to education were no longer sufficient for individuals who lived in complex social and political structures to realize their full potential. Accordingly his second list of human rights, with an emphasis on the importance of social and economic rights, was more comprehensive than the list he provided back in 1897. Mackenzie's improved list of human rights included the rights to protection, franchise, employment, maintenance, and leisure along with the rights to liberty, property, and education.[84]

The first item in Mackenzie's list of human rights in *The Fundamental Problems of Life* was the right to freedom. His preference of a right to liberty instead of a right to life as the first item in his list of human rights can be seen as in line with Green's combination of the rights to life and liberty. As mere life did not constitute a sufficient ground for the individual to act in accordance with his own will, it was not considered to be a right in distinction from a right to free life. And again, in line with Green, the right to freedom was not a right to unlimited freedom. On the contrary, it was dependent on individuals' capacity to use that freedom for the realization of rational and moral ends. In that sense, the right to freedom implied 'the restraint of duty'.[85] This was a right closely connected to individuals' capacity to follow the inner dictates of universal morality and fulfil these moral duties of their own free will. Thus, although it was universal, it was not an 'inborn' right. It was, rather, conditional

---

[83] Mackenzie, *Fundamental Problems of Life*, p. 312.

[84] Mackenzie, *Fundamental Problems of Life*, pp. 312–19.

[85] H. Jones (1883) 'The Social Organism', in Haldane and Seth (eds.) *Essays in Philosophical Criticism*, New York: Burt Franklin, p. 204.

on the fulfilment of certain duties. The most obvious of these duties was that individuals' actions 'must be consistent with the equal freedom of others'.[86] Still another and more fundamental duty required individuals to develop a potential to use this right for the moral end. Mackenzie argued: 'the right to freedom can hardly be one that is inborn. It is rather one that is gradually acquired.'[87] To be a proper subject of the right to freedom, one had to cultivate himself to be 'wise and good' and to be 'accustomed to govern himself by a law within, if he is not to be controlled by the law without'.[88]

The second right on the list, the right to property, was viewed as fundamental by Mackenzie so far as property was used 'creatively' and not simply 'enjoyed'.[89] In other words, the right to property was not related to possession of a thing but to its use in pursuit of the moral end of self-realization. In accordance with the justificatory moral criteria for all rights, the right to property also included its corresponding 'obligation to use what is possessed for the common good'.[90] Again, Mackenzie's approach to the matter was in line with the principle of a just order of ownership within a community that was advocated by both Green and Bosanquet in their earlier works. In his *Lectures,* Green argued that when a man was tempted to steal due to his inability to acquire the basic necessities for his livelihood through honest means, it was the duty of the state to abolish the conditions that gave rise to such temptations and not try to deter people with merely the use of excessive punishment.[91] Similarly, Bosanquet argued when 'starvation is common, some readjustment of rights, or at least some temporary protection of the right to live, is the remedy indicated, and not, or not solely, increased severity in

---

[86] Mackenzie, *Fundamental Problems of Life*, p. 313.
[87] Mackenzie, *Fundamental Problems of Life*, p. 313.
[88] Mackenzie, *Fundamental Problems of Life*, p. 313.
[89] Mackenzie, *Fundamental Problems of Life*, p. 259.
[90] Mackenzie, *Fundamental Problems of Life*, p. 313.
[91] Green, *Lectures*, pp. 193–94.

dealing with theft'.[92] A similar concern for an egalitarian distribution of property was present in Mackenzie's approach to the right to property. Thus, he argued: 'The general principle appears to be that property should, as far as possible, be in the control of those who can and will use it to the best advantage.'[93]

The right to protection was understood to be a safeguard for both individuals' and their possessions' security in a well-ordered society. While Green treated the matter of protection as an inherent part of the rights to life and property, Mackenzie acknowledged it as a right on its own. He argued protection was to be recognized as a right so far as 'the citizen is entitled to expect from it [the state] that he should be adequately protected both in his person and in his property'.[94] The duty implied by the right to protection was not only a negative duty of not harming others but the positive consideration for the maintenance of others' rights by complying with the laws of the state. This included individuals' positive duty to refer any conflict with their fellow men to the courts of the state and to recognize legal punishment as the only legitimate form of coercion in the society. While the conflicts among citizens under a single state were to be resolved through judiciary mechanisms, international conflict in which citizens required to sacrifice their lives proved to be a much more complicated challenge to the right to protection. Like Green, Mackenzie argued that while it was impossible to talk about a morally justified war in which both parties were pursuing a universal good, citizens' right to protection of their lives and possessions could be legitimately suspended for the protection of the social and political order in which they acquired the conditions for a moral life. Thus Mackenzie argued that the maintenance of the right to protection without exception was possible only when the occasions for war became extinct and international problems were

---

92 Bosanquet (1920) *Philosophical Theory of the State*, p. 215.
93 Mackenzie, *Fundamental Problems of Life*, p. 313.
94 Mackenzie, *Fundamental Problems of Life*, p. 314.

settled 'amicably'.[95] He also noted that with the development of an 'international mind' warfare 'would gradually, or perhaps even speedily, come to be regarded as most people in this country regard duelling…'[96]

The right to education was considered by Mackenzie to be essential for individuals' ability to use their other rights in pursuit of supreme values. The importance attributed to this right by Mackenzie as well as by other British Idealists was indicative of their understanding of human rationality and morality as a potential that has to be developed through formal and informal education. After all, the capacity to follow moral laws by ones' own free will without external intervention was dependent on individuals' understanding of the nature and requirements of morality. From this perspective Haldane argued, for example, 'mental freedom actually comes only through freedom from ignorance'.[97] Similarly, Jones wrote that the true purpose of education was to develop the faculties of men so that they can 'apprehend wider and wiser purposes, which is the way to freedom'.[98] Individuals' right to education implied a corresponding duty to form an educational system that served all the components of society. This duty belonged to the state, as it required an extensive reach to various parts of the society as well as a certain level of uni-formity of purpose and considerable resources. Mackenzie argued, from a 'humanistic' point of view, 'the state makes education both its foundation and its crowning achievement' because it 'looks at man as a being developing towards an end, and naturally looks to educa-tion as the means by which this development is to be effected'.[99] While British Idealists, especially after they saw the Prussian example, recognized the possibility that a state could use its educa-tional system to indoctrinate a whole nation in pursuance of false

---

95 Mackenzie, *Fundamental Problems of Life*, p. 314.
96 Mackenzie, *Fundamental Problems of Life*, p. 339.
97 Haldane, *Future of Democracy*, p. 10.
98 Jones, *Principles of Citizenship*, p. 133.
99 Mackenzie, *Lectures on Humanism*, p. 131.

ideals and egoistic ends, they did not take this to be a reason for absolving the state from the duty of serving the development of its citizens.

The right to education was also closely related to the matter of children's rights. According to Jones, children could not be properly considered to be subjects of rights as they lacked the rational and moral capacity to use these rights for universal ends. They were to be considered as 'potentially moral beings' and their rights were in essence 'prospective rights'.[100] From this perspective, a child's right to freedom was limited and conditioned by its parents or caretakers until such time that he acquired the rational and moral capacity to use these rights for his own good and the good of the society. In the meantime, it was the state's and his caretaker's duty to supply the child with education and care. Furthermore, the right to education was not limited to the education of children. Although the state was not judged to have an obligation to ensure adult education, it was important to make sure that willing adults had access to educational facilities. Hetherington and Muirhead argued that important steps were taken in this area through 'University Extension and other classes, and far more strikingly by the spontaneous growth of educational movements among adult-workers—cooperative educational societies, adult schools, working-men's clubs, the Workers' Educational Association, and the like'.[101] While education for children was perceived to be a universal human right by British Idealists, adult education, both vocational and non-vocational, was defined as a moral good that needed to be developed.

Franchise also appeared as a human right in Mackenzie's list of 1928. As it has been discussed previously, the pre-Great War writings of British Idealists were marked by distrust towards a democratic form of government in 'uncivilized' societies. Mackenzie himself defended the necessity of combining democracy with a

---

[100] Jones, *Principles of Citizenship*, pp. 143–44.
[101] Hetherington and Muirhead, *Social Purpose*, p. 217.

certain level of aristocracy for a long time, as he believed that important matters were not to be trusted 'to the care of the man in the street'.[102] Thus he argued, even after the Great War, that uncivilized societies especially were to be 'guided from above by the best and fittest who can by any means be discovered and brought forward'.[103] Mackenzie's concern was that an unenlightened population, unaware of the supreme values that give meaning to human life, would be likely to corrupt a democratic government in favour of egoistic interests. Thus, a right to franchise was to be a right conditional on a people's level of moral development. But this position was in stark contrast with Green's approach to the matter of universal franchise. Green was known as an ardent supporter of the 1867 Reform Act through which franchise was extended to all men living in boroughs irrespective of ownership of property.[104] In a speech he delivered on this matter, Green argued:

> We, who were reformers from the beginning, always said that the enfranchisement of the people was an end in itself. We said, and we were much derided for saying so, that citizenship only makes the moral man; that citizenship only gave that self-respect, which is the true basis of respect of others, and without which there is no lasting social order or real morality. If we were asked what result we looked for from the enfranchisement of the people, we said, that is not the present question. Untie the man's legs, and then it will be time to speculate how he will walk.[105]

It took Green's students a considerably long time to acknowledge that the right to franchise, just like the rights to freedom and property, should be acknowledged as a necessary power for individuals' self-development before its possible consequences could be questioned. For Mackenzie, this realization occurred as late as 1920

---

[102] J.S. Mackenzie (1906) 'The Dangers of Democracy', *International Journal of Ethics*, 16 (2), p. 140.

[103] Mackenzie, *Outlines of Social Philosophy*, p. 185.

[104] Tyler, *Idealist Political Philosophy*, p. 78.

[105] Green, *Works: V. 5 Additional Writings*, p. 234.

when he, for the first time, allocated unconditional support to the ideal of democracy:

> Although it is possible to take different views about political development, and although the future of political institutions is a question on which it would be rash to dogmatize, yet it seems pretty clear that a vigorous development of national life is not possible without free citizens. In this sense most people, especially after the Great War, would admit that democracy must be aimed at, however much they may disagree about the best form of democratic organization.[106]

By the time Mackenzie offered his revised version of human rights in 1928, he had left behind the distinction between civilized and uncivilized nations in regard to their eligibility for a democratic form of government. While recognizing the potential failings of a majoritarian system of democracy, he noted 'the election of representatives is recognized as the only practical method of enabling the underlying purpose to make itself effective'.[107] He argued 'every mature man and woman should at least have the right to vote for a representative'.[108] According to Mackenzie, the only condition that accompanied the right to franchise was the individual's duty 'to inform oneself about questions of national importance and to reflect as carefully as possible about them'.[109]

Further down Mackenzie's list were the social and economic rights to employment, maintenance, and leisure. From the British Idealist perspective, work, be it manual or intellectual, was not only a way to earn money but one of the main activities through which individuals realized themselves and contributed to the world they lived in. Thus, a right to work was not only essential for individuals to accommodate themselves but also and perhaps more importantly to realize their full potential in a meaningful and productive manner. The fruits of man's labour were understood to be valuable not only

---

106 Mackenzie, *Arrows of Desire*, p. 209.
107 Mackenzie, *Fundamental Problems of Life*, p. 315.
108 Mackenzie, *Fundamental Problems of Life*, p. 315.
109 Mackenzie, *Fundamental Problems of Life*, p. 316.

for their use but also as an expression of their will and their contribution to humanity. Jones explained the central importance of work to individual self-realization back in 1909 as follows:

> I cannot doubt that labour is meant to dignify the labourer. He should arise from his daily work a better man. The energies which he sets free upon his handicraft are capable, as every honest workman knows, of coming back to him enriched; bringing with them more skill, the consciousness of a duty well done, and the satisfaction which the artist knows as his best reward.[110]

Clearly, it was not any kind of work that was deemed to be a right from the perspective of British Idealists but work that enabled men and women to express their will in the material world. Thus, Muirhead and Hetherington defended the necessity of labourers' inclusion in the decision-making processes of their workplace.[111] Back in 1918, Mackenzie wrote: 'Labour... in its most perfect and most definitely creative forms, would seem to be the very end of human existence. But to realise this end it must have a certain power of choice and full scope for its exercise'.[112] Thoroughly mechanical labour devoid of creative effort was not considered proper labour by the Idealists. Like all other rights, the right to labour was also accompanied by corresponding duties. The state had the duty to ensure that market forces operated efficiently so that every able person had a chance to find a job. Similarly, individuals had the duty to make sure that they acquired the skills that would enable them to become productive members of the society.

The right to maintenance was clearly related to the right to work so far as the livelihood of an individual and his dependent relatives was to be maintained by earning money through honest work. In light of the nature of industrial organization at the time, what British Idealists considered as conditions of maintenance mainly included a living wage, and a decent house. On this matter, Haldane argued

---

[110] Jones, *Idealism as a Practical Creed*, p. 120.
[111] Hetherington and Muirhead, *Social Purpose*, p. 187.
[112] Mackenzie, *Ultimate Values in the Light of Contemporary Thought*, p. 183.

that it was the responsibility of the state to ensure that in exchange for decent labour nobody is given 'less than that on which he can live decently'.[113] For Mackenzie a right to maintenance bestowed on the state the duty to 'do something to provide suitable house accommodation' to its citizens.[114] He believed such accommodation was to include a 'suitable supply of water and light'.[115]

Lastly, the right to leisure was deemed to be a human right by Mackenzie. In defence of a right to leisure, Mackenzie wrote: 'A human being needs rest and recreation, just as an animal does; and he needs also, as the animal does not, opportunities for the cultivation of the intellectual and more purely spiritual side of his nature.'[116] What Mackenzie thought of as leisure time included the time one spent with his family and friends, or developed oneself in non-work related spheres such as literature, art, and travel. To ensure individuals' enjoyment of their right to leisure, the state should regulate working hours and maintain an infrastructure in which every individual had access to certain services such as libraries, art collections, and means of travel. Obviously, leisure did not mean for Mackenzie purposeless laziness. It was rather perceived as an opportunity for the individual to improve himself in a multitude of spheres that did not necessarily relate to his functions as a worker.

Mackenzie's list of human rights as it was put forward in 1928 offered a minimum set of powers that should be recognized by every state for individuals' pursuance of their self-realization, for the maintenance of well-ordered societies, and for a cooperative and peaceful international order. British Idealists' renewed emphasis on the universal character of the moral end combined with their newly adopted belief in nations' right to self-government culminated in a theory of human rights in Mackenzie's *Fundamental Problems of Life*. In the post Great War period, all British Idealists believed that

---

113 Haldane, *Future of Democracy*, p. 9.
114 Mackenzie, *Outlines of Social Philosophy*, p. 157.
115 Mackenzie, *Outlines of Social Philosophy*, p. 157.
116 Mackenzie, *Fundamental Problems of Life*, p. 317.

protecting individuals' rights and maintaining a peaceful inter-national order were intrinsically related to each other because only those nations which maintained a just system of rights and duties would be of a peaceful disposition towards other states. And most of them — with the exception of Bosanquet — believed that the League of Nations might be instrumental in regulating states' relations with their citizens. A striking example of a possible application of this outlook was present in Hetherington's report on the first Inter-national Labour Conference that was convened in 1919 in Washington.

The internationalist spirit of Hetherington's report was evident in his introductory note to the book. While he put much emphasis on the necessity of introducing universal standards to the conditions of workers in all countries throughout the report, he argued that its actual application was possible only through free participation of states 'in the ways of promoting human good' and not through the arbitrary use of power by an international organization.[117] He argued that the International Labour Organisation in particular and the League of Nations in general provided

> merely the environment within which men's minds and wills may meet and work together, not only in the solution of particular diffi-culties, but to the creation of a more confident, more generous and more universal attitude of mind, that shall be free to create and to sustain a more just and flexible and yet more stable international and national social order.[118]

Based on this sentiment, Hetherington offered insights for possible ways of universalizing workers' rights in the face of apparent variations among nations' interests and priorities, alluding to the economic rights Mackenzie deemed to be universal conditions for human good almost ten years later. Hetherington argued it was possible to agree on 'universal regulation of hours of work', 'observance of a weekly day of rest', and standards for the

---

[117] Hetherington, *International Labour Legislation*, p. viii.
[118] Hetherington, *International Labour Legislation*, p. viii.

'employment of women and children'.[119] He acknowledged the adoption of a convention that prohibited children's employment under the age of twelve by the Conference as a sign of its effectiveness. With much optimism he noted: 'It was a fortunate inauguration of the work of the International Labour Legislature that its first act should have been so wholehearted an effort to secure to the children of the world a prolongation of the days of their youth and of preparation for the duties and responsibilities of industry and citizenship.'[120] Another and much more controversial topic of discussion at the International Labour Conference was the working hours of labourers. Hetherington noted that on this topic, like others regarding unemployment and a minimum wage, it was the tendency of the Conference '*not* to base its standards on the lowest actually existing, but rather to prescribe as high a standard as seemed to be possible, and to admit a system of delays, so that the less advanced could reach the desirable condition not by one leap but by a series of timed and graduated steps'.[121]

The gradualist approach adopted in the Conference was visible in the proposed convention on the working hours. While the ultimate purpose of the convention was to introduce a universal 'limitation of hours of work to eight per day or forty-eight in the week', certain exemptions were guaranteed to states with newly emerging industries.[122] Hetherington was in favour of this approach so far as it did not impose arbitrary standards that were to be applied to all countries irrespective of their specific and economic conditions. He argued that an 'International Conference' was the right medium for the negotiations of working conditions that were to be applied universally so far as it created an arena in which 'beneath the consideration of any particular problem there lay the desire to effect, not only an adjustment, but the largest advance which was seriously

---

[119] Hetherington, *International Labour Legislation*, p. 16.
[120] Hetherington, *International Labour Legislation*, p. 96.
[121] Hetherington, *International Labour Legislation*, p. 19.
[122] Hetherington, *International Labour Legislation*, p. 61.

possible'.[123] According to Hetherington, chances of success at international conferences was dependent on the condition that they did not legislate 'in an abstract, cosmopolitan fashion, but in the full sense of the term internationally'.[124] The international sentiment necessitated that while universal standards were applied to states through international legislation', a full study of the conditions and aims of every State-member' was taken into consideration. Evidently, what Hetherington perceived to be the future of international relations was not cosmopolitan but internationalist in nature. Cooperation in the post Great War world order was to be ensured by the League of Nations, which would not only regulate states' relations with each other but also set standards for their internal affairs.

Mackenzie's and Hetherington's work on human (or international) rights is reflective of the general British Idealist mind-set in the post Great War period. With the exception of Bosanquet, they believed 'that the future well-being of the world depends upon the establishment of a genuine League or Society of Nations'.[125] Establishing a standard level of legal rights protection among states that would be reflective of the already existing universal moral rights was among the most important functions of such a League. With such a system of international cooperation, states would be bound to respect and maintain the rights of their citizens. British Idealists were not designing a utopian world order; on the contrary, they were aware of the possible shortcomings of a system of human rights. Most importantly, they recognized that, even under a perfectly functional human rights system, there were going to be individuals who did not have a reasonable chance to pursue their self-realization. Mackenzie maintained that the best any state could do was to 'provide the fittest conditions for men and women of certain

---

[123] Hetherington, *International Labour Legislation*, p. 73.
[124] Hetherington, *International Labour Legislation*, p. 14.
[125] Mackenzie, *Arrows of Desire*, p. 220.

general types... and even with regard to general types, it can usually only provide opportunities'.[126] He argued that once states ensured the existence of a satisfactory system of rights and duties within their own borders, the rest was to be left to the individuals themselves. Due to the teleological definition of rights from a British Idealist perspective, the existence of a right automatically implied the existence of a corresponding duty. The first and most obvious duty was recognized by almost all rights theorists, and it referred to individuals' obligation to recognize his fellow men as bearers of the same rights he himself enjoyed within a society. The second duty, which was emphasized much more by the Idealists, was individuals' obligation to recognize that they were granted certain rights for the sake of a moral end, and the legitimacy of these rights was dependent on their appropriate use towards the moral end of self-realization.[127] Under an international system of human rights, British Idealists hoped, states would be obligated to make sure that their citizens were bestowed with necessary powers for their self-realization and citizens would be wise enough to recognize that they had the duty to use their rights for the pursuance of a universal moral end.

IV. Conclusion

British Idealists' work on human rights in the post Great War period did not deviate from what they learned from Green on the topic of the importance and nature of rights. On the contrary, this was a period where they distanced themselves from the imperialist vocabulary of 'spreading civilization' and returned to the Greenian vocabulary of universal morality and rights. They dealt with the topic of international cooperation at length and searched for the basis of such cooperation between nation-states in the universal dictates of a teleological morality. Instead of a culturally and politically uniform world order, they advocated liberty at the

---

[126] Mackenzie, *Fundamental Problems of Life*, p. 307.
[127] Mackenzie, *Fundamental Problems of Life*, p. 306.

national and fraternity at the international level. As a concrete example of such an international organization, most of them supported the project of the League of Nations. Furthermore, they all perceived an underlying relation between recognition of rights in independent nation-states and maintenance of a peaceful and cooperative international order. From this perspective they defined the ideal political order as a just 'republic' that had a civic form of patriotism and an international outlook. The most significant indicator of such a political organization was the system of rights and duties it maintained. Although the specifics of each society's system of rights and duties were expected to change due to the particular material and historical conditions in which it evolved, all such systems were to comply with the dictates of universal morality. The universal threshold was individuals' ability to pursue their personal self-realization under the existing system of rights. While Green perceived the most basic liberal rights to life, liberty, property, and family as the minimum requirements for the pursuance of this end, Mackenzie's list of human rights from 1928 included the rights to property, security, education, franchise, work, maintenance, and leisure among those rights without which individuals did not have a reasonable chance of self-realization.

The sense in which rights were independent from the political sanctions of states was the moral end with reference to which their existence was justified. In this universal moral sense, they were antecedent to the existence or recognition of any state. Yet in another and more practical sense, rights' actual enjoyment was very much dependent on states' recognition. Mackenzie argued: 'wherever there is a beneficent force, there is a right of some kind... Nevertheless, it is true to say that the State gives an added force and definiteness to the rights and duties that it finds already existing, and that it introduces new ones.'[128] To the extent that states were vital stakeholders in the maintenance of a system of rights within their own borders,

---

[128] Mackenzie, *Fundamental Problems of Life*, p. 305.

maintenance of a universal system of human rights was also dependent on their willingness and cooperation. It was this internationalist aspect of the younger generation of British Idealists' approach to human rights that was most clearly represented in Hetherington's report on the first Conference of the International Labour Organisation. Especially in regards to the establishment of international organizations such as the League of Nations, these British Idealists foresaw that 'development of international ethics' would constitute a basis for an international order of human rights.[129] Although the international ethics to be developed by the League of Nations was a reflection of already existing universal moral norms, its successful implementation was possible through states' continual cooperation.

---

[129] P. Sutch (2000) 'Human Rights as Settled Norms: Mervyn Frost and the Limits of Hegelian Human Rights Theory', *Review of International Studies*, 26 (2), p. 231.

Chapter 6
Conclusion

Deviating from the general tendencies in contemporary literature, this book focuses on the works of minor British Idealists instead of T.H. Green's to get an insight about what a British Idealist theory of human rights would look like. Admittedly, works of minor idealists up until 1914 did not offer much ethical or political argumentation that can sustain a theoretical basis for a universal system of human rights. On the contrary, their work was dominated by their dedication to the cause of a 'true empire' that would unite all humanity around the values of European civilization. Although these minor figures were not defenders of a militarist form of imperialism in pursuit of larger territories and higher economic benefits, they were willing to forgive the past mistakes of the Empire in the hope that it would be transformed into a civilizing force of humanity. This line of thinking was a very apparent paternalistic approach to non-Western peoples that did not attribute much value to their existing social systems and ethical values. As non-European peoples were perceived as akin to children of humanity in need of guidance and education, their rights were only prospective in nature. In keeping with Isaiah Berlin's famous criticism towards Green in regards to the paternalistic pitfalls of positive liberty, some British Idealists used the interdependence between rights and the moral capacity to justify an imperialist project.[1] This tendency was most obvious in the works of Ritchie and Bradley as they advocated total subjugation of non-

---

[1] I. Berlin (2002) *Liberty: Incorporating Four Essays on Liberty,* ed. H. Hardy, Oxford: Oxford University Press, p. 41.

European peoples for the realization of the supposed moral end of a monolithic high civilization. Muirhead, Mackenzie, Jones, and Haldane appeared to see the British people as benevolent paternal figures to the peoples the British Empire ruled over. Even when they disproved the British Empire's policies—during the Boer War for instance—they did not lose hope in the civilizing power of European empires. In short, their works in this period pointed 'to an important way in which the idealist conception of the self lends itself to paternalistic projects'.[2] While this mind-set was very much in keeping with the general intellectual atmosphere in Britain at the time, it did not constitute a fertile ground for the emergence of a theory of human rights.

The British Idealists' return to the universal ideals of self-realization and the common good corresponds with the massive disillusionment they experienced with the European empires after the outbreak of the Great War. Like many of their contemporary intellectuals, from 1914 onwards, they advocated the necessity of transforming the British Empire into a Commonwealth of Nations and supported the project of establishing a League of Nations. As they were no longer invested in the civilizing project, they looked for an alternative source for international peace and cooperation. Going back to Green's moral and political philosophy, they designated the universal moral end of self-realization as a shared aspect of all humanity and argued that each well-ordered state should maintain a social and political order in which every individual had the means to pursue the universal moral end of self-realization. Furthermore, Bosanquet's work seemed to be effective in reminding a younger generation of Idealists of the vitality of the cultural multiplicity of nations along with the moral universality of humankind. In the post Great War period all British Idealists regarded the principles of liberty and fraternity of nations as basic tenets of a stable and

---

2   G.F. Gaus (1983) *The Modern Liberal Theory of Man*, London: Palgrave Macmillan, p. 178.

cooperative international order. In such an international order each state would be a self-governing political entity free from hostile interventions from other states. Only under such conditions would each unique expression of human potential be incorporated into the overall unity and progress of humankind. Still, their endorsement of cultural multiplicity did not amount to total relativism. Thus, a League of Peace had the immense potential and the duty to facilitate effective communication and cooperation among nation-states to determine the rights that could be upheld universally in every community. Their underlying rationale was that an internally well-ordered nation would not harbour hostile intentions towards other states. Protection of human rights was vital not only for ensuring the conditions for self-realization for every single individual but to make sure that nation-states did not harbour hostile intentions towards each other.

Starting an account of a theory of British Idealist human rights from the 1880s when most of the British Idealists ignored the importance of rights in pursuance of an imperial project seems counterintuitive. Still, doing so is important for multiple reasons. First and foremost, the story of the ideational change and evolution they experienced in less than thirty years is very impressive. Recognizing the existence of this considerable alteration in their thinking lets us know that the British Idealist school of thought was not a monolithic body of thought that floated free from the historical context in which it operated. It was very much influenced by the highly turbulent international order that marked the last decades of the nineteenth century as well as the beginning of the twentieth century. Under the influence of both immensely powerful historical phenomena and shifts in the popular mind-set in Britain, they reacted to questions regarding social, political, and international order and continually modified their positions. Additionally, recognizing the imperialist phase in British Idealist thought shows that, like most other schools of thought, British Idealism was not in itself imperialist, cosmopolitan, nor internationalist. It was possible to use a British Idealist way of theorizing – often accompanied by other popular modes of thought like Darwinism — to support as morally legitimate the dominance of European civilization over all humanity or to advocate the establishment of a league of independent and cooperative nation-states. Recognizing the shifts of emphasis on certain aspects of the theory, for instance the importance attributed to the particular in comparison with the universal, may prove useful in the future to avoid the pitfalls some British Idealists fell down previously.

British Idealists' internationalist approach to human rights in the post Great War period contributes to contemporary discussions by offering a middle ground between cosmopolitanism and communitarianism as a sphere of operation for human rights. While there appear to be contemporary visions for a cosmopolitan political order that would sustain a universal system of human rights, such a project is mostly received with a high level of scepticism. Andrew Linklater, for instance, argues for a cosmopolitan form of citizenship that rejects 'the statists' argument that citizenship, properly so-called, can only have meaning within the confines of the bounded sovereign state.[3] According to Linklater, the project of cosmopolitan citizenship would challenge the idea that 'the interests of fellow citizens necessarily take priority over duties for eliciting their support for global political institutions and sentiments'.[4] Others, however, note that a truly political project of cosmopolitanism that aims at world governance or the 'visions of a doctrinally united global society' are long gone.[5] While, for some, the project of the European Union constitutes an encouraging prospect for some theorists of cosmopolitan citizenship and world governance, others argue that 'one does not become a cosmopolitan citizen because the

---

3   A. Linklater (1999) 'Cosmopolitan Citizenship', in Hutchings, K. & Dannreuther, R. (eds.) *Cosmopolitan Citizenship*, London: Macmillan Press Ltd, p. 49.

4   Linklater, 'Cosmopolitan Citizenship', p. 36.

5   D. Heater (1996) *World Citizenship and Government: Cosmopolitan Ideas in the History of Western Political Thought*, London: Macmillan Press Ltd, p. 209.

state one belongs to is subject to a body of international law'.[6] Such an understanding of cosmopolitan citizenship does not meet the basic tenets of citizenship according to David Miller, and also runs the risk of undercutting 'the basis of citizenship proper'.[7] It would be fair to say that the cosmopolitan project faces increasing criticism, although there is an apparent globalization trend observable today:

> The various cosmopolitan schemas for global transformation currently doing the rounds, whether 'thick' or 'thin', Westphalian or post-Westphalian, are being resisted because they are either seen to be flying in the face of trans-historical international political realities, or the value-amalgam legitimating them should be seen as essentially contested... Although globalization may appear to facilitate the emergence of cosmopolitan global regimes of say, law enforcement or economic regulation, because of their overwhelmingly neoliberal character and the ideological commonalities between the states likely to be pre-eminent within them, their costs and benefits, critics argue, will flow in very particular directions.[8]

On the other end of the spectrum, the communitarian challenge to liberalism has gained prominence as a reaction to the neo-liberalism of the 1980s. According to Newman and De Zoysa, the communitarian challenge to liberalism has established itself against the 'emphasis on individualism and freedom of choice that had arisen since the rise of the Reagan-Thatcher policies in the 1980s'.[9] Against the atomized individual that constituted the basis of the liberal position, communitarians have emphasized the collective societal roots of the individual and the civic moral order that supplies individuals with a moral compass, with 'a set of moral values, that guides people toward what is decent and encourages them to avoid that which is not'.[10] At least some of the proponents of the communi-

---

6   D. Miller (1999) 'Bounded Citizenship', in *Cosmopolitan Citizenship*, London: Macmillan Press Ltd, p. 74.

7   Miller, 'Bounded Citizenship', p. 79.

8   P. Lawler, 'The Good State', p. 432.

9   O. Newman and R. De Zoysa (1997) 'Communitarianism: The New Panacea?', *Sociological Perspectives*, 40 (4), p. 628.

10   A. Etzioni (1993) *The Spirit of Community*, New York: Crown Publishers, p. 24.

tarian position perceive an insurmountable contradiction between 'politics of rights' that prevails in the contemporary order of human rights and a 'politics of the common good' that the communitarians defend.[11] Berger's account of human rights clearly reflects such a position:

> It [human rights/dignity] pertains to the self as such, to the individual regardless of his position in society. This becomes very clear in the classic formulations of human rights, from the Preamble to the Declaration of Independence to the Universal Declaration of Human Rights of the United Nations. These rights always pertain to the individual 'irrespective of race, colour or creed' — or indeed, of sex, age, physical condition or any conceivable social status. There is an implicit sociology and an implicit anthropology here. The implicit sociology views all biological and historical differentiations among men as either downright unreal or essentially irrelevant. The implicit anthropology locates the real self over and beyond all these differentiations.[12]

From the communitarian perspective human rights are taken to be an 'abstractly constituted list' that stands aloof from the social, cultural, and personal specificities of individuals whose very identities are constituted by the community they live in.[13] Thus, the matter of rights are mostly equated with civic rights that are recognized by nation-states and do not have any implications for the international sphere.

Yet from the 2000s onwards, the dichotomy between communitarianism and cosmopolitanism started to attract criticism, mostly because it has been perceived as a false dichotomy operating through undue simplifications that does not do justice to either communitarian or cosmopolitan concerns. In this light, for example, David Morrice asks: 'are individuals said to be wholly constituted, or

---

11 M.J. Sandel (ed.) (1984) *Liberalism and Its Critics*, New York: New York University Press, p. 6.

12 P. Berger (1984) 'On the Obsolescence of the Concept of Honour', in Sandel, M.J. (ed.) *Liberalism and Its Critics*, New York: New York University Press, p. 153.

13 H. Tam (1998) *Communitarianism: A New Agenda for Politics and Citizenship*, Basingstoke: Macmillan Press, p. 224.

only partially shaped by their respective communities? Does not an individual have to exist before or she can be shaped? If so, this pre-existing individual may be possessed of natural rights or human needs which transcend all political boundaries, and which should be recognised, protected and fulfilled by all political communities.'[14] Against this reductionist dichotomy, Morrice offers an alternative that is based on a 'morality of states position'.[15] Similarly, Lawler offers a third way solution to the ongoing intellectual conflict between communitarianism and cosmopolitanism. According to Lawler, this middle-way position is called internationalism, which 'is centred on the seemingly modest, but still demanding idea of the state as a cosmopolitan-minded agent... or a "local agent of a world common good"'.[16] The match between Lawler's 'classical model of internationalism' and the British Idealists' approach to international relations and human rights in the post Great War period is quite striking. It is one of the contentions of this study that this historical approach to the subject matter of human rights may constitute an example of the third way approach Lawler perceives to be a solution to the communitarian–cosmopolitan dichotomy.

Without delving into the details of the British Idealists' inter-nationalist position that has been discussed at length throughout this book, it suffices to attract attention to certain aspects of this position that make it 'internationalist' instead of cosmopolitan or communi-tarian. First and foremost, the idealist approach to human rights takes rights as powers that are recognized and maintained by specific communities. This is most observable in the 'rights recog-nition' aspect of their approach, which acknowledges that for rights to be truly operative, communities, and/or states as their political

---

[14] D. Morrice (2000) 'The Liberal-Communitarian Debate in Contemporary Political Philosophy and its Significance for International Relations', *Review of International Studies*, 26 (2), p. 242.

[15] Morrice, 'The Liberal-Communitarian Debate in Contemporary Political Philosophy and its Significance for International Relations', p. 246.

[16] Lawler, 'The Good State', p. 433.

embodiments, must recognize individuals' claims to certain rights. Without such recognition rights remain as moral claims to certain powers that lack the social/political recognition that is essential for their maintenance. Although such claims are not valueless or non-existent, they cannot practically operate as rights proper. Furthermore, the Idealist position takes rights as the products of the outcomes of an historical process of ethical progress. While the extent and scope of rights are expected to be limited in pre-modern societies, human history is understood to be the process of a continually growing awareness of the worth of every human being and their entitlement to certain rights. Thus, it is acknowledged that specific codifications of rights naturally vary from society to society. This is an outcome not only of societies' level of ethical development but also of the specific natural and historical circumstances in which each society comes to recognize certain rights as necessary powers for individuals. Last but not least, the rights claim and rights recognition processes in every society are understood as political processes with republican implications. Within the British Idealist political theory, individuals are constituted as citizens who are equal participants in the decision-making processes in regard to which rights and duties contribute to the common good of their society. In that light, for instance, the younger generation of British Idealists insists on the necessity of constituting each society in the Kantian 'republican' form so that individuals can become active contributors to the codification of the rights and duties they enjoy within their society. When understood in this way, the British Idealists' approach to human rights complies with the sensibilities of the modern communitarians.

Yet the British Idealists also recognize a universal human nature that constitutes the basis of their moral and political theory. They acknowledge in every human individual the potential for rationality, morality, and sociability. They maintain that it is these universal attributes of humankind that makes ethical life possible and makes it actually prevail to varying extent in every known human society. Most importantly, they argue that in each society exists the moral awareness that for individuals to realize their truly human potentials they must be endowed with certain powers. These powers that enable individuals to pursue the moral end of self-realization without undue constraint are called rights. While the scope of the recognized rights varies from society to society, British Idealists argue for the necessity of the recognition of at least minimum rights for the maintenance of any ethical society. For Green, these minimum rights are rights to free life, property, and family; by the 1920s Mackenzie offered a more comprehensive list that includes rights to franchise, education, maintenance, occupation, and leisure. The underlying justification for the universality of these rights was established by reference to the end they serve, which is the universal moral end of self-realization. The moral end of self-realization was substantiated with reference to the universal human nature that distinguishes human beings from 'lower orders of animals'. The truly human attributes of reasonableness, morality, and sociability substantiate the universal moral end of self-realization irrespective of the race, nationality, and religion of individuals. From this perspective, the British Idealist position seems closer to the cosmopolitan approach to human rights.

The British Idealists brought together these two spheres of morality, the nation-states with their established ethical orders and the universal morality, through their support for international organizations as spheres of communication and cooperation. While their belief in the commensurability of particular ethical orders was justified by reference to the 'metaphysics of self-realization', it did not aim for an homogeneous ethical order worldwide. On the contrary, human rights were construed as a set of minimal powers without which individuals in any society did not have a reasonable chance for self-realization. Yet human rights' specific codification and maintenance within nation-states were argued to be dependent on the particular conditions that prevailed in these communities and were mostly left to the states as political embodiments of truly 'republican' nations. The scope they left for the particular adaptations of human rights within nation-states were most obvious in the emphasis they put on the ideal of self-determination for every nation in the post Great War period. They condoned foreign intervention only in extremely rare conditions when citizens of a tyrannous state lacked all the means of resistance. In an international order that was construed as equal nation-states, human rights were understood to be moral criteria for the assessment of states' fulfilment of their duties towards their citizens. As these rights were claimed and recognized with reference to a universal end, certain basic rights were expected to be recognized by each and every republican form of government. While the list of rights by which all states were expected to abide was open to change and improvement through international communication, the moral end of self-realization was taken as a universal constant. Thus, the seemingly controversial positions of communitarianism and cosmopolitanism were circumvented by the British Idealists' approach to human rights. Arguably, their position was too good to be true.

The realist challenge to any position that prescribes a certain level of morality to international relations can find ample material to argue for the opposing view that the international sphere is in a perpetual 'state of nature'. States' singular interest in their material wealth or military power in opposition to the interests of other states can be substantiated with numerous examples. Yet it is also possible to find, in line with the British Idealist argument that when states are true republics with a healthy form of patriotism, the international sphere can be constructed as a peaceful and cooperative arena that can operate with reference to universal moral concerns. While this proves to be an outcome that requires constant effort on the part of the states as well as their citizens, it is not a utopian position. The relative success of the United Nations in creating a sphere of communication for nation-states on the matter of human rights can be deduced from the high levels of acceptance among states of the

Declarations on Human Rights.[17] While the level of compliance with the terms of declarations varies from country to country, the high number of signatories shows that there exists an ideal of international cooperation in pursuit of the betterment of the human condition in the persons of individuals regardless of their race, nationality, and religious creed. In line with the British Idealists, it seems more productive to focus on the possible ways of improving international cooperation as well as compliance with already existing human rights norms, instead of devaluing the ideal of human rights altogether based on its failures. When human rights are understood as ideals that are in the process of realization, individuals' and states' duties to contribute to the process become more apparent. In his 1918 book, *Some Suggestions in Ethics*, Bosanquet reflects on the future of international relations as follows:

> You do not want mere 'moral' motives, *i.e.* desires for peace and happiness; you want their adequate development into ideas which 'have hands and feet'... The more careful study which is now being devoted to the needs of other countries, and the deep-lying conditions of a peaceful atmosphere, is changing the situation, and bringing with it some promise of a good will adequately furnished for the promotion of peace.[18]

Human rights today turn out to be such an idea, whose hands and feet are the people who continually strive towards its realization. So far as nation-states retain their primacy in world politics, and citizens are dependent for the recognition and maintenance of their rights on their respective states, an international order that enables communication among peaceful and cooperative states constitutes the best possibility for the further advancement of universal human rights.

---

[17] M.J. Perry (1997) 'Are Human Rights Universal? The Relativist Challenge and Related Matters', *Human Rights Quarterly*, 19 (3), p. 481.

[18] Bosanquet, *Some Suggestions in Ethics*, p. 144.

Bibliography

Alexander, James. *Shaw's Controversial Socialism*. Gainesville: University Press of Florida, 2009.

Antony, Anghie. *Imperialism, Sovereignty and the Making of International Law*. Cambridge: Cambridge University Press, 2004.

Beetham, David. 'Introduction: Human Rights in the Study of Politics.' *Political Studies* 43, no. 1 (1995): 1–9.

Bell, Duncan. *Reordering the World: Essays on Liberalism and Empire*. Princeton: Princeton University Press, 2016.

Bell, Duncan. *The Idea of Greater Britain: Empire and the Future of the World Order, 1889–1900*. Princeton: Princeton University Press, 2007.

Bell, Duncan, ed. *Victorian Visions of Global Order: Empire and International Relations in Nineteenth-Century Political Thought*. Cambridge: Cambridge University Press, 2007.

Berger, Peter. 'On the Obsolescence of the Concept of Honour.' In *Liberalism and Its Critics*. Edited by Michael Sandel, 149–59. New York: New York University Press, 1984.

Berlin, Isaiah. *Liberty: Incorporating Four Essays on Liberty*. Edited by Henry Hardy. Oxford: Oxford University Press, 2002.

Bernhardi, Friedrich von, and Allen H. Powles. *Germany and the Next War*. New York: Longmans, Green, and Co., 1914.

Bosanquet, Bernard. 'A Moral from Athenian History.' *International Journal of Ethics* 9, no. 1 (1898): 13–28. In *Social and International Ideals*, 250-70. London: Macmillan Company, 1917.

Bosanquet, Bernard. *Essays and Addresses*. London: Swan Sonnenschein & Co., Lim., 1891.

Bosanquet, Bernard. 'Life and Philosophy.' In *Contemporary British Philosophy: Personal Statements*. Edited by J.H. Muirhead, 49–74. London: George Allen & Unwin Ltd, 1924.

Bosanquet, Bernard. 'Patriotism in the Perfect State.' In *The International Crisis in Its Ethical and Psychological Aspects*, 132–54. London: Oxford University Press, 1915.

Bosanquet, Bernard. 'Review of The Group Mind: A Sketch of the Principles of Collective Psychology with Some Attempt to Apply them to the Interpretation of National Life and Character, by William McDougall.' *Mind* 30, no. 117 (1921): 63–71.

Bosanquet, Bernard. *Selected Essays*. Edited by William Sweet. Vol. 1. Collected Works of Bernard Bosanquet. Bristol: Thoemmes, 1999.

Bosanquet, Bernard. *Social and International Ideals: Being Studies in Patriotism*. London: Macmillan, 1917.

Bosanquet, Bernard. 'Some Socialistic Features of Ancient Societies.' In *Essays and Addresses*, 48–71. London: Swan Sonnenschein & Co., Lim., 1891.

Bosanquet, Bernard. *Some Suggestions in Ethics*. London: Macmillan and Co., Ltd, 1919.

Bosanquet, Bernard. *The Civilization of Christendom, and Other Studies*. London: S. Sonnenschein; New York, Macmillan, 1893.

Bosanquet, Bernard, *The Collected Works of Bernard Bosanquet*. Edited by William Sweet. Bristol: Thoemmes, 1999.

Bosanquet, Bernard. 'The Communication of Moral Ideas as a Function of an Ethical Society.' *International Journal of Ethics* 1, no. 1 (1890): 79–97.

Bosanquet, Bernard. 'The Evolution of Religion.' *International Journal of Ethics* 5, no. 4 (1895): 432–44.

Bosanquet, Bernard. 'The Function of the State in Promoting the Unity of Mankind.' In *Social and International Ideals*, 270–301. London: The Macmillan Company, 1917.

Bosanquet, Bernard. *The Philosophical Theory of the State*. London: Macmillan and Co. Limited, 1899.

Bosanquet, Bernard. *The Philosophical Theory of the State*. Third Edition. London: Macmillan and Co. Limited, 1920.

Bosanquet, Bernard. 'The Teaching of Patriotism.' *Charity Organisation Review* 36, no. 214 (1914): 265–79. In *Social and International Ideals*, 1–20. London: Macmillan Company, 1917.

Bosanquet, Bernard. 'The Wisdom of Naaman's Servants.' In *Social and International Ideals*, 302–21. London: The Macmillan Company, 1917.

Bosanquet, Bernard. 'Three Lectures on Social Ideals.' In *Social and International Ideals*, 195–249. London: The Macmillan Company, 1917.

Boucher, David, ed. *The British Idealists*. Cambridge; New York: Cambridge University Press, 1997.

Boucher, David. *The Limits of Ethics in International Relations: Natural Law, Natural Rights, and Human Rights in Transition*. Oxford: Oxford University Press, 2011.

Boucher, David. 'The Recognition Theory of Rights, Customary International Law and Human Rights.' *Political Studies* 59, no. 3 (October 1, 2011): 753–71.

Boucher, David, and Andrew Vincent. *A Radical Hegelian: The Political and Social Philosophy of Henry Jones*. Cardiff: University of Wales Press, 1993.

Boucher, David and Andrew Vincent. *British Idealism and Political Theory*. Edinburgh: Edinburgh University Press, 2000.

Bowle, John. *Politics and Opinion in the Nineteenth Century*. London: Jonathan Cape, 1954.

Bradley, F.H. *Appearance and Reality*. London: Swan Sonnenschein, 1893.

Bradley, F.H. *Collected Works of F.H. Bradley, Volume 1: A Pluralistic Approach to Philosophy*. Edited by Carol A. Keene. Bristol: Thoemmes Press, 1999.

Bradley, F.H. *Essays on Truth and Reality*. Oxford: Clarendon Press, 1914.

Bradley, F.H. *Ethical Studies*. London: Henry S. King & Co., 1876.

Bradley, F.H. 'Some Remarks on Punishment.' *International Journal of Ethics* 4, no. 3 (1894): 269–84.

Bradley, F.H. 'The Limits of Individual and National Self-Sacrifice.' *International Journal of Ethics* 5, no. 1 (1894): 17–28.

Bradley, F.H. *The Principles of Logic*. London: Oxford University Press, 1883.

Brailsford, Henry Noel. *A League of Nations*. New York: The Macmillan Company, 1917.

Brink, David Owen. *Perfectionism and the Common Good: Themes in the Philosophy of T.H. Green*. Oxford; New York: Oxford University Press, 2003.

Brooks, Thom, ed. *Ethical Citizenship: British Idealism and the Politics of Recognition*. Basingstoke; New York: Palgrave Macmillan, 2014.

Brooks, Thom. 'Introduction.' In *Ethical Citizenship: British Idealism and the Politics of Recognition*. Edited by Brooks, 1–13. Basingstoke; New York: Palgrave Macmillan, 2014.

Brown, Judith M., and Roger Louis, eds. *The Oxford History of the British Empire: Volume IV: The Twentieth Century*. Oxford: Oxford University Press, 2001.

Brown, Stuart. *Dictionary of Twentieth-Century British Philosophers: 2 Volumes*. Bristol: Thoemmes, 2005.

Bryce, James. *Proposals for the Prevention of Future Wars*. London: George Allen & Unwin Ltd., 1917.

Cacoullos, Ann R. *Thomas Hill Green: Philosopher of Rights*. New York: Twayne Publishers Inc., 1975.

Collini, Stefan. 'Sociology and Idealism in Britain 1880–1920.' *European Journal of Sociology / Archives Européennes de Sociologie* 19, no. 1 (May 1978): 3–50.

Dimova-Cookson, Maria. 'Do We Owe More to Fellow Nationals? The Particular and Universal Ethics of Bosanquet's General Will and Miller's Public Culture.' In *Ethical Citizenship: British Idealism and the Politics of Recognition*. Edited by Thom Brooks, 200–23. London: Palgrave Macmillan, 2014.

Dimova-Cookson, Maria. 'Resolving Moral Conflicts: British Idealist and Contemporary Liberal Approaches to Value Pluralism and Moral Conduct.' In *T.H. Green: Ethics, Metaphysics and Political Philosophy*. Edited by Dimova-Cookson and W.J. Mander, 292–315. Oxford: Clarendon Press, 2006.

Dimova-Cookson, Maria. *T.H. Green's Moral and Political Philosophy: A Phenomenological Perspective*. Basingstoke; New York: Palgrave Macmillan, 2001.

Dimova-Cookson, Maria, and W.J. Mander. 'Introduction.' In *T.H. Green: Ethics, Metaphysics and Political Philosophy*. Edited by Dimova-Cookson and Mander, 1–15. Oxford: Clarendon Press, 2006.

Douzinas, Costas. *Human Rights and Empire: The Political Philosophy of Cosmopolitanism*. New York: Routledge-Cavendish, 2007.

Drake, Durant. 'Will the League of Nations Work?' *The International Journal of Ethics* 29, no. 3 (1919): 339–49.

Ellis, John S. "The Methods of Barbarism' and the 'Rights of Small Nations': War Propaganda and British Pluralism.' *Albion: A Quarterly Journal Concerned with British Studies* 30, no. 1 (1998): 49–75.

Etzioni, Amitai. *The Spirit of Community*. New York: Crown Publishers, 1993.

Gaus, Gerald F. *The Modern Liberal Theory of Man*. London; New York: Palgrave Macmillan, 1983.

Gaus, Gerald F. 'The Rights Recognition Thesis: Defending and Extending Green.' In *T.H. Green: Ethics, Metaphysics, and Political Philosophy*. Edited by Maria Dimova-Cookson and W.J. Mander, 209–35. Oxford; New York: Oxford University Press, 2006.

Gouldstone, T. *The Rise and Decline of Anglican Idealism in the Nineteenth Century*. London: Palgrave Macmillan, 2005.

Gowans, Adam L. *Selections from Treitschke's Lectures on Politics*. London and Glasgow: Gowans & Gray, Ltd, 1914.

Green, Thomas Hill. *Lectures on the Principles of Political Obligation*. London: Longmans, Green, and Co., 1895.

Green, Thomas Hill. *Prolegomena to Ethics*. Edited by A.C. Bradley. Fifth Edition. Oxford: Clarendon Press, 1906.

Green, Thomas Hill. *Works of Thomas Hill Green, Vol. 1: Philosophical Works*. Edited by R.L. Nettleship. London; New York: Longmans, Green, and Co., 1885.

Green, Thomas Hill. *Works, Vol. 5: Additional Writings*. Edited by Peter P. Nicholson. Bristol: Thoemmes Press, 1997.

Greenwood, Christopher. 'The Relationship between Ius Ad Bellum and Ius in Bello.' *Review of International Studies* 9, no. 4 (1983): 221–34.

Grey, Edward. *The League of Nations*. New York: George H. Doran Company, 1918.

Hafner-Burton, Emilie. *Making Human Rights a Reality*. Princeton: Princeton University Press, 2013.

Haldane, R.B. *Before the War*. London: Cassell And Company, Ltd, 1920.

Haldane, R.B. *Higher Nationality: A Study in Law and Ethics*. Washington: United States of America Government Printing Office, 1914; reprinted in Haldane, *The Conduct of Life and Other Addresses*. New York: E.P. Dutton & Company, 1915.

Haldane, R.B. 'Introduction.' In Ian Hamilton, *Compulsory Service: A Study of the Question in the Light of Experience*, 9–42. London: Hazell, Watson and Viney, LD., 1910.

Haldane, R.B. *Reign of Relativity*. New Haven: Yale University Press, 1921.

Haldane, R.B. *The Conduct of Life and Other Addresses*. New York: E.P. Dutton & Company, 1915.

Haldane, R.B. *The Future of Democracy: An Address by Lord Haldane*. London: Headley Bros. Publishers, Ltd, 1918.

Haldane, R.B. *The Philosophy of Humanism and Other Subjects*. New Haven: Yale University Press, 1922.

Hann, Matt. 'Double Recognition: Persons and Rights in T.H. Green.' *Collingwood and British Idealism Studies* 21, no. 1 (2015): 63–80.

Hann, Matt. *Egalitarian Rights Recognition*. London: Palgrave Macmillan, 2016.

Hann, Matt. ''Who Is My Neighbour?' T.H. Green and the Possibility of Cosmopolitan Ethical Citizenship.' In *Ethical Citizenship*. Edited by Thom Brooks, 177–99. London: Palgrave Macmillan, 2014.

Heater, Derek. *World Citizenship and Government: Cosmopolitan Ideas in the History of Western Political Thought*. Basingstoke; London: Macmillan Press Ltd, 1996.

Heim, Joseph Charles. 'Liberalism and the Establishment of Collective Security in British Foreign Policy: The Alexander Prize Essay.' *Transactions of the Royal Historical Society* 5 (1995): 91–110.

Hetherington, H.J.W. *International Labour Legislation*. London: Methuen & Co. Ltd, 1920.

Hetherington, H.J.W. *The Life and Letters of Sir Henry Jones*. London: Hodder and Stoughton Limited, 1924.

Hetherington, H.J.W., and J.H. Muirhead. *Social Purpose: A Contribution to a Philosophy of Civic Society*. London: George Allen & Unwin Ltd, 1918.

Hinton, Guy. 'Newcastle and the Boer War: Regional Reactions to an Imperial War.' *Northern History* 52, no. 2 (September 1, 2015): 272–94.

Hobhouse, L.T. *Democracy and Reaction*. New York: G.P. Putnam's Sons, 1905.

Hobhouse, L.T. *The Metaphysical Theory of the State: A Criticism*. London: George Allen & Unwin; New York: Macmillan, 1918.

Hobhouse, L.T. *The World in Conflict*. London: T. Fisher Unwin Ltd, 1915.

Hobson, J.A. *Capitalism and Imperialism in South Africa*. New York: The Tucker Publishing Co., 1900.

Hobson, J.A. 'Is International Government Possible?' *The Hibbert Journal* 15 (1916): 199–203.

Hobson, J.A. 'Socialistic Imperialism.' *International Journal of Ethics* 12 (1902): 44–58.

Hobson, J.A. *The War in South Africa: Its Causes and Effects*. New York: The Macmillan Company, 1900.

Hobson, J.A. *Towards International Government*. New York: The Macmillan Company, 1915.

Hoffmann, Stefan-Ludwig. *Human Rights in the Twentieth Century*. New York: Cambridge University Press, 2010.

Jones, Henry. *Form the League of Peace Now: An Appeal to My Fellow Citizens*. London: The League of Nations Union, 1918.

Jones, Henry. *Idealism as a Practical Creed*. Glasgow: James Maclehose and Sons, 1909.

Jones, Henry. *Old Memories: Autobiography by Sir Henry Jones, C.H.* Edited by Thomas Jones. London: Hodder and Stoughton Limited, 1922.

Jones, Henry. 'Some Unexamined Assumptions That Hinder The Study Of The Conditions Of Social Well-Being.' *Rice Institute Pamphlet – Rice University Studies* 6, no. 3 (1919): 143–65.

Jones, Henry. 'The Fundamental Principle of Good Citizenship Which Social Science Develops and Applies.' *Rice Institute Pamphlet – Rice University Studies* 6, no. 3 (1919): 166–83.

Jones, Henry. 'The Obligations and Privileges of Citizenship — a Plea for the Study of Social Science.' *Rice Institute Pamphlet – Rice University Studies* 6, no. 3 (1919): 119–42.

Jones, Henry. *The Principles of Citizenship*. London: Macmillan and Co. Limited, 1920.

Jones, Henry. 'The Social Organism.' In *Essays in Philosophical Criticism*. Edited by Andrew Seth and R.B. Haldane, 187–213. New York: Burt Franklin, 1883.

Jones, Henry. *The Working Faith of the Social Reformer and Other Essays*. London: Macmillan and Co. Limited, 1910.

Jones, Henry. 'Why We Are Fighting.' *Hibbert Journal* XIII (1914–1915): 50–67.

Kaymaz, Nazli Pinar. 'From Imperialism to Internationalism: British Idealism and Human Rights.' *The International History Review* published online (2018): 1–22.

Kelly, Duncan. *The Propriety of Liberty: Persons, Passions, and Judgement in Modern Political Thought*. Princeton; Oxford: Princeton University Press, 2010.

Kennedy, Thomas C. 'Public Opinion and the Conscientious Objector, 1915-1919.' *Journal of British Studies* 12, no. 2 (1973): 105–19.

Krebs, Paula M. ''The Last of the Gentlemen's Wars': Women in the Boer War Concentration Camp Controversy.' *History Workshop*, no. 33 (1992): 38–56.

Lawler, Peter. 'The Good State: In Praise of 'Classical' Internationalism.' *Review of International Studies* 31, no. 3 (2005): 427–49.

Linklater, Andrew. 'Cosmopolitan Citizenship.' In *Cosmopolitan Citizenship*. Edited by Kimberly Hutchings and Roland Dannreuther, 35–60. Basingstoke; London: Macmillan Press Ltd, 1999.

McCarthy, Thomas. *Race, Empire, and the Idea of Human Development*. Cambridge; New York: Cambridge University Press, 2009.

Mackenzie, J.S. *A Manual of Ethics*. Fourth Edition. New York: Hinds, Hayden & Eldredge, Inc., 1901.

Mackenzie, J.S. *Arrows of Desire*. London: George Allen & Unwin Ltd, 1920.

Mackenzie, J.S. 'Constructive Philosophy.' In *Contemporary British Philosophy: Personal Statements*. Editedby J.H. Muirhead, 231–47. London: George Allen & Unwin Ltd, 1953.

Mackenzie, J.S. *Elements of Constructive Philosophy*. London: George Allen & Unwin Ltd, 1917.

Mackenzie, J.S. *Fundamental Problems of Life: An Essay on Citizenship as Pursuit of Values*. London: George Allen & Unwin, 1928.

Mackenzie, J.S. 'Joad, C.E.M. – Counter Attack From the East.' *Mind* 43, no. 120 (1934): 120.

Mackenzie, J.S. *Lectures on Humanism*. London: Swan Sonnenschein & Co., Lim., 1907.

Mackenzie, J.S. 'Might and Right.' In *The International Crisis: The Theory of the State*, 56–91. London: Oxford University Press, 1916.

Mackenzie, J.S. 'Mr. Bradley's View of the Self.' *Mind* 3, no. 11 (1894): 305–35.

Mackenzie, J.S. *Outlines of Social Philosophy*. London: George Allen & Unwin Ltd, 1918.

Mackenzie, J.S. 'Review of Appearance and Reality, by F.H. Bradley.' *International Journal of Ethics* 4, no. 2 (1894): 246–52.

Mackenzie, J.S. 'Spiritual Values.' *International Journal of Ethics* 33, no. 3 (1923): 248–62.

Mackenzie, J.S. 'The Dangers of Democracy.' *International Journal of Ethics* 16, no 2 (1906): 129-45.

Mackenzie, J.S. 'The Source of Moral Obligation.' *International Journal of Ethics* 10, no. 4 (1900): 464–78.

Mackenzie, J.S. 'The Use of Moral Ideas in Politics.' *International Journal of Ethics* 12, no. 1 (1901): 1–23.

Mackenzie, J.S. *Ultimate Values in the Light of Contemporary Thought*. London: Hodder and Stoughton Limited, 1924.

Mander, W.J. *British Idealism: A History*. Oxford; New York: Oxford University Press, 2011.

Mander, W.J. 'British Idealism and Education for Citizenship.' In *Ethical Citizenship: British Idealism and the Politics of Recognition*. Edited by Thom Brooks, 139–59. London: Palgrave Macmillan, 2014.

Mander, W.J. 'Idealism and the True Self.' In *British Idealism and the Concept of the Self*. Edited by Mander and Stamatoula Panagakou, 287–311. London: Palgrave Macmillan, 2016.

Manela, Erez. *The Wilsonian Moment: Self-Determination and the International Origins of Anticolonial Nationalism*. Oxford; New York: Oxford University Press, 2007.

Mantena, Karuna. *Alibis of Empire: Henry Maine and the Ends of Liberal Imperialism*. Princeton: Princeton University Press, 2010.

Mantena, Karuna. 'The Crisis of Liberal Imperialism.' In *Victorian Visions of Global Order: Empire and International Relations in Nineteenth Century Political Thought*. Edited by Duncan Bell, 113–36. Cambridge: Cambridge University Press, 2007.

Martin, Rex. *A System of Rights*. Oxford; New York: Clarendon Press, 1997.

Martin, Rex. 'Human Rights and the Social Recognition Thesis.' *Journal of Social Philosophy* 44, no. 1 (2013): 1–21.

Martin, Rex. 'Natural Rights Human Rights and the Role of Social Recognition.' *Collingwood and British Idealism Studies* 17, no. 1 (2012): 91–115.

Martin, Rex. 'T.H. Green's Idea of Persons and Citizens.' In *Ethical Citizenship: British Idealism and the Politics of Recognition*. Edited by Thom Brooks, 13–35. London: Palgrave Macmillan, 2014.

Marx, Karl. *On the Jewish Question*. Deutsch-Französische Jahrbücher, 1844.

Mazower, Mark. *No Enchanted Palace: The End of Empire and the Ideological Origins of the United Nations, Lawrence Stone Lectures*. Princeton: Princeton University Press, 2009.

Metz, Rudolf. *A Hundred Years of British Philosophy*. London: George Allen & Unwin Ltd, 1938.

Miller, David. 'Bounded Citizenship.' In *Cosmopolitan Citizenship*. Edited by Kimberly Hutchings and Roland Dannreuther, 60–83. Basingstoke; London: Macmillan Press Ltd, 1999.

Morefield, Jeanne. *Covenants without Swords: Idealist Liberalism and the Spirit of Empire*. Princeton: Princeton University Press, 2009.

Morrice, David. 'The Liberal-Communitarian Debate in Contemporary Political Philosophy and Its Significance for International Relations.' *Review of International Studies* 26, no. 2 (2000): 233–51.

Moyn, Samuel. 'The Continuing Perplexities of Human Rights.' *Qui Parle* 22, no. 1 (2013): 95.

Moyn, Samuel. *The Last Utopia: Human Rights in History.* Cambridge; London: The Belknap Press of Harvard University Press, 2012.

Moyn, Samuel. 'The Universal Declaration of Human Rights of 1948 in the History of Cosmopolitanism.' *Critical Inquiry* 40, no. 4 (2014): 365–84.

Muirhead, J.H., ed. *Bernard Bosanquet and His Friends: Letters Illustrating the Sources and the Development of His Philosophical Opinions.* London: George Allen & Unwin Ltd, 1935.

Muirhead, J.H., ed. *Contemporary British Philosophy: Personal Statements.* London: George Allen & Unwin, 1924.

Muirhead, J.H. *German Philosophy in Relation to the War.* London: John Murray, 1915.

Muirhead, J.H. *Reflections by a Journeyman in Philosophy on the Movements of Thought and Practice in His Time.* London: G. Allen & Unwin, 1942.

Muirhead, J.H. 'J.S. Mackenzie (1860–1935).' *Mind* 45, no. 178 (1936): 277–78.

Muirhead, J.H. 'Recent Criticism of the Idealist Theory of the General Will (I).' *Mind* 33, no. 131 (1924): 233–41.

Muirhead, J.H. 'Recent Criticism of the Idealist Theory of the General Will (II).' *Mind* 33, no. 132 (1924): 361–68.

Muirhead, J.H. *Rule and End in Morals.* London: Oxford University Press, 1932.

Muirhead, J.H. *The Elements of Ethics.* Revised and Enlarged. London: John Murray, 1897.

Muirhead, J.H. *The Service of the State: Four Lectures on the Political Teaching of T.H. Green.* London: John Murray, 1908.

Muirhead, J.H. 'What Imperialism Means.' *Fortnightly Review* LXVIII (1900). Reprinted in *Philosophy and Life and Other Essays*, 79–98. London: Sonnenschein and Co., 1902.

Murray, Gilbert. *The League of Nations and the Democratic Idea.* London: Oxford University Press, 1918.

Nasson, Bill. 'Waging Total War in South Africa: Some Centenary Writings on the Anglo-Boer War, 1899–1902.' *The Journal of Military History* 66, no. 3 (2002): 813–28.

Nesbitt, Darin R. 'Recognizing Rights: Social Recognition in T.H. Green's System of Rights.' *Polity* 33, no. 3 (2001): 423–37.

Nettleship, Richard Lewis, ed. *Works of Thomas Hill Green, Vol. III: Miscellanies and Memoir.* London: Longmans, Green, and Co., 1888.

Nettleship, Richard Lewis. *Memoir of Thomas Hill Green, Late Fellow of Balliol College, Oxford, and Whyte's Professor of Moral Philosophy in the University of Oxford.* London; New York: Longmans, Green, 1906.

Newman, Otto, and Richard De Zoysa. 'Communitarianism: The New Panacea?' *Sociological Perspectives* 40, no. 4 (December 1997): 623–38.

Otter, Sandra M. Den. *British Idealism and Social Explanation: A Study in Late Victorian Thought.* Oxford; New York: Clarendon Press, 1996.

Overstreet, Harry Allen. 'Ethical Clarifications Through the War.' *International Journal of Ethics* 28, no. 3 (1918): 327–46.

Pedersen, Susan. *The Guardians: The League of Nations and the Crisis of Empire.* Oxford: Oxford University Press, 2015.

Pendas, Devin O. 'Toward a New Politics? On the Recent Historiography of Human Rights.' *Contemporary European History* 21, no. 1 (2012): 95–111.

Perris, G.H. 'The New Internationalism.' In *Ethical Democracy.* Edited by Stanton Coit, 30–60. London: Grant Richards, 1900.

Perry, Michael J. 'Are Human Rights Universal? The Relativist Challenge and Related Matters.' *Human Rights Quarterly* 19, no. 3 (1997): 461–509.

Porter, Andrew, ed. *The Oxford History of the British Empire: Volume III: The Nineteenth Century.* Oxford: Oxford University Press, 2001.

Porter, Bernard. *Empire Ways: Aspects of British Imperialism.* London; New York: I.B. Tauris, 2016.

Porter, Bernard. *The Absent-Minded Imperialists: Empire, Society, and Culture in Britain.* Oxford; New York: Oxford University Press, 2004.

Porter, Bernard. *The Lion's Share: A Short History of British Imperialism, 1850–2004*. 4th ed. Harlow; New York: Pearson/Longman, 2004.

Rawls, John. *Political Liberalism*. New York: Columbia University Press, 1993.

Ritchie, D.G. 'Another View of the South African War.' *The Ethical World*, January 13, 1900. In *Collected Works of D.G. Ritchie, Vol. 6: Miscellaneous Writings*. Edited by Peter P. Nicholson. Bristol: Thoemmes Press, 1998.

Ritchie, D.G. *Collected Works of D.G. Ritchie Vol.6: Miscellaneous Writings*. Edited by Peter P. Nicholson. Bristol: Thoemmes Press, 1998.

Ritchie, D.G. 'John Brown's Body,' *The Ethical World*, September 9, 1900. In *Collected Works of D.G. Ritchie, Vol. 6: Miscellaneous Writings*. Edited by Peter P. Nicholson. Bristol: Thoemmes Press, 1998.

Ritchie, D.G. 'Mr. Hobson's Book and the Coming Settlement.' *The Ethical World*, March 10, 1900. In *Collected Works of D.G. Ritchie, Vol. 6: Miscellaneous Writings*. Edited by Peter P. Nicholson. Bristol: Thoemmes Press, 1998.

Ritchie, D.G. *Natural Rights: A Criticism of Some Political and Ethical Conceptions*. London: Swan Sonnenschein, 1903.

Ritchie, D.G. 'On the Conception of Sovereignty.' *The Annals of the American Academy of Political and Social Science* 1 (1891): 385–411.

Ritchie, D.G. 'The Moral Problems of War – in Reply to Mr. J.M. Robertson.' *International Journal of Ethics* 11, no. 4 (1901): 493–514.

Ritchie, D.G. *The Principles of State Interference: Four essays on the Political Philosophy of Mr. Herbert Spencer, J.S. Mill, and T.H. Green*. London: Swan Sonnenschein & Co., 1891.

Ritchie, D.G. 'The Rationality of History.' In *Essays in Philosophical Criticism*. Edited by R.B. Haldane and Andrew Seth, 126–58. New York: Burt Franklin, 1883.

Ritchie, D.G. 'The South African War.' *The Ethical World*, February 3, 1900. In *Collected Works of D.G. Ritchie, Vol. 6: Miscellaneous Writings*. Edited by Peter P. Nicholson. Bristol: Thoemmes Press, 1998.

Ritchie, D.G. 'War and Peace.' *International Journal of Ethics* 11, no. 2 (1901): 137–58.

Ritchie, D.G. '1792 – Year 1.' *International Journal of Ethics* 3, no. 1 (1892): 75–90.

Robbins, Peter. *British Hegelians 1875–1925*. New York: Taylor & Francis, 1982.

Sandel, Michael J., ed. *Liberalism and Its Critics: Readings in Social and Political Theory*. New York: New York University Press, 1984.

Smuts, J.C. *The League of Nations: A Practical Suggestion*. London: Hodder and Stoughton, 1918.

Stamos, David N. *Myth of Universal Human Rights: Its Origin, History, and Explanation, Along with a More Humane Way*. London; New York: Routledge, 2015.

Stapleton, Julia. 'Political Thought and National Identity in Britain 1850–1950.' In *History, Religion, and Culture: British Intellectual History 1750–1950*. Edited by Stefan Collini, Richard Whatmore, and Brian Young, 245–70. Cambridge: Cambridge University Press, 2000.

Stawell, F. Melian. 'Patriotism and Humanity.' *International Journal of Ethics* 25, no. 3 (1915): 292–306.

Sutch, Peter. 'Human Rights as Settled Norms: Mervyn Frost and the Limits of Hegelian Human Rights Theory.' *Review of International Studies* 26, no.2 (2000): 215–31.

Sweet, William. *Idealism and Rights: The Social Ontology of Human Rights in the Political Thought of Bernard Bosanquet*. 2nd edition. Lanham: University Press of America, 2005.

Sylvest, Casper. 'Continuity and Change in British Liberal Internationalism, c. 1900–1930.' *Review of International Studies* 31, no. 2 (2005): 263–83.

Sylvest, Casper. 'Interwar Internationalism, the British Labour Party, and the Historiography of International Relations.' *International Studies Quarterly* 48, no. 2 (2004): 409–32.

Tam, Henry. *Communitarianism: A New Agenda for Politics and Citizenship*. Basingstoke: Macmillan Press, 1998.

Thompson, J. Lee. *A Wider Patriotism: Alfred Milner and the British Empire*. London: Routledge, 2008.

Tinker, Hugh. *Race, Conflict and the International Order*. London: Macmillan Education UK, 1977.

Tufts, James H. 'Ethics and International Relations.' *International Journal of Ethics* 28, no. 3 (1918): 299–313.

Tyler, Colin. 'Contesting the Common Good: T.H. Green and Contemporary Republicanism.' In Tyler, *Common Good Politics: British Idealism and Social Justice in the Contemporary World*, 61–101. Switzerland: Palgrave Macmillan, 2017.

Tyler, Colin. *Idealist Political Philosophy: Pluralism and Conflict in the Absolute Idealist Tradition*. London; New York: Continuum International Publishing Group, 2006.

Tyler, Colin. *The Metaphysics of Self-Realisation and Freedom*. Exeter: Imprint Academic, 2010.

Tyler, Colin, ed. *Unpublished Manuscripts in British Idealism: Political Philosophy, Theology and Social Thought, Volume 1*. 2nd edition. Exeter: Imprint Academic, 2008.

Weeks, H.T. 'An International War Chest.' *International Journal of Ethics* 29, no. 1 (1918): 26–28.

Wells, H.G. *The Idea of a League of Nations*. Boston: The Atlantic Monthly Press, 1919.

Williams, Chris. ''Our War History in Cartoons Is Unique': J.M. Staniforth, British Public Opinion, and the South African War, 1899–1902.' *War in History* 20, no. 4 (November 1, 2013): 491–525.

Winkler, Henry R. 'The Development of the League of Nations Idea in Great Britain, 1914–1919.' *The Journal of Modern History* 20, no. 2 (June 1948): 95–112.

Woolf, L.S. *International Government*. New York: Brentano's, 1916.

Woolf, L.S. *The Framework of a Lasting Peace*. London: George Allen & Unwin Ltd, 1917.

Yearwood, Peter J. *Guarantee of Peace: The League of Nations in British Policy 1914–1925*. Oxford: Oxford University Press, 2009.

Zimmern, Alfred. *The League of Nations and the Rule of Law, 1918–1935*. London: Macmillan and Co., Limited, 1936.

Index